from Loyalists to
Loyal Citizens

From Loyalists to Loyal Citizens

The DePeyster Family of New York

Valerie H. McKito

excelsior editions

State University of New York Press
Albany, New York

Published by State University of New York Press, Albany

© 2015 State University of New York

All rights reserved

Printed in the United States of America

No part of this book may be used or reproduced in any manner
whatsoever without written permission. No part of this book may be
stored in a retrieval system or transmitted in any form or by any
means including electronic, electrostatic, magnetic tape, mechanical,
photocopying, recording, or otherwise without the prior permission in
writing of the publisher.

Excelsior Editions is an imprint of State University of New York Press

For information, contact State University of New York Press, Albany, NY
www.sunypress.edu

Production, Jenn Bennett
Marketing, Kate Seburyamo

Library of Congress Cataloging-in-Publication Data

McKito, Valerie H., 1977–
    From loyalists to loyal citizens: the DePeyster family of New York / Valerie
H. McKito.
        pages cm. — (Excelsior editions)
    Includes bibliographical references and index.
    ISBN 978-1-4384-5810-6 (paperback : alk. paper)
    ISBN 978-1-4384-5812-0 (e-book)
    1. History—United States—Revolutionary Period (1775–1800).   2. History—
United States—State & Local—Middle Atlantic (DC, DE, MD, NJ, NY, PA).

10 9 8 7 6 5 4 3 2 1

For my Sister,
Renae

Contents

Acknowledgments

There are many people and institutions to whom I owe a debt of gratitude for their support in the creation of this work. To the New-York Historical Society and the wonderful librarians and staff of the Patricia D. Klingenstein Library, many thanks for allowing access to, and graciously allowing me permission to quote from, your collections. My special thanks to Ted O'Reilly of the Manuscripts Division whose patience and kindness while I repeatedly searched through the entire DePeyster Collection was overwhelming. To the Gilder-Lehrman Institute, for generously granting me a fellowship that allowed this project to take root, and then grow wings.

For their kindness, expertise, and generosity I heartily thank the librarians and staff of the American Antiquarian Society. As a Kate B. & Hall J. Fellow at the American Antiquarian Society, I was permitted access to the impressive collections at that institution. This allowed me to study a wide array of Loyalist material and begin asking important questions that informed this study. The Maryland Historical Society likewise contributed to the formation of this project by granting me access to their collections as a Lord Baltimore Fellow.

Texas Tech University, along with its faculty and staff, deserve special thanks for their gracious and unwavering support throughout the creation and revision of this manuscript, especially Gretchen Adams who served as advisor and guru throughout the dissertation process, Catherine Miller whose keen insights and comments helped to shape this project, and Randy McBee and Jorge Iber both of whom supported and believed in my abilities while a graduate student.

To the University of Nebraska, Kearney I offer great thanks for supporting and encouraging me to submit this manuscript for publication, especially Vernon Volpe, Mark Ellis, and Pam Proskocil. Eastern New Mexico University deserves more thanks than I can muster for its support and encouragement throughout the revision process. For two years, ENMU, its faculty, staff, and students encouraged me to make this manuscript the best I could make it, sending me to conferences, listening to ideas, and offering kind suggestions. Suzanne Balch-Lindsay, Dale Streeter, Donald Elder, and Simon Chavez deserves special thanks for knowing when to encourage, when to prod, and for being supportive through the entire process.

I am also indebted to many individuals who offered insights and made this a better manuscript in the process, many of whom may not have even realized their contributions at the time. Dolly Wilson, Jeffrey Mosher, and Allan Taylor, all of whom served on my dissertation committee. Joseph C. Miller, who once took the time at an annual meeting of the AHA to ask a graduate student about her dissertation and whose questioning provoked deep consideration about the ways in which wars end. Caroline Sloat of the American Antiquarian Society whose questions opened up the study in new directions. Ellen Dunlap of the American Antiquarian Society, who convinced the Colonial Timothy Bigelow Chapter of the DAR to open its headquarters, the home of a former Loyalist, to exploration. Peter C. Messer, Daniel Killbride, Jeannine DeLombard, and Peter P. Reed, all of whom asked great questions and offered critical insights during our time in residency at the American Antiquarian Society. George Van Cleve, who offered insight on the world of politics in the early years of the U.S. Republic while waiting for the New-York Historical Society to open in the mornings. Kim Richardson and Laura Jarnagin Pang without whose helpful comments and insights the Brazil section would suffer. And to Bruce C. Daniels, whose advice first pointed me in the direction of the Loyalists, thank you.

A heartfelt thanks to Amanda Lanne-Camilli, acquisitions editor with State University of New York Press, thank you for believing in the potential of this manuscript, championing it through the approval process, and for all of your patience in between. And to Jenn Bennett, production editor extraordinaire, thank you for applying your expertise and keen insight to this manuscript. Your encouragement and hard work made the editing process smooth and painless, a truly amazing feat.

I also owe thanks to several organizations without whose support, this project would not have been possible. The American Antiquarian Society, the Gilder-Lehrman Society, Texas Tech University, and Eastern New Mexico University all provided financial support for the creation of this manuscript. The Rocky Mountain Council For Latin American Studies and the Georgia Association of Historians whose members graciously and kindly offered encouragement and insight while working on the manuscript. The Library of Congress, Manuscripts Division, whose collections allowed me to create a more accurate understanding of the Loyalist experience.

I owe the largest debt of gratitude to my family. My husband, Jeff McKito, unfailing supported me at every turn. My parents, Evelyn and Lincoln Clabo, whose love of learning across all fields of knowledge infected me at an early age, and whose love and support has never wavered. My sisters, Renae Cooper, Angela Wiering, Pamela Ruble, and Michele Cole, along with their families, whose encouragement is a thing of beauty. My brother Chad, who (in addition to encouragement) selflessly read through the manuscript with a fine-toothed comb and offered good cheer. Without you, this book would not have been possible.

Introduction

The Disappearance of the Loyalists

*I*n 1819, Washington Irving published the story of a lazy but lovable farmer named Rip Van Winkle. One day, while wandering in the mountains, Rip met the ghosts of Henry Hudson and his crew. Hudson invited Rip to join himself and his men for a round of ninepins, after which Rip took a nap. Upon waking, Rip returned home only to discover that his wife, family, friends, and just about everyone he knew were dead. His return coincided with an election day. When asked which side he voted for, Rip, confused and ignorant of the Revolution that passed by while he slept, replied that he was a loyal subject of the King. Cries of "tory! spy! refugee!" rang out; the townspeople were ready for blood. Rip was saved from a terrible fate when an old man confirmed Rip's strange story, telling the townsmen that he remembered Rip from the days of his boyhood. When the townsfolk properly understood that Rip was ignorant of the Revolution, and that he was misguided in his allegiance to the King, they forgave him, and Rip went on to live a quiet life much like the one he left behind years before. Although Rip Van Winkle was a fictional character, was his predicament all that different from real-life Loyalists who found themselves in a new world at the end of the Revolution? Could it really have been that easy for the Patriots to move on and, more importantly, forget the sins of the Revolution, especially when it was all too clear that the former Loyalists were not ignorant of the issues surrounding the Revolution and many would make no apologies for their loyalty? In some places, and depending on the individual's status and vocation, the answer is yes.

1

Rip's sleep finds its real-life parallel in the ten-year Canadian exile of Frederick DePeyster. One of four brothers in a prominent New York family who retained their allegiance to England when Independence was declared, Frederick also served as an officer in the British army. Like others who found themselves on the wrong side when peace came in 1783, Frederick moved to Canada.[1] Away from the controversies and turmoil of post-Revolutionary New York, Frederick reemerged in a time when people were more concerned with their own day-to-day existence. While Rip benefits from being known in his small village, so, too, does Frederick DePeyster, only his "village" was his social and economic circle of New York City. Just as Rip avoided the most contentious phase of post-Revolutionary settlement, so, too, did Frederick DePeyster and others like him. With varying degrees of difficulty, they made the transition into their old homes in a new country. Like Rip Van Winkle, Frederick DePeyster not only survived this transition, but thrived.

American Loyalists, in the context of the Revolutionary War, have long been a subject of study for historians because their decision to remain loyal to Great Britain is inexorably intertwined with the founding of the United States as well as the development of Canada. There are numerous studies (both general and state- or county-specific) that discuss the questions of who the Loyalists were, why they made the decisions they did, and how they were treated during the American Revolution. Generally, the studies agree that Loyalists came from every sort of background in the colonies at that time: some were wealthy, while others were poor; some were recent immigrants, while others had roots reaching back to the establishment of their colony. Their reasons for remaining loyal to Great Britain were likewise as varied. Some believed that whatever the differences the colonies had with their mother country, the Americans were better off in the fold of the Empire than on their own in a hostile world. For others, the decision was purely that of self-interest as the British had promised land to anyone who served in the Loyalist ranks. And for still others, the decision was made for them by suspicious neighbors who pronounced their loyalty for them. These studies usually end with the Treaty of 1783, the repeal of anti-Tory laws, or the evacuation of New York in 1783. They do not usually examine the fate of those Loyalists who chose to remain in the United States following the end of the Revolution, nor do they discuss the return of the Loyalists to their former homes.

Although most traditional studies of the American Loyalists wave good-bye to the Loyalists with the sailing of the evacuees from New York in 1783, there are some historians who have followed the Loyalists into exile in Great Britain, Florida, and the West Indies. Wallace Brown provided a general overview of the Loyalist diaspora in *The Good Americans*. More specific studies quickly followed. In 1972, Mary Beth Norton examined the Loyalist community in London while that same year Wilbur H. Sieburt followed the Loyalists to the West Indies. In 1975, J. Leitch Wright Jr. explored the Loyalist experience in Florida. *Liberty's Exiles* by Maya Jasanoff is the most recent contribution and provides a more detailed overview of the Loyalist diaspora. These studies reveal that while the Loyalist refugees may not have had the easiest experiences in their new homes, most were determined to make the situation work as they were no longer welcome in their former homes. These studies also contain the odd line about Loyalists who decided to take the risk and return to their former homes in the United States. Some studies even mention that the returning Loyalists enjoyed a position of prominence in their former communities, despite their Loyalist past. However, as those studies examined the lives of Loyalists who stuck it out in their new homes, we are left to wonder about those who did return.

Not surprisingly, histories of Loyalists in Britain's other North American colonies abound, tied as they are to the settlement and founding of what we think of today as Canada. In these studies, the mention of Loyalists returning to their former homes is not odd by any means; rather, those notices of Loyalists leaving their Canadian homes for their former American homes is a running theme throughout the early years of the Loyalist settlement there. Neither is this surprising given the frontier state of the Canadian colonies at that time. Life was hard, the weather was cold, supplies were low, everyone was poor, and the land promised to the Loyalists by the government was not partitioned for their immediate use.

The reasons for the Loyalists to leave Canada were many, yet not everyone who wanted to return to their former homes was willing to risk an attempt, and so most remained where they were. Threats of violence issued at some places during the Revolution continued to hold their force in the postwar era. Despite this, many Loyalists successfully returned to their former homes, as did Rip Van Winkle. In "The Rehabilitation of Loyalists in Connecticut," Oscar Zeichner stated that while some Loyalists had difficulties in returning to a normal life in their former homes, Connecticut actually tried to attract Loyalists from other areas if they could prove to be of some financial benefit to the state. Likewise, David E. Maas in *The Return of the Massachusetts Loyalists* states that although Massachusetts discouraged the return of Loyalists to the state, if the Loyalists were members of a profession with limited numbers, say a medical physician, the state would tolerate their return. In both cases, while these states allowed, and in some cases encouraged, the return of Loyalists to their territory, local counties and towns did not always abide by the State's ruling, and many who returned expecting smooth sailing ran into troubled waters. But while "forgetting" was not so easy in those states, it became the order of the day in New York, where *Rip Van Winkle* is actually set.

In 1940, Oscar Zeichner addressed the specific concerns of New York in "The Loyalist Problem in New York After the Revolution."[2] Zeichner focused on Loyalists in general rather than on returning Loyalists. Nevertheless, his analysis is important for understanding the situation in New York at the end of the Revolution. Zeichner noted that, in addition to being the last colony to declare independence, New York (the whole state, not just the city) boasted a high Loyalist population throughout the War.[3] As a result, the Patriot population of New York, determined to demonstrate their commitment to the Revolution, passed some of the harshest anti-Tory laws in any of the states. Yet continued enforcement of these laws was impractical given the scope of the problem, and soon New Yorkers decided that as long as those with Loyalist pasts kept those affiliations quiet and went along with the new government, it was best to "forget" the past and get on with life.

Judith Van Buskirk both confirms and complicates Zeichner's study with *Generous Enemies*.[4] By demonstrating that the boundaries of loyalty were, by necessity, blurred in New York during the Revolution, Van Buskirk's work provides a better, more nuanced understanding for the return of the Loyalists to that state than Zeichner suggests. Loyalty was not so much a matter of Patriot and Loyalist for many in New York, but rather a matter of survival. As a result, many in New York who may genuinely have considered themselves to be Patriots had dealings in British-occupied New York City. The opposite was also true: those who thought of themselves as Loyalists had dealings with the Patriots outside the British lines. Given the difficulty in defining boundaries of loyalty in New York, it becomes clear why, in New York, "forgetting" the past was the most prudent way to move into the future. It also helps to explain why Loyalists would return to New York despite the severity of their anti-Tory laws, and why the state of New York was not overly concerned with the strict enforcement of those laws.

While Zeichner and Van Buskirk laid the foundation for an examination of the return of the Loyalists to New York, the need remains for a close, systematic examination of the mechanics of this process for this largely understudied group. One of the reasons for this gap in scholarship is the difficulty in identifying records for returnees, many of whom left behind few records to document why or even when they returned. While this was certainly due to a fear of retaliation in some places, in other cases it appears to be much more simple; returnees wanted to get on with their lives in familiar surroundings even if it was in a new country whose formation they initially opposed.

My approach has been to use a case study of one individual family whose public and private activities can be traced over the tumultuous period of war, exile, return, and assimilation into the new political order. Frederick DePeyster of New York offers such an opportunity. His father, James DePeyster was, throughout the Revolution, considered a "dangerous tory [sic]." His four sons and one son-in-law not only shared his politics but took up arms for the British.[5] After the Revolution, James remained in New York while his sons relocated to New Brunswick, Canada, and other locations in the Empire. By 1794, one of James's sons, Frederick, returned to New York and established himself as a successful merchant. Frederick's success was so great that his own sons were able to use the family name, as well as business and social networks, to launch themselves into business and to establish various charities and societies, such as the New-York [sic] Historical Society, home to the DePeyster Collection. By the 1820s this generation not only was completely established within the highest circles of New York society, they also could not be considered less than thoroughly "American."

Frederick left no documents behind to explain his decision to return to New York, but in reconstructing his life, it seems that he really did not need to. Throughout the massive mix of correspondence, both personal and business, and assorted papers spanning hundreds of years in the DePeyster Collection, housed in the archives of the New-York Historical Society, there is no hint that Frederick, or any of his family, felt the need to look over their shoulders for Patriot mobs armed with pitchforks and torches. Frederick DePeyster did just what we would expect him to, given his family name and colonial reputation. The fact that he was able to do this despite his Loyalist background makes him an ideal example of what the physical reality was in New York for Loyalists versus what the state portrayed through its laws.

Chapter 1 of this study considers the DePeyster family in colonial New York and examines why they chose to remain loyal to Great Britain during the Revolution. The DePeysters were prominent in both the Dutch and British colonial governments. Although they held office in those governments, they were also prominent merchants and landowners. As one of New York's elite families, the DePeysters married into most of the other elite families, creating and reinforcing bonds of mutual interest across the colony. When the Revolution finally came to New York, it made sense for the DePeysters to remain loyal to Great Britain. It was both the conservative position and one that suited their interests. As a result, Frederick, his brothers, and his brother-in-law (all young men), served in the King's forces during the war, and were forced to leave New York thereafter.

Chapter 2 follows Frederick DePeyster and his brothers into exile in New Brunswick, Canada, and examines their attempts to re-create their New York lives and status in their new home. According to the Treaty of Paris, 1783, those who bore arms for the King could not stay in the United States; they had to leave. Although Canada was largely a frontier area, a small group of Loyalists established themselves as the elite of their new home. Their maneuverings created a new colony that they intended to use to cement their position as the social, economic, and political elite. Throughout all of the turmoil of those early years, Frederick DePeyster consistently sided with the Loyalist elite and was himself counted among their numbers. Yet for all of their efforts, New Brunswick remained economically depressed, and after ten years, Frederick DePeyster made the decision to return to New York to achieve the economic success that eluded him in New Brunswick.

Chapter 3 examines the inward focus of the DePeyster family by exploring the relationships Frederick had with his brother Abraham, who remained in New Brunswick, and his sister Margaret James, who lived in England. Upon his return to New York, Frederick became the head of his family, despite being the sixth child and fourth son. His relationships with his brother Abraham and his sister Margaret James reveal the expectations and responsibilities of DePeyster family members, despite the physical distance between them. These relationships also reveal familial attitudes toward wealth and society and the role of the DePeyster family therein.

Chapter 4 considers Frederick DePeyster's economic success in New York following his return from Canada. Frederick was able to utilize his vast familial network and business contacts to establish himself in New York as a merchant. In addition to importing wine, rum, and spices from Europe and the West Indies, Frederick continued to do business in New Brunswick (not all of it strictly legal) and invested in various projects like canals and roads, all of which contributed to his increasing economic standing in New York. By 1820, Frederick had managed to build a fortune sufficient to cement himself and the DePeyster name in the upper echelons of New York's economic elite.

Chapter 5 examines the social reintegration of Frederick DePeyster into New York society as reflected in the lives and opportunities of the next generation of DePeysters. Frederick's sons, nephews, and nieces were provided with every opportunity to mix with the elite of New York. They were sent to the most prestigious schools and had apprenticeships with the most respected individuals and firms, none of which would have been possible without either Frederick's financial success or his extensive familial and social network.

Chapter 6 follows this next generation of DePeysters after Frederick's retirement from his merchant activities in 1820. It examines whether they were able to maintain the DePeyster status, both social and economic, established by Frederick after his return to New York from his Loyalist exile in Canada. While all strove for success, the results of their efforts were not equal. In general, those who were most successful were the ones who were able to innovate and adapt to their circumstances, much as Frederick himself had done.

In the end, the picture that emerges of the DePeysters is that of a successful, wealthy family, concerned with both familial and business matters, whose focus was internal rather than external, a family that benefited both from New York City's conflicted relationship with wartime enthusiasm and from their wealth and family ties. Given New York City's unique occupied status during the war and the necessity of blurred boundaries during that time, it makes sense that, in New York at least, people may not have wanted to call too much attention wartime activities, lest their own activities should fall under that same scrutiny. In this sense, the DePeyster experiences are representative of those faced by many returnees of the same socioeconomic status in both New York State and in the City.

Chapter 1

The DePeyster Tradition

$\mathcal{D}$uring the Revolutionary War, loyalty was complicated. Often the financial, political, and familial concerns of an individual and community overlapped and created contradictions, which could be reconciled only with difficulty, if at all. In New York, this was especially true. There, the inhabitants participated in their local economy while also playing a part in the economy of the British Empire. The produce of New York found a good market in the British West Indies, where it was shipped via New York–owned ships. This economic relationship was complicated by multilayered political relationships. The great landed families of New York vied for control of the government with each other and with the great merchant families of New York City. In this contest, each side utilized their tenants and employees against each other. Another complication was that most of these families were interrelated through marriage to one another. Due to these complicated relationships, the loyalty of a person to either side of any contest was rarely such a clear-cut issue. For the DePeysters this is especially true. It is possible, however, to identify one overriding factor governing their choices throughout the war and thereafter. Decisions regarding loyalty, politics, and money were made with one question in mind: Would it be good for the DePeyster family?

The DePeysters were prominent in New York under both Dutch and English rule. Johannes DePeyster (1626–1699),[1] as the family's American patriarch, can be found in almost any history of New Amsterdam or early colonial New York. Arriving in New Amsterdam around 1647, Johannes DePeyster made his mark on the colony as a successful import merchant and through his service to the colony under Dutch rule as *Schepen* and *Burgomaster* and later under English rule as Alderman and Deputy Mayor.[2]

Johannes's son Abraham (1657–1728) was likewise well known. From his father, he inherited land and the connections of business and society. Like his father, Abraham held many government positions including alderman, mayor, Supreme Court judge (and later chief justice), member of the King's Council, acting governor for a short time, and treasurer for the provinces of New York and New Jersey. In addition to the many positions he held in government, he also held the rank of Colonel and commanded the city and county militia. During his life, Abraham was one of the wealthiest merchants in his generation, known particularly for wine importation.[3]

Abraham also associated with the elites of colonial society. Among his particular friends were the Earl of Bellomont, governor of New York and Massachusetts, and William Penn, proprietor of Pennsylvania. In 1695, while serving as the mayor, Abraham built the DePeyster mansion in the heart of the merchant community, near the East River, on Queen Street (later renamed Pearl Street). As demand for space grew, New Yorkers filled in the waterfront, pushing the DePeyster mansion farther from the docks. The area, however, remained socially desirable until after the Revolutionary War. The house itself stood until 1856. The house boasted spectacular gardens, which encompassed a large area, part of which were later donated to the city for the building of City Hall. The grounds likewise included detached buildings that housed stables, kitchens, and slave quarters. The mansion itself was 59 by 80 feet and three stories tall, not including the attic area. It boasted double-arched windows across the front as well as a balcony that extended the full length of the house. The home soon became a favorite gathering spot for political dignitaries and the social elite. In fact, colonial governors would review their troops from the balcony of the DePeyster mansion. As was common at the time, the mansion also contained an office for Abraham's merchant activities.[4]

In addition to Abraham's political positions, his siblings, children, nephews, and nieces also furthered the interests of the family by intermarrying with the other elite families of New York City. Soon the DePeysters were related by marriage and blood to families like the DeLanceys, Axtells, Jays, Schuylers, Beekmans, Hakes, Bayards, DuBoises, Reades, Clarksons, Ogdens, Hammersleys, Charltons, and Livingstons, just to name a few. These types of connections provided succeeding generations with a readymade network to establish themselves in both society and business. After families Anglicized, younger generations were expected to utilize these contacts to build their own fortunes; those who could not, were not usually trusted with as large a share of inherited wealth. This was contrary to Dutch traditions where all children, including females, inherited equally. This is, however, typical of New York merchant families who wanted to safeguard the family wealth and status.[5]

Near the end of his public career, Abraham DePeyster served the colonies of New York and New Jersey as treasurer; however, in 1721 he suffered a mental breakdown, the specifics of which are not recorded, which prevented his further participation in public life.[6] His son Abraham Jr. (1696–1767) then took over the position of treasurer for New York as well as the family's shipping interests at the age of 25. Unlike his father, Abraham Jr. did not pursue a variety of political positions; apart from being treasurer, he held no other political positions. This did not detract from the family's standing. In fact, throughout Abraham Jr.'s lifetime, the family's status and prestige continued to grow. Abraham Jr. expanded his shipping interests to include smuggling and privateering and was consistently listed among the wealthiest inhabitants of New York.[7] Smuggling at this time was more or less socially acceptable; people knew who did it and purchased their goods, but generally did not go so far as to speak of it in polite company.[8]

In 1722, Abraham Jr. married Margaretta Van Cortlandt, daughter of Jacobus Van Cortlandt, former mayor of New York City. Together they had eleven children, five of whom lived into adulthood. Their oldest surviving son, James (1726–1799), followed his father into shipping. James DePeyster was also known as James Abraham, James A. or Jacobus. There is very little relating to James DePeyster in the DePeyster Collection at the New-York Historical Society; it could be that his documents fell victim to servants' fires, that he destroyed them during the Battle of Long Island, or that he simply was not a "saver." Either way, it makes determining his relationships with his children difficult. While Abraham was known for importation, smuggling, and privateering, James focused primarily upon the latter two activities and owned, in part or whole, a large fleet of vessels for those purposes.[9] The shift in shipping tactics makes sense, given the time in which James operated. With Great Britain and the colonies involved in a series of wars encompassing both Europe and the Americas, there was ample opportunity for privateers and smugglers to operate profitably.[10]

James's marriage in 1748 to Sarah Reade, daughter of Joseph Reade and member of the King's Council, brought another change to the family as they moved their membership from the Dutch Reformed Church to Trinity Episcopal.[11] This is not too surprising as "Anglicanism was a faith based on nationality," and the Reades were conspicuously English.[12] Additionally, according to Dutch tradition, the groom would take on the religion of his bride. This is part of the reason Dutch traditions persisted so long in New York after the English took over. While the Dutch Reformed Church maintained a large amount of influence in New York City and probably ranked second to the Anglican church in the wealth of its parishioners, the dilution of the Dutch community and the splitting of the congregation over which language to hold services indicated its declining importance. Trinity was the church of New York's political elite, and it attracted the affluent and influential; the DePeysters' move to Trinity had the potential to benefit more than just their souls.[13]

James and his wife Sarah continued to live in the house on Queen Street with his father and mother,[14] but he also built a country house called *Ranelagh* (located at what today is Broadway and Worth Street) for his family to retire and entertain "dignitaries of state and celebrities from abroad."[15] The house was castle-like and handsomely furnished, and it contained a large library of rare and valuable books. The gardens were extensive, with groves and wooded walks, lawns, and flower gardens.[16] James was known as a gentleman of leisure during this time, despite his shipping interests, and took little interest in politics. The couple's family grew rapidly; out of thirteen children, nine lived into adulthood. The family's wealth allowed the children of James and Sarah to have an ideal childhood. Reminiscences of the siblings from later in life depict idyllic carriage rides through tree-lined roads and along river banks, long walks with "pals," and the family's good company.[17]

This idyllic situation changed, however, when James's ships were swept from the seas as casualties of the French and Indian War. While some of his ships undoubtedly fell prey to the French Navy, James also faced losses from the British Navy, which aimed to put an end to illegal trade with the French West Indies. In *Defying Empire*, Thomas M. Truxes described some of the problems James ran into during the French and Indian War. For instance, when an informant turned him in for loading flour without the proper certificates, for loading ships with naval stores bound for neutral ports, and for importing French goods disguised as British goods, James and his partner faced fines and criminal charges for subverting the law and supplying the enemy in a time of war.[18] This is the specific reference to the observed illegal activity; however, Truxes returns to the incident throughout the book, including the report and arrest of James DePeyster and his partner as well as their revenge upon the informant. The revenge on the informant extended beyond just James DePeyster and his partner; just about everyone involved with merchant activities in New York, including investors, participated in ruining the reputation and life of the informant, George Spencer. This elite group roused the rabble against the informer, trundling him through the streets in an open wagon while the populace threw vegetables and insults at the man. When that torment proved insufficient to deter Spencer, the group conspired to buy one of his debts and then threw him in jail when he failed to pay. Spencer's credit, name, and reputation were ruined in New York City, but rather than back down from his accusations, Spencer persisted in hopes of a reward. The trial turned into a bit of a farce as the jury of DePeyster's peers refused to convict. This type of trade and smuggling could be considered treason under the Treason Act of 1351, which prohibited providing "aid and comfort" to the enemy; however, officials rarely prosecuted these cases as such because the Act also required proof of intent to secure the enemy's victory.[19] Many prominent New York City residents were involved with this type of trade, "the mayor, several aldermen, the families of Supreme Court justices, in-laws of two lieutenant-governors, members of the provincial assembly and the Governor's Council" as

well as the merchant elite.[20] Additionally, the difficulty of obtaining testimony against members in these groups forced British officials to level
lesser, but still severe, charges for trading with the enemy. Regardless of
the method of loss, by the end of the war James was left a debtor. With
incessant demands from creditors mounting in the postwar depression,
Abraham Jr. took out a series of loans, some quite large, from friends
and family to cover his son's debts.[21] Backed by his father, James's
shaky financial situation seemed well-secured. Consequently, very little
changed for the DePeysters immediately.

The same could not be said for New York. The years following the
French and Indian War were politically tumultuous for the colonies,
and New York City was no exception to this phenomenon. The chaotic
atmosphere exacerbated tensions already present in politics. In the
1750s, two leading factions in New York politics were represented as the
"country party" and "court party."[22] The priorities of the groups were
markedly different. The country party was concerned about maintaining their holdings, and focused on strengthening New York through
greater settlement of the colony and the proliferation of farms. They
emphasized the "power of the elected assembly" over that of the "governor and council."[23] The city-based court party believed that trade
was the key, and, as a result, they could count much of the merchant
community among their supporters.[24] They emphasized the legitimacy
of the governor and the prevalence of government officials within their
ranks.[25] The court party had yet one more title, the "Episcopal Party,"
as many constituents were also members at Trinity Church.[26] Given
the divergent aims of the parties, the court and the country parties
jockeyed for position within the government of colonial New York.[27]

When the British government passed the Sugar and Stamp Acts,
the merchants of New York, many of whom belonged to the Court
party, protested the measures because they feared the Acts would harm
business. Many of those who signed these protests, and indeed some
of whom even served initially as delegates to the Continental Congress,
turned away from the radical direction some colleagues were taking
toward armed rebellion. For Loyalists it was one thing to protest a
measure formally that they thought unfair; it was quite another to
take extra-legal steps to remedy the situation. This point in particular

became a matter of pride for the Loyalists in Canada after the Revolution who, despite their points of contention with the government, never resorted to armed resistance to make their point. Although New York was not the most radical in its protest, it has been described as the "loudest," both in 1764 and thereafter, up until the actual Declaration of Independence.[28] Given New York's economic dependency on Atlantic trade, both with Great Britain and other nations, many found it was in their best interest for the relationship with their parent country to remain the way it was prior to the French and Indian War. That does not mean that they desired separation from Great Britain, but rather that they may have wanted simply a return to normalcy. Michael Kammen states that while New York may not have been the "cockpit" for the Revolution like Massachusetts, its self-interest in—and reactions to—the issues made it a fulcrum.[29] For example, New York's initial protest resulted in the calling of the Stamp Act Congress in 1765 at New York City from October 7th to the 22nd. After the Stamp Act Congress adjourned, the situation in New York quickly deteriorated for traditional leaders and elites. As the general populace became involved in the various protests, traditional leadership eroded and found itself forced to compromise more and more with radical elements who wanted more decisive action. The leading families attempted to restrain the crowds to prevent unprincipled actions, but they did so to the detriment of their own influence.[30] Nevertheless, the residents of New York City, never the easiest group to deal with due to their diversity, mostly shied away from radical action. If separation with Great Britain occurred, or the port was heavily restricted, the financial loss would affect everyone. The result was that during the ensuing months, radical leaders rarely got their way either. For the most part, the activities of the mobs in New York were fairly tame as mob activities go, taking out more wrath on effigies than on actual persons or properties. One exception to this was the destruction of Major Thomas James's house. This incident terrified the traditional leadership into a more conservative position, favoring paper protests to more popular protests.[31]

Major Thomas James was the commander of the British Artillery at Fort George in New York and future son-in-law of James DePeyster.[32] Major James made himself particularly obnoxious to the protestors when he announced that he would "cram the Stamps down their throats."[33] Rumors circulated that should violence break out, Major James "was to be buried alive."[34] When the riots finally did break out on October 31, 1765, the mob did not bury the Major but made its way to his newly renovated estate near *Vaux Hall*, on the outskirts of town.[35] The mob carried off what treasures they could, including liquor, books, clothes, and linens. What they did not want or could not carry, they destroyed. The mob cut open beds, smashed glass and china, and built a fire on the grounds to burn other items.[36] The house itself they "beat to Pieces all the Doors, Sashes, Window Frames and Partitions in the House, leaving it a mere Shell."[37] To the city's elites, this action was a blatant destruction of property, and they feared their property might be next. Thus, many of New York's elites reconsidered their association with the more radical elements, and party affiliation became fluid. In other words, class now played a more significant role in determining what side individuals chose.[38]

Two years after the Stamp Act Riots, Abraham Jr. passed away. His will is simplicity in itself. He directed that all of his "just debts" be paid, and the rest of the estate go to his wife until her death, after which his children would share equally, as was the Dutch tradition.[39] Despite the simplicity of his will, Abraham Jr.'s estate was large. He owned a great deal of property including about half of the northern side of Wall Street. Despite his vast land holdings, Abraham Jr.'s executors soon found his estate owed £50,000 to the Colony of New York. Upon the death of Abraham Jr., the Council of New York undertook an audit of his office's accounts. The figure of £50,000 comes from the records of the colonial government of New York during their deliberations on how to proceed with the estate of Abraham Jr. and whether or not they would allow creditors to take the separate estates of both his wife and son as well.[40] As Treasurer for the Province, Abraham DePeyster Jr. was personally responsible for collecting the import duties of the colony. If he failed to collect, the fees were to come out of his personal funds.[41] At least part of Abraham Jr.'s debt came from unpaid duties. Another part of the debt came from uncollected quitrents, but what percentage they represented of the total £50,000 is unknown.[42] After the estate of Abraham DePeyster Jr. was divided and sold,[43] £30,000 still remained outstanding to the colony.[44] Up until his death, Abraham DePeyster Jr. was considered one of the wealthiest men in New York and was certainly a man of great consequence. This changed upon his death when Abraham Jr.'s executors were forced to turn the estate, lock, stock, and barrel, over to the Colony of New York. However his wife, Margaretta, was allowed to keep her considerable dowry.

To complicate the settlement of Abraham's estate, his son James, named as an executor, was also deeply indebted to the estate. Prior to his death, Abraham Jr. took out a number of sizable loans for James from family and business partners. In 1770, the Assembly decided to enforce the codicil of Abraham Jr.'s will, which stated that acting as an executor did not cancel any debt owed by that person to the estate. James, despite being described as an "insolvent debtor" in 1768, was responsible for the loans Abraham Jr. took on his behalf from friends and family.[45] James could not repay his debt to his father's estate, much less claims from other creditors, and as a result he was forced to seek relief through bankruptcy. James was ordered to turn over a complete inventory of his estate, including books and china, to the Assembly. He was allowed to keep from the inventory any bedding and clothing for his family.[46] James's reputation suffered as a result of the liquidation. Although still a member of the elite socioeconomic circles of New York by virtue of blood and familial relations, James's family lost considerable respect within those circles.

Evidence of this can be seen in the marriage of James's daughter Margaret to Colonel (formerly Major) Thomas James of the Stamp Act Riots. Colonel James did not come from a family of similar social status; rather, his respectability came from his military career and the fortune he acquired in that profession. Had the family maintained their status after Abraham Jr.'s death, Colonel James would not have been considered a suitable match since Margaret would have been paired with someone from one of New York's other leading families who had status, wealth, and family respectability. However, given the family's change in circumstance, Colonel James was considered a "good" match for this DePeyster daughter. Of James's other daughters, Ann (also known as Nancy) did not marry, and the other two, Mary Reade and Elizabeth, married respectable men, but not necessarily men of elite status. The same patterns are also present with James's sons: Joseph Reade married the daughter of the sheriff for Jamaica, Long Island, certainly respectable but of no money and nowhere near the status of the DePeyster family. James Jr. never married, focusing instead on a military career. Frederick's first marriage to Helen Livingston Hake also reflects this aspect in some respects. Because Helen carried the "right" familial names, this assertion requires some explanation. Helen's mother was a Livingston; however, her great-grandfather, Robert Livingston, was a disgraced member of the family. While his son Robert Gilbert, Helen's grandfather, did much to restore honor to his branch of the family, his father's disgrace lingered like a bad stench in the air. This taint would most likely have been forgotten but for the fact that Helen's father, Samuel Hake, who, despite an impressive English lineage, was a ne'er-do-well whom people would have preferred to ignore but for his wife and children (for a fuller description of his activities, please see chapter 2). Abraham seems to be the only one of James's sons to make a match that would have been considered "good" prior to change in status: he married Catherine Livingston, whose father was John Livingston, a Tory who, during the British occupation of New York, remained in the city rather than fleeing to Livingston Manor to take refuge as so many of the Livingstons did.

Despite the bankruptcy and their reduced circumstances, the DePeysters still had some resources to draw on. Although not explicitly stated, James's wife Sarah had a separate estate, part of which was the estate in Jamaica, Long Island, to which the family moved after the unhappy proceedings.[47] It was common practice for both the Dutch and the wealthy in general during this late colonial period to preserve familial wealth through separate estates. Although not a legal term, the documents refer to these types of estates as "dowry estates." This was the case with Abraham Jr.'s wife Margaretta and other female members of the DePeyster line who made out individual wills separate from their husband's estates. This practice was displayed again in the next generation when Frederick DePeyster's wife, Helen Hake, died prior to her husband and left her "dowry estate" to be divided among their children. However embarrassed or upset extended family members were over James's financial demise, they remained supportive of his wife and children. In the years immediately following the bankruptcy, several relatives remembered James's children in their wills, although not always equally. As individuals without children of their own, or with their children already provided for by their husband's wills, those family members were thus able to dispose of their wealth without restriction, and in so doing, displayed their preference for certain individuals or their displeasure with others. Family members with the same name were often thus favored as were individuals with pleasant dispositions, while troublemakers and those who did not bother to flatter were excluded.[48]

James's younger, unmarried brother Frederick (1731–1773), a snappy dresser known as the "Marquis," generously remembered his brother and bequeathed to him a riding chair, double sleigh, and his choice of two plate pieces.[49] Frederick was called the "Marquis" partly because of his penchant for fancy clothes and partly because he inherited a sizable estate in Rouen, France, from his great-aunt, Madame Van der Hulst de Peyster. The estate did not come with a title, but the pretention of the dress and estate provoked the nickname. John Watts DePeyster reports in his autobiography that these French lands were somehow "lost" to the family, although the specifics are not given. Frederick, the Marquis, died in New York, so we simply do not know whether those lands were part of his estate at the time of his death and therefore part of his nephew's inheritance. To James's son Joseph Reade (1754–before 1803), then 19 years old, Frederick left £100, a gold watch, a silver-hilted sword, a dozen fine shirts, six pairs of laced ruffles, and two dozen neck cloths. The bulk of Frederick's considerable estate, however, went to his namesake and nephew, James's son Frederick (1758–1834), then 15 years old. Interestingly, James's oldest son, Abraham (1753–1798), then 20, was not included in the will, nor many of the others that followed. No reason is given for the exclusion of Abraham; he simply was. Reading through his correspondence, one gets the impression that Abraham had a rather imperious attitude, and that he tended to take his superiority for granted. This attitude is also present in stories of Abraham related to his military service during the Revolutionary War, particularly in the Battle of King's Mountain. During this battle, Abraham's unit was forced to surrender to the Patriots.

Unhappy that Patriot officer Colonel Campbell was not able to stop his men from firing quickly enough, Abraham refused to dismount his horse and instead called out, "Colonel Campbell, that was d—d unfair!" twice before Campbell ordered him down.[50]

Female relatives were particularly generous with James's children, establishing trusts for them, but excluding James from receiving any fringe benefits one might expect a parent to receive. Anne Chambers, for instance, sister of James's wife Sarah, left to each of James's daughters £500; to his son, Frederick, all her lands in Ulster County; and James Jr. (1757–1793), £200. More generally, Anne established a trust fund for all of the DePeyster children, over which James was excluded as an executor.[51] A similar pattern appears in the will of Ann (Johanna) DePeyster (1701–1774), sister to Abraham Sr. Ann left a portion of her estate to her sisters and to the children of James DePeyster. Once again, James was excluded as a trust executor. At this time, executors of trusts or estates were entitled to fees for administering the inheritance. While executors were compensated for their troubles, they were also financially liable for any mishandling of the fund. Ann, however, took the matter a step further. Just to show her displeasure with her nephew, she explicitly stated that her nephew James was to receive £5 "and no more" from her estate.[52]

Although no specific reason is stated in any of the wills for the exclusion of James DePeyster, it is probable that those mentioned earlier were among his many relations who were embarrassed by his insolvency and were themselves exposed to scandal by his downfall. If this was indeed the case, then his obvious exclusion makes sense as a way to display their dissatisfaction with his actions and the situation to which he exposed the whole family.

While the family's circumstances were reduced as a result of James's bankruptcy, their family name and familial relations continued to benefit the family. In fact, those social networks, and the goodwill of the extended family, were very likely more valuable to this branch of the DePeyster family after the bankruptcy than before. Consider again the marriage of James's oldest child Margaret (1749–1819) to Colonel Thomas James, the former Major of the Stamp Act fame in 1776. Colonel James came from a family that was not of equivalent social status to the DePeysters before the bankruptcy. This is not to say that he was of a lowly status; indeed, his commission indicates that either his family had some influence and money, or the Colonel had a patron wealthy enough to purchase his commission for him. Rather, the Colonel was not of the elite status the DePeysters were prior to the bankruptcy. Colonel James, however, was himself wealthy. The destroyed contents of his house from the Stamp Act Riots indicate wealth, and later, when the Assembly reimbursed Colonel James for the damages, they awarded him over £1,745, no small sum for the contents of a house.[53] For Colonel James, the marriage provided access to the close-knit elite social networks of New York. For Margaret, her social status and connections allowed her to make a respectable match despite the disruptions of war and economic concerns. Those relations were more than likely the reason Abraham, James's oldest son, secured his commission as a Captain with the King's American Regiment after the infamous "shot heard 'round the world," signaled the start of an entirely different game in 1775.

After the Battles of Lexington and Concord, local Patriots began taking steps to diminish the influence of Loyalists in their communities. This was especially true in New York City, which had long "been regarded on both sides of the Atlantic as a nursery of loyalty," even prior to 1775.[54] This does not mean that New Yorkers were submissive to any and all measures proposed by Parliament; rather, it means that New York had more to lose by parting ways with the Empire due to its dependence on trade. Therefore, New Yorkers worked harder and longer than the other colonies did to come to an equitable settlement with Parliament that would repeal those Acts that were harmful to business than did other colonies. One could argue that New Yorkers were not so much Loyalists as compromisers. Politicians and merchants were afraid that the city's heterogeneous population would unravel without the steadying hand of Empire and that a "revolution might end in chaos."[55] Those factors were some of the main reasons that New York was the last of the thirteen colonies to declare its independence in 1776. As a result of this reluctance to embrace the rebellion wholeheartedly, New York Patriots became even more determined in their efforts to marginalize the Loyalists. This was one of the reasons that Queens County, a Loyalist stronghold, initially had been a place of heavy contestation. Supporters of the Crown counted half the city's merchants among their numbers. This group "tended to be wealthier than their patriot counterparts," and as a general rule they were also Anglican, but as in anything, they chose their sides based on individual experiences and beliefs. As a result, the dividing line between the two sides was often quite thin.[56]

In January 1775, the colonial Assembly for New York adjourned, and with that, New York's colonial government ceased to be an effective, functioning body within the colony. Ad hoc revolutionary committees were already in place throughout much of the colony and took charge of as many duties as they could. In New York, however, both power structures continued for a time to operate simultaneously, although it was clear the revolutionary committees were in charge. That New Yorkers allowed both governments to continue to function points to their reluctance to join the revolutionary movement with enthusiasm. For example, on June 25, 1775, the city held simultaneous celebrations for George Washington (who recently had been appointed commander to the Continental Army) and William Tryon, the Royal Governor (who returned to the colony after a year-long absence).[57] Despite the fact that the Assembly was no longer effective, it continued with the motions of governance throughout these tumultuous years. Another example of this overlap of bodies occurred on February 14, 1776, both the Royal Assembly and the Provisional Congress met in City Hall. Members of the Royal Assembly arrived only to discover that their traditional meeting hall was occupied by the Congress. In order to hold their meeting, the Assembly simply moved 100 feet away and met in the chambers of the New York City Common Council. The Royal Government kept up the pretense until April of 1776, when Governor Tryon returned to London. At that point the Assembly quit meeting altogether, and the Courts also ceased operations.

With the Assembly in recess in January 1775, the Committee of One Hundred (as the revolutionary committee was known at the time) asserted its authority without opposition.[58] As colonial authority and the influence of the elite diminished, many prominent Loyalists fled the city, and some left the colony altogether. The Committee of

One Hundred made arrests and imprisoned those it considered public enemies.[59] By April 1775, the colony convened its first meeting of a provisional congress. Because of New York's known sympathy for the Crown (or at least its commerce), and its reluctance to declare its independence along with the other colonies, the Continental Congress recommended that pressure be maintained on the Loyalists there. Despite this, the Provincial Congress maintained "moderate" treatment of its Loyalists at this point in comparison to other colonies.

After the American Army was in full occupation of New York City in June 1775, the situation for Loyalists deteriorated. The army's presence boosted the Patriot cause, and those inhabitants suspected of Loyalist sentiments "were forced to recant in public, then tarred and feathered, ridden through town on rails, or forced to parade the streets."[60] Episcopal Churches were boarded and stripped of the monarchial trappings; prayer books were burned and clergy scattered. Local persecutions and fear flooded New York City so that by July 1776, only about 5,000 of the City's original 25,000 inhabitants remained.[61]

It appears that James DePeyster avoided the majority of recriminations from his Loyalist stance due in part to his location. The family's estate in Jamaica, Long Island, was a far cry from the City, and also happened to fall within the bounds of Queens County, a Loyalist stronghold.[62] Although repeated attempts were made to bring Queens County into the Patriot fold, Queens County continued to ignore or successfully contest the demands of the New York Provincial Congress.[63] Despite James's location, his Loyalism did not go unnoticed. The Provincial Congress created the "Committee for the Detection of Conspiracies" to track down, disarm, and put on trial "disaffected persons" whose activities might endanger the American cause.[64] In June 1776, the Committee submitted James's name as one of fourteen inhabitants of Jamaica who fit that description. The report went on to state more specifically that James DePeyster "is said to be a dangerous Tory. His son has been pursued several times, but can't be taken."[65] One can only imagine they meant Abraham, who was the first of James's sons to serve and was the most likely to be in the service at this time; however, his other sons, Joseph Reade, James Jr., and Frederick also served with the King's forces.

When the British finally made their appearance in early July 1776, Loyalists from New Jersey, Long Island, Manhattan, and Staten Island rushed to join their ranks.[66] Among them was Abraham DePeyster. In December, at the age of 23, he was commissioned as a captain in the King's American Regiment. Under his commanding officer, Ferguson, Abraham spent much of his time fighting in the southern colonies, most notably at the siege of Charlestown, North Carolina, and most infamously at the Battle of King's Mountain in what today is Tennessee. During this battle, Ferguson was killed and DePeyster forced to surrender. His reputation came under immediate fire for this move, and he applied for and was granted parole. After statements were obtained from witnesses and casualty reports obtained, it seems his reputation, at least among his ilk, was cleansed.[67]

In 1779, William Axtell, member of the King's Council, was given the commission of Colonel and charged with the creation of a company to patrol Long Island. He was also brother-in-law to James DePeyster. Axtell was born in the West Indies and went directly from there to New York, unmarried, to settle an inheritance. While there he met Margareta (Nancy) DePeyster, James's sister, and married her. The couple had no children of their own but brought in "wards," including Elizabeth Shipton and, for a short time, James's son Frederick. At the start of the Revolution, Axtell and his household left New York City and resettled at the Axtell estate, Melrose, in Flatbush.[68] The regiment Axtell created was called the "Nassau Blues,"[69] and he recruited his nephew, Frederick DePeyster, then 18, to serve under him. Frederick went into the position as a captain-lieutenant. He served in the Nassau Blues until 1780 when he accepted a captain's commission in the King's American Regiment at age 22. An oft-repeated but undocumented story of Frederick's military service states that while crossing a river on horseback, Frederick came under fire. The bullet passed through one of his legs and the horse, and then, through his other leg. The bullet killed the horse but Frederick was able to get himself to safety.[70] Regardless of the story's veracity, it stands as an example of the way people thought of Frederick and his approach to the events in his life, with straightforward determination, letting nothing stand in the way of his success.

DePeyster's son, James Jr., also joined the King's American Regiment and was commissioned a Lieutenant in 1776 at the age of 19. James also saw action in the southern colonies and was promoted in 1781 to captain-lieutenant, at age 24. James seems to have been ideally suited for the soldier's life and made a career out of it, staying active even after the Revolution by joining the Royal Artillery under the command of his brother-in-law, Colonel Thomas James. James's second oldest son, Joseph Reade, also fought in the king's forces, but unlike his brothers, he was not commissioned as an officer.

Throughout the war, Loyalists had little reason to believe in anything other than a complete eventual victory over the rebellious colonists. They were certain that when the final victory came, the British government would fulfill its promises to reward the honest Loyalists who took up arms for the mother country and to punish with leniency the rebels. In New York, the sons of the leading families took commissions in newly formed Loyalist regiments with the promise of land, money, and title. Middle- and lower-class New Yorkers also took up arms for the King on the promise of land. Throughout the war, the Loyalists, civilian and military, complained of maltreatment by British officers and soldiers citing among other things, property destruction, and verbal and physical intimidation.[71] They endured these hardships with growing frustration but stayed the course, looking forward to their promised reward.

When the Treaty of Paris, 1783 officially ended open warfare between Great Britain and her former thirteen North American colonies, for those who had remained loyal to Great Britain throughout the Revolution it was just one more in a long series of disappointments. According to the treaty, "real British subjects . . . who have not borne arms" had the right to return without interference and reclaim confiscated property, while "persons of any other description" had one year to move freely in the United States to reclaim property and set their affairs in order. Additionally, the treaty prevented further confiscation of property, protected Loyalists from harm to body and property while in the United States, and ordered the immediate release of any Loyalist "in confinement."[72]

The treaty, with its clauses respecting the Loyalists, caused a major upset in the newly formed United States. In New York, the legislature declared that until England offered to compensate the Americans for their losses, it would not allow the Loyalists to reclaim their lost property.[73] Furthermore, New Yorkers let it be known that any Loyalist attempting to return to their former homes, much less reclaim property, faced insults, tar and feathering, whippings, and other violence; when one or two Loyalists tried this, they quickly discovered the Americans were not spewing idle threats. Loyalists had placed their trust in the fact that Great Britain would win the war, and now the lack of enforcement of the provisions of the 1783 treaty regarding Loyalists was a bitter pill indeed.[74]

Throughout the Revolutionary War, each state had passed some sort of restrictive legislation relating to Loyalists. In some cases, the laws were light, requiring simply an oath of allegiance to the revolutionary government. But in many other cases, the laws were compounded with stern restrictive measures. Those accused of holding Loyalist sympathies faced disenfranchisement, barring or suspension from political office, excessive taxation, property confiscation, quartering of Continental troops, banishment, and execution. Despite the treaty clauses respecting Loyalists, each of the new states refused to retract their anti-Tory legislation. They wanted to remind the Loyalists that only through their acquiescence to the new regime would their presence be tolerated. Those states with a strong or vocal Loyalist presence tended to have the harshest laws. Wallace Brown, in *The Good Americans*, presents the following breakdown: "Harshest"—New York, South Carolina; "Harsh"—Massachusetts, New Jersey, Pennsylvania; "Light"—Rhode Island, Connecticut, Virginia, North Carolina; "Lightest"—New Hampshire, Delaware, Maryland, Georgia.[75]

Enforcement of anti-Tory laws and the level of vigilante action varied from state to state and indeed from community to community; adherence and "Tory-baiting" tended to be most severe directly following the evacuation of the British from an area. In Massachusetts, for instance, immediately following Evacuation Day on March 17, 1776, Loyalists faced tar and feathers, beatings, and imprisonment, among other punitive measures if they remained within the state. By the time the Treaty of 1783 was announced, Massachusetts was no longer as vigilant as it had been. Part of the reason for this was that the overall Loyalist population was, by then, so small in comparison to the larger population that the state could afford to be lenient in its enforcement of the law. David E. Maas has even argued that the introduction of the Treaty revived anti-Tory sentiment, which had largely died down in the state.[76] Pennsylvania also passed severe laws relating to the Loyalists and, after the British left Philadelphia in 1778, became the only state to actually execute Loyalists for treason.[77]

In New York State, those laws that were detrimental to the lives, safety, and property of those who failed to support the Revolution were enforced rigorously throughout the war. Later, when the British withdrew from New York City, those Acts, along with a few new additions, came into force in the city as well. While New York's radical Whigs were determined to enforce the laws just as enthusiastically in the city as in the state at large, they often found this difficult. Throughout the war, so many people in New York City blurred the line of loyalty that full prosecution or even persecution was impossible. As a result, in the immediate aftermath of the war, many people were accosted for Loyalism whether they were guilty or not. Thereafter, once the precedent for harsh treatment was established, only the most obvious or obnoxious Loyalists were thus singled out. In general, if one had not actually taken up arms against the revolutionaries, and if he was willing to remain silent on the issue of his former allegiance, then he was allowed to stay. For those who had taken up arms for the King, who were too outspoken, or who had already fled, the laws were brought fully to bear.[78]

The State of New York deprived Loyalists of their right to vote and hold office, allowed for the banishment of persons of suspected loyalty, and, perhaps most famously, paved the way for the confiscation of Loyalist properties. Under that same spirit, the state also passed an Act of Attainder, which declared fifty-nine leading Loyalists guilty of treason, their property and lives forfeit.[79] As Loyalist property began to accumulate in the state's hands, the legislature acted again and in 1780 authorized the sale of that property.[80] All of the attainted were Episcopalians. William Axtell, brother-in-law to James DePeyster, was one of the fifty-nine. His Flatbush estate was confiscated and sold to Colonel Aquila Giles of the Continental Army.[81]

The estate was a gift to Giles's wife, Elizabeth Shipton, the adopted daughter of William and Margareta Axtell. Although on the surface this transaction appears to be one of convenience to keep the fortune in the family, upon closer inspection it is clear that it was not. Elizabeth met Giles while he was a prisoner of war, possibly at Melrose, which served for a time as a prison. When the Axtells discovered the blossoming relationship, they acted quickly to separate the two. Giles was relocated several times; each time farther and farther away from Elizabeth. The Axtells even returned to their city residence to keep the two apart. Despite these precautions, the two managed to keep up a covert correspondence. Axtell finally threatened to send Elizabeth away from New York in late September or early October 1780, and at that point she agreed to an elopement with Giles. Just a few days later, Axtell's wife Margareta died. When Elizabeth and Giles finally returned to Melrose to ask Axtell for his blessing, he turned them away. Elizabeth was disinherited and was cut out of the will and out of Axtell's life. For the remainder of the war, Elizabeth lived with Giles' family in Maryland. After the confiscation, William Axtell settled in England and never returned to his former home; he died in Surry at 75, in 1795. For $4,500 Giles purchased the Axtell estate and enjoyed life as a prominent family for about twenty years. Eventually, the Gileses were forced to sell the estate and move to a house in the city. In 1822, Giles died followed shortly thereafter by Elizabeth.

When the state was all but certain British tenure in New York City was at an end, it passed the Citation Act (1782) and the Trespass Act (1783). The Citation Act prevented Loyalists from suing any Patriot indebted to them, while at the same time the Trespass Act allowed Patriots to sue Loyalists for damages done to their property while occupied by the British. Former residents descended upon the City expecting payment soon, and "[b]rawls and even organized attacks on [Loyalists] . . . became common."[82]

Of the thousands who fled New York City with the British between 1782 and 1783, most were from "Connecticut, New Jersey, Pennsylvania, and other colonies."[83] Many New York Loyalists were able to blend back into the general population, where the line between the moderates of both sides was a bit fuzzy. James DePeyster, his wife, and their three young daughters remained. The fact that James's fortunes did not revive during the war must have contributed to his acceptance in postwar New York. He came from a prominent family but had neither the wealth to be a target for the confiscation committees, nor the influence to sway others toward his political views. In the end, although labeled a "dangerous tory [sic]," being a resident of Queens County once again benefited James DePeyster as the people there were more concerned with getting events back to normal than extending a conflict that had disrupted their lives.

Despite the fact that New York quite often disregarded the Treaty of 1783 with respect to Loyalist safety and property, and also the fact that many communities countenanced Loyalists in their midst, there was one aspect of the treaty the state was determined to enforce. All who bore arms for the King must go. For many Loyalist soldiers and officers this was not such a hardship. If they had owned property before the war, chances were that it was now long gone, confiscated by local Patriot committees or new governments. Additionally, those who served the King were promised land, and they were still to receive it, just not where they had originally expected. During the war, they thought they would assume ownership of their Patriot neighbors' lands; now those Loyalists learned they would acquire frontier property in Canada. This promise of land actually attracted many Patriots to convert to the British cause at the last moment so that they might participate in the land distribution. The sons and son-in-law of James DePeyster could not stay because they had born arms as officers against the independence of the American states. Thus when the last of the British fleet sailed out of New York harbor on November 25, the DePeysters were among their numbers.

They could not stay; they had to go. With regard to family fortunes and whether or not going would benefit the family, clearly the answer was yes. Abraham DePeyster had no property in New York, nor was he likely to inherit anything of significance in the near future. His prospects in Canada, however, were bright. Officers were promised good land and positions in authority. Thus Abraham, whose prospects were dim in New York, had the chance to be the gentleman he was raised to be in Canada. Frederick's situation was similar to Abraham's but differed in significant ways. Frederick did own land in New York, land he had inherited from relatives at the age of 15 in New York City (lots on Broadway near Cortlandt Street); Bergen County, New Jersey; Bedford, New York; and Ulster County, New York. But once again, his conspicuous activities as an officer in a Loyalist regiment prevented his remaining in New York. He would receive the same benefits as Abraham in Canada for being an officer and perhaps increase the family's fortunes while increasing his own. Throughout Frederick's minority and during his time in Canada, it seems that James DePeyster managed his son's property. For Joseph Reade DePeyster, Canada was also the best option. Joseph Reade had no land in New York, and his marriage to a woman outside his elite circle meant that he would not be able to rely upon his wife's fortune to sustain the family as his father and grandfather had. Additionally, Joseph Reade had served as a soldier in a Loyalist regiment, which meant that he was unable to remain in New York. His service, however, still entitled him to land in Canada, which was more than he could hope for if he attempted to remain in New York. James Jr. chose to remain in the British Army at the end of the war and served with the artillery division. Not only would attempting to stay have endangered the lives and well-being of the family, but leaving provided significant benefits in the form of land and status. In this new arrangement, the DePeysters would continue to be a family of respectability and status.

Chapter 2

Canadian Exile

*I*n the twenty years or so after the British gained control of what we now think of as Canada from the French, the area remained a sparsely settled frontier backwater of the British Empire. Canada had few residents and little business. Life was difficult there. With short growing seasons, farming was both more tenuous and more critical to survival. Winters were harsh, arriving early, leaving late, with temperatures dropping to extreme levels. Despite this, thousands of Loyalists looked to Canada, more specifically Nova Scotia and the frontier, as a refuge when they could, or would, not return to their former homes, and when expense put Britain out of reach. Among these were DePeyster brothers Abraham, 32; Joseph Reade, 29; and Frederick, 25. The majority of refugees just hoped for land and basic starter provisions. For a select group of Loyalists, however, settling in Canada represented an opportunity to shape the world to their wishes. The aspirations of this group triggered political maneuverings and intrigues throughout the small Loyalist world and caused ripples, which affected not only local politics but created such a stir that Parliament was forced to intervene. Throughout the first years of tumultuous settlement, Abraham and Frederick used this chaos, their family name, and their military status as officers to establish themselves among the social elite.

Joseph Reade presents an interesting juxtaposition to his brothers, due to his enlisted status. While lacking the advantages his brothers had militarily, Joseph Reade also worked to improve his situation using the tools available to him. Despite the differences in these brothers, they all had the same goal: to reclaim to one degree or another the prestige and wealth associated with their ancient family name. In this

31

respect, the story of the brothers' time in Canada is not so much the story of exiled Loyalists as it is the story of status, wealth, power, and what those individuals did to achieve what they thought of as their due. Of the brothers, Frederick was the most successful. As a result of his time there, Frederick was able to successfully launch himself into business as a wholesale merchant, among other things, and eventually become the patriarch of his family.

Although the Treaty of Paris, 1783, allowed for noncombatant Loyalists to remain in their former homes, those who had served the King were required to leave. Throughout the thirteen former colonies, many civilian loyalists remained; however, in many locations they were forced to leave. Throughout the war, they left their respective homes, in trickles and in floods, the fortunes of many dependent upon the success of the British Army.[1] The first and perhaps most famous, evacuation of Loyalists occurred in Boston on St. Patrick's Day in 1776. In Massachusetts, the day the Loyalists left, willingly or otherwise, was commemorated as "Evacuation Day" well into the 1860s, and, to this day, remains a secondary cause for celebrating on St. Patrick's Day in many areas of the Bay State. Evacuation Day still remains a legal holiday in Massachusetts. When the British troops were no longer able to protect the Loyalists, many moved behind British lines, often to New York but sometimes to other locations within the British Empire, in order to safeguard their lives. Other, lesser waves of Loyalist evacuations occurred out of New Jersey in 1777, Philadelphia in 1778, Rhode Island in 1779, Virginia in 1779, 1780, and 1781, and South Carolina in 1781 (which Frederick most likely helped facilitate, given the company in which he served).[2] New York would follow with its own waves throughout 1783.

As news from the peace talks filtered back to the United States, it became clear that those who left would not be returning, and soon even more would be forced to leave. While many Loyalists attempted to slip out of New York City and go back to their former homes to live in peace with the results of the Revolution, other Loyalists, from the areas surrounding New York were forced into the city for protection against their angry Patriot neighbors.[3] For those Loyalists who could not return to their former homes, and for those who had borne arms for the Loyalist cause, the decision of where to begin their new lives was at hand. For the majority of fleeing Loyalists, who were overwhelmingly from "humble economic origins,"[4] Canada (most prominently Nova Scotia) was the destination of choice (Alan Taylor states that the Canadian provinces received at least 50,000 Loyalists in all),[5] due to both proximity and cost of travel.

Since the time of the American Revolution, historians assumed that Loyalists tended to be from elite backgrounds and took their wealth and knowledge with them when they left the United States. This idea has some appeal given the economic depression the United States slipped into following the conclusion of the war. The first historian to challenge the "elite background" assumption was Esther Clark Wright in *The Loyalists of New Brunswick*, originally printed in 1955. Wright systematically challenged and overturned the common theory by compiling a list of the Loyalists of New Brunswick. This list details the names, occupations, former homes, Revolutionary service, and land grants for each household head Wright could track down. The list demonstrates that the majority of household heads were working men; while the list is incomplete and historians have since found numerous errors, historians of Loyalist Canada still agree that those inadequacies do not overturn her thesis that the majority of Loyalist settlers to New Brunswick were working-class, not the elite. In fact, corrections and additions only seem to reinforce her initial findings that most Loyalists were farmers or tradesmen prior to the Revolution. According to Condon, "only eight percent of New Brunswick Loyalists had the motive and the means to seek compensation for property losses from the Loyalist Claims Commission."[6]

For the wealthiest of Loyalists, like William Axtell, brother-in-law to James DePeyster, the destination of choice was Great Britain. For most Loyalists, however, that option was simply too expensive, and many who did move to London soon relocated in frustration. Their fortunes, which had put them in the elite echelons of colonial society, were not enough to support them in a similar manner in Britain. Some Loyalists chose to resettle in the British West Indies. This also was an expensive venture. Additionally, not everyone favored a new home so far from, or so much warmer than, the old.[7]

By 1782, Nova Scotia, particularly Halifax, had already received thousands of evacuees from various locations in the thirteen colonies. The situation there was dire as winter arrived that year (just as it was during the next few years), and the frontier communities of that colony struggled to accommodate new arrivals. Houses were overcrowded, people were stuffed into every standing structure, and still there was not enough room for everyone.[8] The refugees looked to newly appointed Governor John Parr for a solution to their woes. Unfortunately for Parr, his patron, Lord Shelburne, fell from power in London. Shelburne's political career followed a path similar to that of many of his contemporaries. The tempestuous political situation in Great Britain following the American Revolutionary War meant that many politicians rose and fell from power in a matter of months when they failed to provide George III with the answers he wanted. Shelburne returned to power a few years later when William Pitt the Younger became Prime Minister. At this point, however, he was out of power and had no influence to protect John Parr from attack. This made Parr cautious in his approach to the problem of Loyalists for fear of losing his position by angering the British government, the Loyalists, members of his own government, or some combination of the three.[9] To further complicate the position of both Parr and the Loyalists, instructions from Britain regarding the Loyalist resettlement were slow to nonexistent in their arrival as new leadership in London preferred to direct its attention to other neglected areas of the Empire.

In an attempt to limit the chaos of the arrival of the Loyalist refugees, the military embraced the idea of allowing the civilians to organize themselves into "associations." The military actually preferred working with associations, rather than individuals, because it streamlined the process of removal. Each association had a board of agents who negotiated with the government of Nova Scotia for "provisions for one year, clothing, medicine, building material, farm utensils, mill equipment, . . . weapons," and land for each family in order to smooth the transition of the Loyalists into their new homes.[10] It was also the responsibility of the board of agents to organize their members' removal from New York and work with the military. Two of the more prominent groups were the Port Roseway Association and the Bay of

Fundy Adventurers.[11] At the same time, the more closely the associations worked with the military, the more they restructured themselves along military lines. Members were broken down into "companies," each with a designated spokesman, which were then assigned to a ship and a departure date.[12] It should come as no surprise that those members with higher "rank" in the association were also those with greater wealth and social stature. These associations, and their organization, came to dominate the politics of early Loyalist settlement in Saint John (the settlement at the mouth of the Saint John River); people stayed in their associations, and their agents continued to negotiate with the government on their behalf as well as their own. This military-style organization of the civilians further reinforced the social dominance of the military officers such as Abraham and Frederick DePeyster.[13]

Despite the best efforts of these associations to make the move as painless as possible, the Loyalists still encountered many hazards. Having little space in which to travel, the majority of evacuating Loyalists were forced to sell their goods as quickly as possible before the move, retaining only a precious few items for themselves. Although the poor had precious little to transport in the first place, all those but the wealthiest of the Loyalists found themselves in this situation. The majority of Loyalists were neither dirt-poor, nor were they extremely wealthy; today we would probably refer to them as middle class. To complicate matters, the new American authorities were gripped with paranoia, and carefully monitored what possessions the Loyalists carried off with them.[14] There was a great fear among New Yorkers that the evacuating Loyalists would tear down their houses, and those of the Patriots, and transport them to Canada, although only 10 percent of the Loyalist families would have had enough money to hire private transportation to accomplish such a feat. This fear resulted in the confiscation of a number of legitimately owned goods. As a consequence of both space restrictions and confiscation, Loyalist refugees arrived at their new homes on the frontiers with little to begin their new lives.[15]

When the first groups of refugees evacuated from New York in 1783, they found very little was actually prepared for their arrival in Nova Scotia. Even worse, previous waves of refugees from prior years occupied every available house, hovel, shed, chicken coop, and tent.[16]

As a result, despite their best efforts, many of these association refugees had no place to go. Nevertheless, the early arrivals in 1783 often fared better than those who came later in the year (there were at least six different waves of refugees and military companies during 1783),[17] since they had enough time to construct small huts for themselves to help make it through the winter. As later waves of refugees arrived, conditions became more and more crowded.[18] By necessity, lots claimed by early arrivals were divided and subdivided to make room for the newcomers. With the arrival of each succeeding wave of refugees in 1783, resources and provisions became more and more scarce. Thus when the last arrivals made it to Canada, they met with evacuees who had arrived during the war and who, by 1783, were desperate to hold on to what little they had scrounged up. Meanwhile, others had given up, exhausted by the effort required to eke out any type of living on the Canadian frontier. Even as waves of refugees from the New York evacuation arrived, earlier evacuees fled Canada for other locations— sometimes within the Empire, usually not in Canada, most often to return to their former homes, come what may.[19] Clashes over shelter, food, and employment characterized the early years of Loyalist settlement in Canada. First-person accounts from this time read like those of Jamestown during its early years, minus the cannibalism. The suffering the Loyalists endured and survived became a badge of honor for later generations who styled themselves the most loyal of all British subjects, but at the time, Loyalists who had left their civilized homes for the frontier saw their predicament as one more betrayal by the British government.

One of the principal problems Governor Parr faced was the need to quickly distribute land to the Loyalists and settle the Loyalists on that land. For those Loyalists who wanted to settle near Halifax or in the part of Nova Scotia by the mouth of the Bay of Fundy, near the Saint John River (such as the military, the Bay of Fundy Adventurers, and the DePeyster brothers) the process was a long, drawn-out, contentious affair.

The area of Nova Scotia north of the Bay of Fundy was densely wooded and sparsely settled. The land was riddled with lakes and streams that flowed through flat, fertile land; providing easy transport across the territory and a multitude of fish to compliment the rich wildlife that inhabited the woods. To further enhance the land, the coastline was dotted with deep harbors that could accommodate even the largest of ships. Despite these attractive qualities, the region was sparsely settled for a reason: the climate was severe with long winters and short growing seasons. The amount of snow the region received meant that settlers would remain isolated for a good part of the year, not only from each other, but also from game and fish. To complicate matters, while the harbors were deep, the bay itself was treacherous to navigate, with extreme tidal fluctuations, strong, unpredictable currents, dense fog, and large rocks.[20]

Yet the area was not devoid of population. It is estimated that in 1783, before the arrival of the Loyalists, the area north of the Bay of Fundy had about 3,600 inhabitants; including Native Americans, Acadians, and British Americans.[21] For the most part, the Native American and Acadian populations tried to stay out of the way of the British American residents (both new and old) and often retreated in the face of encroachment. The British Americans lived in four population centers. Of the two most substantial settlements, one was at the mouth of the Saint John River and the other was farther up the river at Maugerville.[22] With the exception of the settlement at the mouth of the Saint John River (which was a commercial enterprise), these British Americans were former residents of New England who had moved north during the land rush in the 1760s following the French and Indian War.

Although many Loyalists viewed the sparsely populated area as ripe for the taking, the land was not unclaimed. Following the French and Indian War, large grants of land were made to speculators who tried to lure British settlers to the newly acquired territory. Although some brave souls relocated to the area, generally land speculation north of the Bay of Fundy was a bust. Many men of wealth, whether from England, Nova Scotia, or the other American colonies—men like Thomas Hutchinson and members of the Nova Scotia government—invested in the land only to see no return. The lands were left wild and undeveloped as the owners turned their attention to more pressing and more profitable matters. According to the terms of most land grants made for Canada in the 1760s, the land needed to have at least one person to every 200 acres within ten years or be subject to forfeiture, a legal process known as escheat. By 1783, the majority of those lands claimed in the 1760s should have been escheated to the government years before. But with the demand for this land low, and with many of the owners holding important positions in the governments in Nova Scotia and in London, it was less trouble for Nova Scotia simply to allow the land to remain as it was. When Loyalists fled to Nova Scotia after the War, the land was suddenly in high demand, and those still in possession of their title to the 1760s grants meant to make their investment profitable at last. At the same time, Loyalists were not willing to pay the high prices suddenly demanded for the frontier land, and they demanded the escheat process begin immediately to invalidate earlier claims.[23]

When Governor Parr learned that both the military and the civilian groups had focused on the St. John River Valley for their settlements, he was alarmed. For new settlers to get valid title, they had to either buy the land from the original claimants or challenge those claimants with legal action to seize the earlier titles. And because the government had promised the Loyalists free land, there was very little likelihood of their actually paying for the land. Parr tried to redirect the Loyalists to parts of Nova Scotia that he thought might more easily (or less controversially) be developed, like southern Nova Scotia or the area just north of the St. Croix river, the boundary with the United States. Nevertheless, Parr knew that the Loyalists could not stay in Halifax and as a result he allowed them to move on to their intended destinations, even that of the Saint John River Valley.

This, then, was the situation in Nova Scotia at the start of New York evacuations. Governor Parr, without a patron or instructions to protect him, was forced to grapple with a difficult situation that was about to get worse. The British government not only subsidized the transportation of the Loyalists to Nova Scotia, but they also decided to subsidize the voyage to Nova Scotia for those Loyalists who fled to Britain to avoid the war.[24] The majority of Loyalists in Britain were individuals who had wealth and status in the colonies prior to the war. Upon their arrival in Britain, most stayed in London, hoping to have some influence on the government over the prosecution of the war. Because they did not expect to remain there long, they did not pursue, and were not seriously considered for, employment in government positions, new investment opportunities, or any endeavors that required some degree of permanence. Once in Britain, however, these Loyalists were separated from their wealth in the colonies, and as their debts mounted they began to agitate for government compensation of their suffering. The government responded by granting "pensions" to the Loyalists in London; however, while the Loyalists viewed this as compensation for their suffering, the government saw the pension as a handout. By providing them with passage to Nova Scotia, the government would no longer have to pay these Loyalists, some of whom received a large monthly amount. These Loyalists would become the problem of Governor Parr. It should be noted that removal to Nova Scotia was voluntary and a good number of the London Loyalists chose to remain in London rather than live in the wilderness of Canada.

The evacuation of New York in 1783 was the largest of its kind, with the military population alone conservatively estimated near 10,000, necessitating that it take place in waves throughout the spring, summer, and fall of 1783.[25] General Sir Guy Carleton, commander-in-chief of the British forces of North America, was in charge of the British evacuation of New York. Guy Carleton had a long military career, and early on he participated in the Jacobite Rebellion and the War of the Austrian Succession. During the Seven Years' War, Carleton served in Germany, Canada, France, and Havana. In 1766, Carleton was appointed acting governor of Quebec, and he became the official governor in 1768. While he was serving as governor, the American Revolution broke out; Carleton organized the Defense of Quebec in 1775 and the counteroffensive into New York in 1776. Carleton was knighted in June of 1776, and was raised to the peerage as Lord Dorchester of Oxford County in 1786. In 1782, Carleton was appointed commander-in-chief of the British forces of North America. It was in that position that he oversaw the Loyalist evacuation of New York. In this position, Carleton experienced not only difficulties with former Patriot residents of New York City returning to find their property destroyed or taken over by others, but also problems involving the two opposing military forces now confined within the same city. There was one other element where perhaps he did not expect so many problems, but from which he received a multitude: the evacuating Loyalists themselves.

While on one level all Loyalists shared the experience of leaving home, family, and friends, not all Loyalists were equal.[26] There was a small group of men who, prior to the war, ranked as men of consequence in their former homes in terms of position and status, both economic and social. This small group of men, which included the DePeyster brothers, was determined to regain some of their former glory, and they believed they had the political acumen and contacts within the British government to do so.[27] The first and primary way they believed they could do this was through large land grants. With large amounts of land, these men could lease the property, gaining tenants (who in their vision would be rightly deferential) and saving themselves from physical labor while still reaping a profit. This plan to become great landlords, remaking themselves in the ideal image of the landed English gentleman, was wrought with pitfalls. To begin with, the government limited land grants to a maximum of 1,000 acres, while it required at least 5,000 acres to become the great landlords of their dreams. Further, these men knew that turning the frontier lands into profitable farmlands would be neither quick nor easy, which meant they would be cash-poor until significant profits could be generated. To remedy the situation, these men decided the tried, true, respected, and profitable route of government service was in order.[28] No doubt this was a course they would have pursued anyway; however, the threat of being cash-poor meant that government positions were imperative to maintaining the elite status they desired. This would also prove problematic, for it was far easier to imagine the glory of a government position than to actually obtain one. Not only did an individual have to curry favor with the government in Britain (and following Yorktown, the British government was very unstable), but there also needed to be offices to fill. For all of these variables to come together in perfect alignment, these elite Loyalists would need a new colony.

The idea of a new colony in North America was not original to the Loyalists. As early as 1779, Lord North asked William Knox, Undersecretary of State for the American colonies, to prepare a plan of government for the establishment of a Loyalist colony in the region that is now the state of Maine to be called New Ireland. The idea of a separate province came up again at the end of the war in conjunction with the question of what to do with the Loyalist soldiers who had been promised land in exchange for their services. The government preferred to keep the men in close proximity to one another, should their services be required once more. Edward Winslow, member of the Loyalist elite and officer in the King's army, became the champion for a separate Loyalist colony. If he and his cohort could convince the British Government that its goals of keeping the American regiments together could best be served by the creation of a new colony, and at the same time further their own interests, so much the better. A new colony would create government positions, and with the Loyalist elite in charge, perhaps the restriction on acreage might be modified and their hopes for the future fulfilled.

This struggle to create a separate Loyalist colony is referred to as the "Partition Movement" because in order to create a new colony, Nova Scotia must be divided into two separate colonies. It should be noted that Loyalist officers and the civilian Loyalist elite did not want partition for partition's sake; they wanted the partition of Nova Scotia in order to create an environment conducive to maintaining the status quo hierarchy. Thus, the Partition Movement was about more than just the division of Canada.

Both contemporaries and historians identify the first action in the Partition Movement as having occurred in March of 1783, before the evacuations of New York. Officers of the Provincial Regiments, including Muster Master General Edward Winslow, Major John Coffin, Lt. Col. George Turnbull, Lt. Col. William, Lt. Col. Isaac Allen, and Colonel Gabriel G. Ludlow (all of whom would go on to serve in prominent positions in New Brunswick), drew up a petition and presented it to General Sir Guy Carleton, who then forwarded the petition to Governor John Parr of Nova Scotia.[29] This petition, signed shortly before official word of the Treaty arrived in New York, recognized the fact that as soldiers for the Crown, they would not be permitted to remain in the United States. It also proposed that those men should be rewarded thus: 300 acres to each private, 350 for corporals, 400 to sergeants, 5,000 acres to field and staff officers, and to each an allowance of clothing, arms, building tools, and half-pay for life. The officers were not so crass as to state such an outrageous difference outright; instead, they couched the 5,000 acres in polite terms, stating that they should receive the "same allowance" that had been granted at the conclusion of the last war (Seven Years').[30] Neither Abraham nor Frederick DePeyster signed this petition, but several of the signers were among their close friends and acquaintances. For instance, George Turnbull named Frederick DePeyster as executor to his estate, and often during their time in Canada the two associated with the others mentioned above.[31] It is important to note that this petition, which preserved the hierarchy established by military life, was not protested by the enlisted men, who knew of the terms and were grateful to know that their officers were working to secure more land for them than they currently owned. One would not expect, therefore, that a similar civilian petition would be the cause of much trouble, yet it was.

The civilian counterpart to the military petition is now known as the Petition of the Fifty-five.[32] This petition was brought before General Carleton in the summer of 1783 and was signed by fifty-five men, prominent in their local communities as landowners, and political and social leaders, men like attorney Ward Chipman and clergyman Charles Inglis, who would also go on to play prominent roles in New Brunswick. These men did not serve in the military during the war. The petition requested that these men be granted 5,000 acres of land each by virtue of their prewar status and so that they would become the landed gentry of Nova Scotia, which would help to preserve the system of deference and more closely tie the remaining North American colonies to Great Britain.[33] General Carlton thought this petition very reasonable and forwarded it on to Governor John Parr.[34] It makes sense that some of the agents for the Loyalist associations were signers of the Petition of the Fifty-five,[35] but it is also for this very reason that many Loyalist settlers would look skeptically upon the efforts of the associations and their agents and eventually view their actions as one more element in the Partition Movement.

When the petition's contents were made known, however, attorney Elias Hardy and merchant Samuel Hake immediately drew up a counterpetition to the fifty-five that represented the interests of a larger number of men of lesser status. This counterpetition was "signed" by 600 men, but usually it is referred to as the "Counter-Petition" or the "Counter-Petition to the Fifty-five" rather than the "Counter-Petition of the 600." The fact that a good percentage of these men used Xs to sign their names reveals their lower status. The counterpetition was not about loyalty to the Crown, although they couched their protest in terms of loyalty; rather, it was about land and other advantages in what would be their new home. The counterpetition stated that the fifty-five had no right to take such preemptive measures when all Loyalists sacrificed for the King, and all understood they would receive the same compensation. The counterpetition charged that if the fifty-five were granted their land, those fiefdoms would engulf the most fertile spots of Nova Scotia, leaving everyone else to suffer on barren and remote lands or to become a tenant "to those most of whom they consider as their superiors in nothing but deeper art and keener policy."[36] One of the 600 signers of the counterpetition was Joseph Reade DePeyster, who as an enlisted soldier was entitled to at least 300 acres under the military petition. Members of the Loyalist elite charged that Hardy and Hake were simply taking out their frustrations as two men who were "failed" at their chosen careers and had been marginalized by the elite.[37] Nevertheless, those two men succeeded at motivating and organizing the nonelite Loyalists. Carleton immediately backed down, stating that the Petition of the Fifty-five exceeded government guidelines for land allotment, and that he was sure Parr would turn it down. Further, Carleton promised to forward the counterpetition to Governor Parr with all haste. As D. G. Bell states, the Petition of the Fifty-five "reveals the fragile unity of the Loyalist community, in New York as at Saint John."[38] Although neither the military petition nor the Petition of the Fifty-five went into effect, the fissures revealed by their creation would only grow wider throughout the first years of Loyalist settlement in Canada.

Thanks in part to their status as officers, Abraham and Frederick DePeysters' situation was not as dire as that of other Loyalist refugees, including their brother Joseph Reade. While Frederick DePeyster's personal wealth was substantial thanks to the various inheritances he received from relatives, Abraham DePeyster was not as wealthy as his brother. Many of the relatives who favored Frederick with land and legacies omitted Abraham from their wills. Abraham's marriage may have mitigated his financial situation, as his wife came from the Livingston family. However, the exact date of his marriage to Catherine Livingston is unknown; most histories simply state that he was married around the time that he left for Canada.[39] Thus in Abraham's case it seems that his military commission and family name, not wealth, made the difference to his position in Canada, while for Frederick, wealth could have come into play. Assuming Frederick and Abraham sailed with their companies, they would have sailed with either the July or fall fleets. Joseph Reade, who was not an officer, had very little money, but did have a wife and a child: he would have sailed with the October Fleet, very late in the season, with prospects not quite as bright under the plan of the elites.[40]

By the time the British military fully evacuated New York on November 21, 1783, and its personnel arrived in Saint John, the land was much divided, though titles were not firmly established. The British government had decided, upon the recommendation of General Carleton, to settle the regiments together on land along the Saint John River rather than at the mouth of the river, with the regiments receiving their settlement north of Fredericton.[41] They also decided upon the amount of land to be granted for civilians and military alike. Each civilian head of house was to receive 100 acres, and an additional 50 for each family member. The civilian allotment was also granted to military personnel, who also received their military allotment. The military allotment mandated that privates would receive 100 acres; officers the rank of subaltern and below would receive 500 acres each; captains would receive 700 acres; and field officers would receive 1,000 acres.[42] This meant that Frederick DePeyster was entitled to 800 acres, Abraham 850 acres, and Joseph Reade 300 acres. However, no one was to receive more than 200 acres until everyone had received his basic grant.[43]

Despite this proclamation, neither soldier nor civilian could get title until the earlier land grants were rescinded throughout the area. But many individuals staked their claims anyway, especially where owners were absent, leading later to conflicting claims and overlapping boundaries. In areas where land was settled and landowners in residence, as in the Maugerville area, the Loyalists accused them of disloyalty in order to nullify their existing land titles. Many early settlers were displaced in this process. During this time, Abraham and other leading Loyalists like Lt. Col. Gabriel Dveber and Major John Coffin were appointed as magistrates for Sunbury County, Nova Scotia. As a result, Abraham moved his family to the area to fulfill his duties.[44] While he may have received title to his 850 acres, that title could not have been clear because the escheat process had not yet begun. Abraham was also granted the rank of Colonel when he agreed to serve in the Nova Scotia militia. In addition, the position of magistrate came with the promise of an income. While the Loyalist officers of Canada would eventually receive half-pay from the British government, this was not granted until after the separation of New Brunswick from Nova Scotia and Governor Carleton's arrival in 1784. There is no more specific date for his arrival except the vague statement that the Governor arrived before winter arrived in 1784. Abraham must have felt secure in his new position, and was no doubt somewhat dismayed as the situation north of the Bay of Fundy deteriorated into chaos over the winter of 1783 to 1784.

Despite the eagerness of some Loyalists to get to their lands, many others remained at St. John, squatting on whatever patch of land would support a tent. Before long, the order and deference that the elite Loyalists touted as the true evidence of the people's loyalty to the Crown began to break down. More and more people, including Governor Parr, were urged by Elias Hardy and his men to question the authority of the Loyalist elites, recalling the divisions created by the Petition of Fifty-five. This was significant for there was a certain amount of risk in opposing the accepted authority; from charges of disloyalty to acting in a manner similar to that of the Americans often followed such opposition. Accusations of fraud against the company agents and the Loyalist elite began to circulate throughout the settlement of Saint John. Governor Parr further delayed the process of escheat north of the Bay of Fundy, as he was now convinced that the Loyalist elite would use their land to challenge his government. This delay only served to keep the Loyalists in Saint John in overcrowded conditions and off their promised lands, to the further detriment of deference toward the Loyalist elite, and law and order.[45] It should be noted that Governor John Parr was extremely helpful and prompt in the settling of the Port Roseway Association; the escheat process began immediately, and Parr cut through much red tape for this particular group. He also took the liberty of renaming their settlement Shelburne after his patron.

Throughout this time Joseph Reade DePeyster's name often appears on the petitions of the nonelites to protest the maneuverings of the elites. Although we do not know much about Joseph Reade's life in Canada, it seems clear that he shared the experience of most Loyalist refugees who were poor and scrabbling to hold on to the little they had to begin with. The incident of the damaged blankets provides key insight to the difference in perspective with which the various sides, Loyalists (both elite and nonelite), the government in London, and the military, viewed the situation. Unexpectedly in 1783, blankets arrived at Saint John, however, the Loyalists discovered the blankets were hole-ridden. The Loyalists felt that once again their government, for whom they sacrificed so much, had turned its back on them, giving them second-hand, worthless blankets. The Loyalists assumed this was a reflection of the government's opinion of them. Petitions of protest were drawn up, signed by a large number of people, and forwarded to the Army who had initially sent the blankets. Unbeknown to the Loyalists, the blankets sent to Saint John were Army castoffs, destined for incineration until someone thought that the desperate refugees might appreciate even a damaged blanket, for many of the refugees had not even that to their name. This act of charity was misunderstood by the Loyalists and their protests were resented by the Army. There would be no more blankets from the Army, and the Loyalists would retain hard feelings at the suspected slight.[46] For a civilian (and overwhelmingly poor) population that already felt ill-used by the government in being sent to a frontier area and given few or shoddy provisions, the blanket incident was the last straw. While the Partition Movement initially grew out of the Loyalist elite's desire for land and offices, in the end, it was the problems of the nonelite and the seeming inability of Nova Scotia to administer the St. John area from Halifax that moved the government in London to separate the territory north of the Bay of Fundy from Nova Scotia, creating the new colony of New Brunswick on June 18, 1784. One month after this, Joseph Reade DePeyster's name last appears in any official record; he was 31.[47]

Throughout the winter of 1783 to 1784, the situation in St. John deteriorated. The carefully laid plans of the Loyalist elite and their military counterparts to maintain order based on deference fell apart. The refusal of Governor Parr to begin the escheat process meant the Loyalists were forced to stay in St. John, wasting time and resources on shelters they did not intend to remain in for long. The nonelite were particularly upset and placed the blame for the situation squarely on the shoulders of the Loyalist elite, whose maneuverings had stalled the process of escheat and settlement to the detriment of all. They began to question the authority the Loyalist elite claimed to have. Their anger and frustration at the situation often took physical form; rioting was commonly reported back to London, raising more than a few questions as to what was going on in the American colony. Although the Loyalist elite were not happy about the situation, they used it to their advantage; they sent representatives and petitions to both the government and their friends in London claiming that Parr's refusal to begin the escheat process proved he was unequal to the task before him. In his attempt to thwart the designs of the Loyalist elite, Parr unwittingly gave them a legitimate grievance against himself and lent credence to their argument that a partition of Nova Scotia was indeed necessary.[48] These elite Loyalists still retained the friendship and influence of General Carleton, whose opinion London still considered authoritative on matters relating to North America, and they effectively used that friendship for their own purposes.[49] This is not to say that Carleton was an unwitting participant. Carleton had his own designs for the remaining North American territories, and partition fit into his own plans rather nicely. Carleton hoped to convince the British Government that the remaining colonies needed to be united under a Governor-General. Once united, the Governor-General would handle the day-to-day issues of those colonies, lessening the burden on the government in London. Having solved the dilemma of the remaining American colonies so nicely for the British government, Carleton hoped to be granted the peerage.

As General Sir Guy Carleton and the Partition Movement seemed to be gaining ground, Governor Parr moved quickly to head them off. In February 1784, Parr sent the Chief Justice of Nova Scotia, Bryan Finucane, to St. John to mediate property disputes and restore order. While Finucane's visit was largely successful in calming the general populace, he also garnered the contempt of the elites. In his urgency to restore order, Finucane "applied the principles of *equality* to all the matters under dispute,"[50] giving the same weight to the claims of the nonelite as he did the elite, often deciding in favor of the nonelite and further endangering the elite's carefully laid plans of hierarchy and deference. The elite also blamed Elias Hardy for Finucane's actions, as they believed Hardy's rhetoric had an undue influence on the Chief Justice. The elite Loyalists, who at every turn emphasized hierarchy and deference, threatened open revolt against Finucane's decisions. The elite were committed to their vision of the Loyalist settlement as laid out in early 1783, that theirs would be "the most gentleman-like government on earth" and "the envy of the American States"; but as Ann Gorman Condon states, "Finucane's visit . . . revealed, with shocking clarity, how insubstantial their actual authority was, so long as they were subject to the government of Nova Scotia."[51]

The hopes of the Loyalist elite seemed to crumble in early 1784 shortly after William Pitt the Younger, assumed the offices of Prime Minister. While Pitt seemed not to care much about the American colonies one way or the other, his ascension brought Lord Shelburne, a patron of Governor Parr, back to power.[52] The situation in St. John had gone too far, however, and had come to the attention of too many in Britain; the government in London had to act. Many Loyalists living in London gave testimony during the public hearing on the North American colonies; the elite Loyalists were hopeful that all of their recommendations would be passed without question, especially as Governor Parr's appointed advocate, Bryan Finucane, did not arrive in time to testify. Yet they were disappointed in many aspects. While the partition of Nova Scotia was granted, and the colony of New Brunswick was established on June 18, 1784, the British government did so on the basis of administration (i.e., efficiency), not on the idea of creating "the most gentleman-like government on earth." In other words, the government in London agreed that events proved that Nova Scotia as one colony was just too large to administer properly from Halifax. Nevertheless, the government in London was ever-practical and realized that a new colony would have many posts to fill. However, they did not give those positions to Edward Winslow and his cohort, but instead gave them to London Loyalists who were drawing large pensions and had so far resisted leaving London. Still, there were consolations for Saint John's elite. One was that the British Government officially decided to continue the navigation system, thus locking the United States out of the West Indies, and giving those in the Canadian colonies a huge financial opportunity. No doubt this particularly pleased Frederick DePeyster, who established himself as a merchant in St. John. Perhaps he even decided to enter into business because of this decision. Another consolation was that General Carleton's brother, Thomas Carleton, was named as the governor of the new colony and he was determined to get the Loyalists of New Brunswick on their land as quickly as possible. In doing so, Carleton eased the resentment of both elite and nonelites at having been delayed so long in claiming their just rewards. An added benefit of settling the Loyalists on their lands was that the population of St. John would drop and there would be less threat of civil disorder from that quarter as a result.[53]

Governor Thomas Carleton was, like his brother, a career military man. He was a man of action who made decisions and stuck to them; he did not tolerate people who questioned his authority, and he expected results. By the time Governor Carleton arrived in New Brunswick in the fall of 1784, he and his advisors already had a plan in mind for the direction of the new government. Carleton accepted, almost without deviation, all of the plans laid out by the Loyalist elite for the structure of the colony's government, everything from governing structure to economic measures and the location of the capital. Under Governor Carleton's direction, the government of New Brunswick was established over the winter of 1784 to 1785, and the measures instituted during that time dominated the colony and helped establish its character. One of the first things Governor Carleton instituted was military half-pay for life. This action alone demonstrates a key different between Parr and Carleton. Parr followed orders and waited for permission before acting, whereas Carleton tended to act first and, if necessary, ask for forgiveness later. The government in London did not give prior approval for the half-pay, and had it balked at Carleton's provision, the governor would have been on the hook for the funds himself. As it was, London gave its blessing to the measure. For Frederick and Abraham, this meant a much-needed additional source of cash. Perhaps more than anything else, the newly appointed Governor bypassed the problems with former grants by requiring that all existing grants be reregistered within three months or be forfeited, a decision that bypassed traditional legal order and favored resident owners over nonresident owners. Again, his actions were blessed after the fact. The Governor also began the escheat process against the old land grants of the 1760s. These two devices quickly cleared up many land disputes and freed up vast amounts of land, and by the end of 1785 the government of New Brunswick closed the books on land distribution and settlement.[54] Under the new government, military personnel received first consideration when they divided once and for all the vast Canadian landscape. Abraham's grant at Maugerville in Sunbury County was renewed, and in 1785 Abraham was granted the position of Sheriff of Sunbury County.[55] Later, in 1786, Abraham was also granted a town lot on the western side of Saint John, but he most likely leased this property as his primary residence was at Maugerville.[56]

There, at Maugerville, Abraham and his wife, Catherine Livingston (1759/60–1839) began their family.[57] The two married around the time of Abraham's departure for Canada, but the exact date is unknown. Most reports place the wedding date just prior to Abraham's departure from New York while a few others place the marriage date in 1785. Catherine was the daughter of John Livingston who was a prominent Loyalist throughout the Revolutionary War. He spent the duration in New York City, rather than retreating to Livingston Manor as various other family members did. Regardless of his Loyalist status, his Patriot family members used his position in New York to obtain items across enemy lines. Although it is unlikely that John Livingston went to Canada after the war, his sons, who served with Abraham during the war, did resettle in Canada. Prior to the war, John Livingston was quite successful as a merchant, but we do not know whether or how his wealth survived the war. Likewise, we do not know what type of wealth Catherine brought with her into the marriage. If Catherine did bring wealth into the marriage, mounting bills indicate that it was quickly spent, and as their family grew (five children before 1793[58]) the compensation from his government position became less and less satisfactory.

Abraham did not work the land himself. In keeping with the ideals of deference and hierarchy of the Loyalist elite, which also happened to be DePeyster family ideals, he used hired men.[59] Unfortunately for Abraham, in the chaotic, poverty-ridden days of early settlement, cheap labor was hard to come by; most men had their own land, which required their attentions to ensure that their families did not starve. It is possible that Abraham leased his lands as the Loyalist elite planned, but there are no records that indicate this was the case. If he did lease his land, he did not see a large enough return to sustain his family financially. Abraham also utilized his slaves in maintaining the household. Although the British did free the slaves of Patriots during the Revolutionary War, Loyalists were allowed to retain their slaves and transport them with their other belongings. Many Loyalists lost their slaves during the evacuation process as returning Patriots kept a close eye on any black individual leaving with the British, both those who were slaves and those who claimed freedom. Although it is uncertain whether Abraham brought his slaves with him out of New York, we know through surviving bills of sale that Abraham purchased at least two slaves while in New Brunswick.[60] Thus, while not living at the standards to which he believed himself entitled, Abraham was not poor and was certainly better off than many Loyalists.

While New Brunswick seemed to be coming together, it was not what the Loyalist elite had dreamed of. The hoped-for deference and unity did not show up on cue. As soon as Carleton and his advisors established the functioning parameters for the government, factions began to emerge, partly due to the location of the capital. Although Saint John was by far the largest settlement within the colony, Carleton and his advisors consciously decided not to locate the capital of the province at that place. Rather, they chose the city of Fredericton in York County. Part of the reason for this was the central location of Fredericton within the colony, which, they hoped, would "encourage wide-spread settlement."[61] Another reason was the military advantage offered by an upriver location, which was close to the former soldiers whose land grants began just north of the town. Carleton and his advisors also hoped that the Fredericton location would emphasize an agricultural economy as opposed to a commercial economy, not to mention that life in a commercial city could become explosive, as the events of the winter of 1783 to 1784 had shown.[62]

Politics in the city of Saint John very quickly became defined by two opposing forces, the "Lower Covers" and the "Upper Covers," also referred to as the opposition party and the government party, respectively. The Lower Cove faction was led by Elias Hardy. This group questioned the high-handed manner in which Governor Carleton set policy and succeeded in frustrating many of his efforts in the newly established Colonial Assembly. The Upper Cove faction often looked to the likes of Ward Chipman for leadership and tended to support Governor Carleton's programs for the colony.[63] While initially these sides closely resembled the lines drawn by the Petition of the Fifty-five, alliances began to blur as many from the merchant community, who had initially sided with the Upper Covers, drifted toward the Lower Covers. It is important to remember that in New York, before the Revolution, those counted among the most wealthy were merchants, not necessarily large landowners. Nevertheless, merchants and landowners often worked together for the benefit of their bottom line. This is different from the situation in New Brunswick where the merchants and landowners often found themselves at odds. While the two groups initially found their interests aligned in New Brunswick, this situation eventually began to change. Additionally, the old merchant community at the mouth of the Saint John River, prior to the Loyalist settlement, supported the interests of the Loyalist elite until their goals were no longer compatible, at which point they threw in their lot with the merchants. Again, the reasons for this go back to the decision to locate the capital at Fredericton, away from Saint John, the most developed city in New Brunswick. Most of the business of the colony was transacted in Saint John, yet businessmen would have to travel to Fredericton in order to register contracts. In a place where deep snows made travel inconvenient for so much of the year, this often meant that the cost of business was higher, and in a cash-poor economy, this was less than ideal for the merchant community.[64]

It is not easy to predict where Frederick DePeyster would have aligned himself in this situation. For one thing, upon his arrival in Canada, Frederick embraced the profession that had initially brought wealth to his family in New York, the varied and multilayered profession of the merchant. Because of this, Frederick was granted a water lot in Saint John in 1784. Water lots were plots of land, which during high tide were half submerged by the river or sea. The idea was that those granted water lots would build them up, lending stability to the water front and allowing for an easier transfer of goods from ship to warehouse.[65] As part of his military settlement, Frederick, along with his fellow officers from the New York Volunteers, also received land in York County, in the township of Fredericton.[66] Frederick knew what a boon having land located near the capital of the colony could be to his fortunes. Frederick and the others even sent a letter to Governor Carleton, praising him for his decision. In the letter they also requested that Carleton reconsider his strict building guidelines for the city, which would prevent the subdivision of lots.[67] It is likely, given his success, that Frederick strategically placed himself within the political factions and utilized them all to his best advantage during his time in New Brunswick, a feat that most merchants were unable to attain as the factions dug in to their respective sides.

Frederick's status as a single man with no troubling debt enabled him to lease out his properties in Saint John and York County, launching himself into business as a successful merchant and landlord in the province. Leases were preferred to regular renting because they were generally long term and thus encouraged tenants to improve the property with buildings while ensuring a long-term financial commitment. Renting was short term and tended to encourage the use and abuse of the land, high tenant turnover, and uncertain income. As a result of these practices, Frederick gained the wealth his brother lacked while still maintaining a high social position, thanks to his military rank, connections, and family name.

The good will that Frederick continued to cultivate among the Loyalist elite (the pro-government faction or the Upper Covers) came in handy during the drawn-out legal dispute over Sugar Island. One month before the separation of New Brunswick from Nova Scotia in 1784, Governor Parr made a grant of Sugar Island to Chief Justice Bryan Finucane. Sugar Island lies within the Saint John River, 8 miles north of Fredericton, the soon-to-be capital of New Brunswick, and clearly within the territory set aside for dispersal among the Provincials.[68] In 1787, Andrew Finucane brought suit as his brother's heir to gain control of Sugar Island, which had by then been settled by Provincials, former Loyalist soldiers. The suit listed Frederick DePeyster as the primary defendant although whether Frederick actually owned all of the land himself is unknown.[69] Part of the land was divided into 10-acre lots and was settled with men of the New York Volunteers. At any rate, the suit was brought against Frederick DePeyster, and, in his defense, he recruited Ward Chipman to represent him, while Andrew Finucane recruited Elias Hardy. The old lines of the Petition of the Fifty-five were once again replicated and with as much passion. With Chipman on Frederick's side, Edward Winslow, Jonathan Sewell, and Colonel Allen quickly fell in line and threw their support behind Frederick. Andrew Finucane found himself an outsider in the world of the Loyalist elite. By the time of Finucane's lawsuit, New Brunswick was a separate colony from Nova Scotia and its Chief Justice, G. D. Ludlow, presided along with Justices Putnam and Upham, all members of the Loyalist elite. The court rejected Finucane's case on the grounds that the land in question had been allotted to the soldiers in recognition of their service in the late war. Finucane appealed, and in February 1793 the case was once again before the court. Finally, after being appealed to the King in Council, the matter was decided in favor of Frederick DePeyster.[70]

As for Abraham, there was no question as to his political allegiance. In 1792, the New Brunswick Assembly offered Abraham the position of Province Treasurer. Traditionally the individual holding this position was responsible for the collection of customs. It was a position with which Abraham was familiar, as his grandfather DePeyster held the post in New York prior to the Revolution. Certainly the Assembly would not have made this offer had there been a question about his allegiance to the Loyalist elites. Abraham happily accepted the post and moved his family to Saint John, where he hoped other opportunities would present themselves. Once there, Abraham built a house on fashionable Prince William Street[71] while occasionally investing in Frederick's ventures. There is no indication that Abraham himself became an import-export merchant. While in Saint John, Abraham and his family kept company with the elite of New Brunswick society: Edward Winslow, Jonathon Sewell, Ward Chipman, Judge Putnam, the Ludlows, and so on. This group did well, meaning they had no overwhelming debts, as long as the Navigation System kept the West Indies closed to American commerce.[72] This type of prosperity, for those who considered themselves the landed gentry, was short-lived. As the French embarked on their Revolution and rumors of a Continental War began to spread, fear began to spread through New Brunswick that the British government would seriously reconsider the Navigation System.

When war with France did come, Britain abruptly dropped the Navigation System in 1793, in respect to the West Indies, welcoming trade with the United States, which was better prepared to fulfill the needs of a country at war. This move diverted the majority of ships away from New Brunswick and toward ports in the United States. To compound the problem, crop failures and poor harvests thwarted the New Brunswick agricultural market. Thereafter, Abraham and the rest of the Loyalist elite slipped further into debt in order to keep their standard of living at a respectable level. Abraham's situation of "living in debt" is not quite as we would think of it today. At the time, men of wealth did not keep much cash at the ready, preferring, instead, to make their money work for them. When money was at hand, it was quite often lent out to someone else, to be repaid with interest. Similarly, if cash was needed, one would borrow it from another. This arrangement was generally considered sensible as it provided a place for investment and would "grow" wealth. This arrangement was generally beneficial to both parties so long as all contracts were kept and creditors did not press for early payment. Requiring early payment from one debtor in turn required that debtor to press their debtors before the agreed-upon time. In a healthy economy this would be an inconvenience but in a bad economy, as was the case with early New Brunswick, this could lead to financial ruin.[73]

As Abraham's fortunes diminished, several disputes between the political factions virtually shut down the finances of the colony and left even those with government appointments, like Abraham DePeyster, without a vital part of their income. The Loyalist elite now had status and land but were cash-poor, and they resented the politically cantankerous and wealthy merchant class who flipped their allegiance to the Lower Covers and were mostly excluded from the elite ranks.[74] After his move to Saint John, Abraham began to rely increasingly on his younger brother Frederick for assistance and credit.

By 1793, Frederick, age 35, was doing well. His property holdings expanded to include almost 2,500 acres of land, several city lots in Saint John, and large herds of cattle and sheep. He owed no money on his properties and was owed money by others.[75] Frederick used the profits from his leases to fund his mercantile adventures, the profits of which he reinvested into property, mercantile business, and money lending. It was a pattern common to the merchants of his day,[76] and one that Frederick DePeyster would follow for the rest of his life, bringing with it success, money, and prestige along with some resentment and jealousy from neighbors, family members, and business associates who did not fare quite so well in their endeavors.[77]

As early as 1790, Frederick DePeyster's business ventures led him back to New York on purchasing trips. During these visits, Frederick took the opportunity to visit his parents, James and Sarah Reade DePeyster, at their home in Jamaica, Long Island, and inquire into his New York properties, which his father had managed for him from the time of his minority. Throughout the Revolutionary War, Frederick's father, James, somehow managed to keep tabs on, and make sure title was clear on, the properties Frederick had inherited from his various relatives, including the properties from his great aunt Ann DePeyster in 1774.[78] During his visits to New York, it seems that Frederick slowly began to assume control over the various properties left him, and he established himself in business at New York under his own name.[79] Given the distance from the Revolution, many New Yorkers were willing to forget the past and allow former Loyalists to reestablish themselves, especially if doing so would increase the wealth of New York. In that spirit, and under the influence of Alexander Hamilton, New

York slowly repealed its anti-Tory laws, the last of which occurred in 1792.[80] Frederick DePeyster thus became one of many merchants to utilize their contacts both in New York and in Canada.

Facilitating Frederick's transition from Saint John to New York was Frederick's social status. In New York, Frederick, although not among the wealthiest of New York's citizens, was wealthy enough that his family name allowed him access to the highest social circles. Frederick associated with Aaron Burr, the Jays, and the Beekmans, in addition to the prominent families to which he was connected by birth.[81] While Frederick's past might have proved a hindrance in another state, in New York, people were more willing to overlook that bit of unpleasantness, especially given the blurred lines there between Patriot and Loyalist during the late war and Frederick's wealth and pedigree, which tied him to the most prestigious homes there.

By 1793, Frederick was able to make an advantageous match with Helen Livingston Hake, daughter of Samuel Hake, Commissary-General of the British Army in North America.[82] Helen had been left a rather large estate by her grandfather, Loyalist Robert Gilbert Livingston (1712–1789), and had grown up a near-neighbor of the DePeysters before James's bankruptcy and the Revolution. Helen lived in New York City under the protection of her guardians, while her father resided in Saint John in order to carry out his duties to the British Army. The proposed union was welcomed by their friends, Helen's New York guardians, and Frederick's family; however, Helen's father proved suspicious of his daughter's suitor and, according to Frederick, claimed that he (Frederick) was not "possess'd of a single shilling of property."[83] We do not know for certain why Hake opposed the union. As Commissary-General of the British Army in North America, and a resident of Saint John, he would have had easy access to information about land grants made in New Brunswick. His objections, nevertheless, could have stemmed from a number of other sources, and the accusation of poverty may have been just a convenient excuse. Hake may have been concerned that Frederick would squander his daughter's estate through the bad business practices his father and brother had displayed. Another possible objection may have been Frederick's illegitimate son, Frederick Augustus (Augustus). Augustus was born before 1792 and his mother's name was not listed in the family Bible. Perhaps Hake objected to the marriage on the basis of "loose" morals. And, of course, the objection could have been related to the political alliances of the two men. Throughout the tumultuous years of resettlement and establishment, the sympathies of the two men seem to have been consistently on opposite sides; Hake was identified with Elias Hardy in leading the opposition to the Petition of the Fifty-five.

Hake himself is one of those opportunistic individuals who pops up all over the world of the Loyalist diaspora and was called by contemporaries "a busybody, a fraud, [and] even a damned scoundrel."[84] Hake was born to a prominent New England clothier and later moved to New York to establish himself as a wholesale merchant, where his shop was next to that of Robert Gilbert Livingston. Shortly after his arrival in New York, Hake was married to Helena Livingston, Robert Gilbert Livingston's daughter. By late 1773 or early 1774, Hake was in "embarrassed" circumstances. Loved by his working-class customers for liberally extending credit, Hake was unable to collect on the debts owed him, and his father-in-law was said to have "paid many thousands" to keep Hake's family from poverty.[85] Not long after the wedding, rumors circulated that Hake treated his wife poorly. The couple had two children, Helen and Samuel Jr. At the onset of the war, Hake sailed for England in an attempt to placate London merchants to whom he owed extensive debts. In his absence, he sent his wife and children to the Livingston estate at Rynbeck. There, in 1777, the house was attacked by Patriots and set afire. The children safely escaped the encounter, but Helena was forced back into the burning structure and perished.[86]

Hake later returned and attempted to send British goods over enemy lines, whereupon he was captured and the goods confiscated. Later, he was released on parole to New York City. As the war drew to an end, Hake involved himself in many seemingly contradictory endeavors. For instance, Hake joined, and became chairman for, a Loyalist association bound for Abaco in the Bahamas. At the same time he promoted the Abaco Association, he also became involved in drafting the Counter-Petition to the Petition of the Fifty-five.

Hake's behavior gained him few friends among the social elite. First of all, most association boards had members who had signed the

Petition of the Fifty-five. Those board members were usually prominent in their various worlds and petitioned for extra land in an effort
to maintain that elite status in their new homes. If the petition had
been successful in Nova Scotia, it would have established precedent
for similar indulgence in other areas of Loyalist settlement. By helping to organize the Counter-Petition, Hake may have set himself up
as a friend to the working man, just as his credit policies had, but
doing so garnered him no fans among the elite to whose circle his
wife's family belonged. This move is probably the reason his name was
later removed from the Abaco association's petition to Carlton.[87] Hake
himself never did arrive in Abaco, for another matter soon consumed
his attention.

While promoting his plans for Abaco, Hake developed yet another scheme. For a small fee, Hake said he would collect the claims of
Loyalists and deliver them personally to the Loyalist Claims Commission in London.[88] He also promised to shepherd the petitions through
the Commission, thus ensuring a speedy resolution and prompt compensation. Unfortunately, Hake was unable to follow through on his
promises and later sent his apologies to those who had contracted with
him; he was unable to act as their emissary with the Commission due
to problems with his own petition.

In an attempt to resolve his own petition to the Loyalists Claims
Commission, Hake hastened to London to meet with the Commission
immediately.[89] In his petition, Hake had claimed great wealth. Of all
the petitions brought before the Commission, Hake's petition received
some of the most intense scrutiny of any case and was eventually rejected for fraudulent claims, at which point the matter was handed over to
the Lords of Treasury. More than twenty witnesses testified that Hake
was either bankrupt or embarrassed before the war began and that the
property he tried to claim in his petition had actually been signed over
to his father-in-law, Robert Gilbert Livingston, when Hake was unable to
repay the many loans extended to him. Hake escaped formal charges
only because his loyalty to the Crown was beyond reproach, whatever
his personal standards.

Hake continued to live in infamy among the elite circles of New
Brunswick, Nova Scotia, and New York as a result of his behavior.

Nevertheless, his uncontested Loyalty was rewarded by the British Government with the position of Commissary-General of the British Army in North America. Exactly when Hake received this position is unknown, but it was after December 1784, the date the Loyalist Claims Commissioners ruled on his petition (there is no mention in the petition of Samuel Hake being anything other than a merchant), and before November 1785, when Hake was located in Canada, just as Benedict Arnold decided to make Saint John his home. Of the occasion, Lieutenant H. M. Gordon of Halifax wrote to Edward Winslow in New Brunswick that "General Arnold arrived yesterday and I understand means to visit your province. Mr. Hake and he will be good company."[90] Hake's tenure in the position eventually ended in disgrace, as controversy remained his constant friend.

Whatever Hake's reasons for refusing his blessing to the union of his daughter and Frederick DePeyster, whether his moral or political objections, true financial concern, or the possibility of exploiting the situation in some way for his own benefit, the result was that Frederick was forced to call upon his extensive network of connections in New Brunswick to secure his marriage to Helen Hake. Frederick wrote to G. D. Ludlow, Chief Justice of New Brunswick, requesting an impartial inquiry into his property holdings in the province. With his engagement and veracity on the line, Frederick urged Ludlow to expedite the inquiry, so that the truth of matter might be revealed before further damage to his reputation occurred.[91] Frederick DePeyster also wrote Isaac Allen Esq., a judge in New Brunswick, and repeated his requests for urgent inquiry into the matter. Their affirmation of Frederick's good character and economic standing would force Hake to rescind the grounds for his objection to the marriage. So dire and delicate did Frederick consider the situation that he sent the letters by personal carrier to his brother Abraham for hand delivery to the intended recipients.[92]

The situation resolved quickly in Frederick DePeyster's favor, and the two married April 1, 1793. Helen brought into the marriage with her, as her own separate estate, the inheritance from her grandfather: three farms in Otsego County, New York, and extensive lands in Duchess County, New York.[93] With their marriage, the repeal of the last anti-Tory legislation in New York, and, no doubt, the opening of trade within the British Empire to the United States, after ten years in Canada, Frederick DePeyster made his home once more in New York.

Abraham, the oldest son, remained in New Brunswick. It is doubtful this was lightly considered, especially as Abraham and his wife had five children by 1793: Catharine Augusta (Augusta), Harriot Charlton (Harriot), Sarah Caroline (Caroline), James, and William Axtell.[94] Abraham's correspondence reveals that he greatly missed his former home and family and worried about the future of his children. No doubt the stymied market in New Brunswick, the decision of the Assembly not to pay salaries, the bad harvests, and his compounding debt were all reasons for Abraham to take his family and move to greener pastures where his family might be of some comfort. Yet would his situation really be best served by relocating to New York? In New Brunswick, Abraham was an owner of a large tract of land, he was a Colonel in the local militia, and he had genteel status and access to coveted government positions. What was there for Abraham in New York besides family and old friends? Unlike Frederick, Abraham did not inherit large amounts of land in the United States. Abraham had no cash to bring with him to New York, and given the poor state of his credit, he would have had a difficult time finding a line of credit based on his holdings in Canada. In New Brunswick, he may have been cash-poor and struggling to make ends meet, but at least he could have the illusion of living like a DePeyster. In New York, there would have been no such illusion. In order to maintain what status he did have, necessity demanded that Abraham remain in New Brunswick to preserve his family's social status, and he did so.

The ten years immediately following the American Revolution spent in New Brunswick were formative for the DePeyster brothers. During that time, the three brothers carefully calculated their actions, monitored the alliances they made, and utilized their resources in order to further their own interests. They also manipulated their identities to gain the best possible advantage. Despite the fact that they were all Loyalists, they did not, and in some cases could not, present themselves in the same fashion. All three were DePeysters, and all three of the brothers used the weight of their familial name to gain entrance into the upper levels of their social circles. For Joseph Reade DePeyster, who served as a regular enlisted soldier during the war, this meant working to protect his interests against the elites of New Brunswick who wanted to dominate the colony, politically, economically, and socially. He signed every petition to thwart the actions of the elites up until his death. For Abraham and Frederick, both of whom served as officers in the British Army during the American Revolution, the DePeyster name granted them entrance into the ranks of the Loyalist elite of New Brunswick. At that point, however, the brothers utilized different identities in conjunction with that of the DePeyster name to further their interests. Abraham presented himself as a member of the landed gentry in line with the expectations of the Loyalist elite, and in doing so, gained a government position in New Brunswick. Frederick, while a landowner in his own right, emphasized instead his identity as a merchant. Although he had no government position, he did not need one; his success as a merchant provided him with an income more than sufficient to support himself in New Brunswick and launch himself into the merchant world of New York.

Chapter 3

Sibling Relations

*F*rederick DePeyster's success in building his fortune in business after the Revolution (discussed in the next chapter) provided him with the financial wherewithal to support the prestige of his family name. This equilibrium between wealth and name, missing from this branch of the DePeyster family since just before the American Revolution with the bankruptcy of Frederick's father, James DePeyster, was not achieved by Frederick's siblings, but they desired and felt entitled to it. As a result, the family often looked to Frederick to smooth over the differences in their own affairs through extending credit, giving presents, or acting as a financial agent. While these demands on Frederick had the tendency to add strain to the familial relationships, they also kept the growing family closely tied to one another and to the ideal of what it meant to be a DePeyster and how a DePeyster ought to live. The relationships of Abraham and Margaret to their brother Frederick are particularly important in exploring these complicated binding ties as the elder two siblings better remembered the stature of the family prior to the Revolution, during the family's golden colonial days.

The relationship between Frederick and his older brother Abraham is particularly complex. Both served the King during the Revolutionary War, both moved to New Brunswick, Canada, and both received settlements in Saint John for their service. While the brothers' situations were decidedly different by the time Frederick returned to New York, initially they were not divergent. As members of the military gentry, both men moved in the highest circles of New Brunswick society, holding company regularly with Edward Winslow, Governor Thomas Carleton, and church officials, among others.[1] Frederick, however, chose to pursue a merchant's life and used that enterprise to build up his fortune, while Abraham pursued the life of the landed gentry, and entered into business only as a secondary line. The difference in their respective choices made all the difference in the fortune of these two brothers.

Once in Canada, the two brothers received land allotments for their military service to the British government during the American Revolution. Already part of the military gentry, Abraham settled his land near Maugerville in 1784 and hoped to add to his prestige by positioning himself as one of the landed elite. There he hired laborers to work his land along with his slaves. Abraham himself was appointed to and served as sheriff of Sunbury County, collecting debts, fines, fees, bails, and bonds. In this position, Abraham was financially responsible for any monies that he failed to collect. Various accounts from this period reveal that Abraham spent liberally on items for his household. During the Maugerville period, Abraham gained status and respectability among the Loyalist elite, all the while undermining his own financial stability. In 1792, the government of New Brunswick offered Abraham the position of treasurer, which he accepted. Abraham then moved his family to the port city of Saint John, where he built a house on fashionable Prince William Street, and opened a store in an effort to increase his wealth. No doubt Abraham began conducting business with his brother Frederick at this time.

After Frederick returned to New York, correspondence reveals that the two brothers maintained a close social and business relationship. Abraham also made clear his trust and respect for his younger brother Frederick in a 1793 letter, prior to Frederick's marriage and permanent resettlement in New York. An unspecified illness took the life of their young acquaintance, Miss Smith. Abraham found the incident particularly disturbing as he found himself suffering from the same illness. In his distress, Abraham wrote to Frederick asking him to care for his wife and children in the event of his death. As the eldest son, Abraham also told Frederick that he would be responsible for the care of their beloved parents. Abraham also told Frederick that, should he want it, Frederick could have Abraham's position with the government in order to properly fulfill his duties.[2] In the early years of New Brunswick it was not uncommon for the military elite to form a sort of hereditary elite as well. Government positions defaulted into lifetime appointments with children or siblings taking over the position in instances of death or incapacity.

In addition to requesting that Frederick look after his family, Abraham also placed other responsibilities upon Frederick. These responsibilities began as small requests, at different times, for Frederick to perform small services for Abraham so that his family might be able to maintain the coveted lifestyle of the Loyalist elite. Abraham also requested small extensions of credit, gifts for his children, and gifts in general. For instance, Abraham requested expensive items such as smoked hams and tongue, revealing the elite status Abraham's family tried to maintain in New Brunswick.

Frederick complied with his brother's wishes to the best of his abilities, but Abraham's requirements were not always easy to meet, especially as the years began to pass, and Frederick's other obligations required more of his attentions. One of these other obligations was family. By 1795, Frederick and his wife, Helen Hake, had two sons, James Ferguson (1794–1874) and Robert Gilbert Livingston (1795–1873), in addition to Augustus, then about 5 years old.[3] In 1796 the couple added another child, Frederick Jr. (1796–1882).

Despite Abraham's position with the government as treasurer and his store, he found himself deeper and deeper in debt. Although the position of treasurer initially came with a small salary, by this time the Assembly was in a battle of wills with the Governor and the Council, resulting in the financial paralysis of the colony. This meant that salaries were greatly reduced, and in the case of the treasurer, not paid at all. One can only imagine that Abraham stayed with the position, despite not being paid, for the prestige and status it offered.[4] Whether Abraham's debts arose from overextension for the purposes of keeping up appearances, the generally poor economic situation in New Brunswick, the burden of maintaining a large family, or because he was "truly an unfortunate man," we do not know, but by 1795, Abraham was unable to make payments to his creditors, and asked Frederick to extend him credit to pay his debts and advance him money for store items.[5] In 1797, Abraham requested that Frederick make a gift of paint and oil so that he would be able to paint his house, both inside and out, in preparation for its sale.[6] Although this is not necessarily an indication of a financial demise, other events quickly followed that indicate an overall decline in fortune. For instance, Abraham began asking Frederick the value of certain household goods (fur muffs, English silver, sugar and milk pots) and what prices they might fetch in New York. That same year, Abraham began petitioning Frederick to sign over his Saint John water lot. Abraham believed that the water lot would help his business venture, and as Frederick was now established in New York, the water lot, apart from the income it generated through rent, was no longer vital to Frederick's interests. Abraham reasoned, why should Frederick not sign the property over to him, since he could benefit so greatly from it? What Frederick's intentions were regarding the Saint John water lot, we do not know, but in the end the lot remained in Frederick's hands. If he did intend to act, he did not do so quickly enough, and Abraham was forced to give up his store.[7]

During 1797, Abraham's requests for gifts and extensions of credit grew frequent and arbitrary. Abraham, still hopeful of opening another store, continued to draw upon his brother for credit. By the end of May, Frederick was forced to write a firm letter reminding his brother of the rules and financial constraints that governed the world of business, both for merchant and moneylender.[8] Frederick asked Abraham to be more cautious in his business dealings to keep them both from ruin. Before Frederick had time to seal the letter, however, he received another missive from Abraham informing him, rather offhandedly, that he had once again drawn upon Frederick to satisfy his creditors. Frederick's irritation at the situation was palpable in his hastily written postscript; "can you conceive I am made of cash or that I am rich neither [accusations] are just."[9] From Abraham's position and point of view, however, Frederick was both. Frederick and his wife now were raising four children. He was successful in business and was living near family who could offer assistance if needed. Additionally, Frederick's household included both servants and slaves, a clear mark of wealth and status. Abraham's efforts, on the other hand, always seemed to come up short of satisfactory; his business deals fell through, and he did not choose the right investments at the right times, among other short comings. Additionally, his physical remoteness from the extended family took its toll through the successive waves of illness that swept the family. His inability to care for his family in the manner he believed them due, both physically and financially, wore on his mind, and his reply to Frederick's reprimand display his frustration.

> I cannot help thanking you for accepting my orders, tho
> am sorry to find it put you to so great an inconvenience
> I shall not do the like again unless from mere necessity,
> which God forbid should be the case, nor shall I ever apply
> to you further Sir[10]

Clearly upset with his brother, Abraham followed through on his promise for at least a short time by placing orders on other New York merchants.[11]

The brothers soon patched up their relationship, although we are not privy to the details due to a gap in the correspondence. What we do know is that by the time the brothers began working together again, their business relationship was a much more structured one than before. Abraham, however, was more open about his financial limitations than he had been, directing Frederick as to when he could or could not participate in certain shipments and deals. He also advised Frederick as to the current prices of goods in New Brunswick to help facilitate Frederick's business there. Despite these changes, the brothers' relationship still suffered from Abraham's impatience and the resultant misunderstandings.

In July 1797, Abraham informed his brother that two of his sons, James and William were ill, James dangerously so. William was sent away to recover, but they thought it too dangerous to move James immediately.[12] Abraham was hopeful that James would pull through, but just two days after he wrote to Frederick regarding the illness, James died.[13] Soon, both Abraham and his wife were ill, and it was not until August 2 that Abraham was able to convey the news to the family in New York.[14] With the loss of his son, Abraham entrusted his brother with the charge of procuring a tombstone for the "dear Lamb." Abraham promised to pay any amount so long as Frederick attended to the task "immediately."[15] At the beginning of September 1797, Abraham asked

Frederick to buy gold earrings for two of his daughters, Augusta and Caroline.[16] When neither the earrings nor the tombstone had arrived by the end of that month, Abraham complained, "how could you be so cruel, as not to send me the tomb stone for my heavenly babe; it is unpardonable in you" and "Why did you not send the ear rings . . . the dear babes are much disappointed that they have not arrived."[17]

Despite incidents such as these, Abraham continued to trust Frederick, and Frederick continued to act for his brother, protecting his interests and smoothing the way with creditors. For instance, in November 1797, Abraham wrote to Frederick regarding a business deal gone awry. Abraham had arranged for the purchase of a farm in Maugerville for £180 from a John Thompson, before Thompson's resettlement on Long Island. The deed was not delivered until later by Thompson's brother Cornelius, but at that point Abraham found the deed altered to reflect a sale price of £200. Perhaps if Abraham had not sold the farm to another person already, he might have walked away from the deal. As it was, Abraham needed to secure the agreed-upon price in order to pay for the farm and make a profit. Abraham had no recourse other than to apply directly to John Thompson for a redress of the situation, but he was afraid that Cornelius might hear of it and write as well, tainting the situation. To prevent this, Abraham beseeched his brother to go in person to Long Island and visit Thompson in order to determine covertly what was really going on. Abraham seems to have kept Frederick in the dark about this particular plan until it all went very, very wrong and he had no choice but to call upon his brother for assistance. Abraham presented the situation to Frederick in one long letter, begging his brother to act on his behalf.[18]

Despite the fact that Abraham continued to fall further behind in his financial obligations, he increased the amount of business he sent to his brother. When people came to Abraham wanting advice on New York contacts for business, or simply wanting to place orders, Abraham continually pointed them toward Frederick. While Abraham fancied that Frederick, "in time [would] have all the business from this place," his continual practice of utilizing Frederick as a safeguard for his credit, and his general criticism of Frederick's efficiency, lent a constant strain to the relationship.[19]

Yet when Abraham, so prone to illness, died on February 19, 1798, at age 45, Frederick did what his brother asked of him and made certain that Abraham's family was taken care of. Catharine Livingston, Abraham's widow, was 38 at that time and had six children to look after, in addition to settling her husband's estate. Once Abraham's estate was settled, Catharine took the children, Augusta, Harriot, Caroline, William Axtell, Charlton, and Ann Eliza Sewell, and moved back to New York. She probably lived near the DePeysters at Jamaica, Long Island, although it is possible she settled near the Livingstons for a short time. Frederick took in Abraham's oldest daughter, Augusta, for schooling as agreed upon prior to Abraham's death, and in 1802, Frederick, along with his brother-in-law, Dr. William Hammersley, accepted financial guardianship for the children.[20] Frederick and Hammersley managed the estates left to Abraham's children by their grandmother Sarah Reade DePeyster and their aunt Sarah (Sally) DePeyster, both of whom had died that year, in addition to the inheritances that defaulted to them upon their father's death.[21]

Although Frederick and Abraham did not always agree on business matters or even what was required of the other in their relationship, in the end Frederick continued to fulfill his brothers requests and demands, if not always in as timely a fashion as Abraham would have preferred. Even after Abraham's death, Frederick continued to fulfill his brother's wishes in taking financial responsibility for, and a personal interest in, Abraham's children. The financial situation of Catharine, Abraham's widow, is not clear following his death. Abraham was bankrupt upon his death, and his estate was sold off to pay his creditors. We do not know if Catherine was allowed to keep whatever property she brought into the marriage, although it is likely that his creditors would have tried to obtain it given the dismal state of Abraham's financial affairs. Likewise it is equally unclear whether Catherine was allowed to retain Abraham's half-pay upon his death. Having survived the war, but not being career soldiers, the DePeyster brothers were not entitled to half-pay when their services were completed; it was only by a special act of Parliament that the Loyalist soldiers were able to retain half-pay for life, and even then, only due to the financially strapped environment of Nova Scotia and New Brunswick. Whether this benefit continued after his death is unknown but unlikely. While Abraham was in Canada, Frederick did what was necessary to make sure that his brother's family maintained a certain standard of living, and perhaps most significantly, that the DePeyster name was not embarrassed by a financial *faux pas*. That Abraham did not make this an easy task speaks to the attitude of Frederick and his siblings toward family.

Perhaps even more contentious than the relationship of Abraham and Frederick was that of Frederick and Margaret, eldest of the DePeyster siblings. Margaret married Thomas James of the Royal Artillery in 1776. James was his wife's senior by many years. Although we do not know when he was born, we do know that he entered the military in 1737 and served for more than forty years. Most young men entering service were usually 13 to 17 years old.[22] After the siege of Charleston in 1780, Colonel James retired and the couple moved to London. There, Margaret gave birth to a daughter, Margaretta Sarah. Two years later, the Colonel died. There is no direct mention of any estate belonging to Colonel James or of its passing to Margaret James, and there is no mention of annuities. In 1800, Margaret lived off a pension (whether from her husband's estate or from the government for being a Loyalist is unknown), and an inheritance from her grandmother, Margaret Van Cortlandt, both of which she considered too small to maintain her status. That is not to say that Margaret was destitute. On the contrary, from her letters we know that she spent more on rent for one year's lodging than most workers made in total wages during the same period. Margaret's main concern was that she be able to keep up the level of affluence to which she was accustomed; her inability to do so left her convinced that she was nearly penniless and in a wretched situation.

Although we do not know for sure, it seems likely that Margaret returned to her family in New York for a short time. We do know that in 1800, Margaret was settled in London and was none too happy about it. She wrote her brother:

> I may say without Vanity—I have first proved my affection
> to my Husband—by leaving my Relation & Country [New
> York] for his Sake—then as a Parent—I left all for my
> Daughters Sake . . .[23]

Margaret's only child Margaretta (Peggy) had married Mr. Edward Martin Esq., of Moretonhampstead, Devonshire; the couple resided in South Wales, not in London.[24] Mr. Martin and Margaret James were not on the friendliest of terms. A definite reason for animosity between the two was money. While Margaret's income was small, her daughter's husband often required funds from Margaret to help keep the couple from ruin; although Mr. Martin was a lawyer, he was not the most industrious soul, and his intemperate spending habits often left his family destitute. As such, Mr. Martin often found himself at odds with Margaret, who had definite ideas about how she, as a DePeyster, her daughter, and her granddaughters should live.[25]

Margaret clearly saw herself as a woman belonging to the economic and social circles of the gentry. The DePeyster name granted her access to those circles in New York and opened doors in England as well. With her DePeyster connections, Margaret was invited to social parties with elite personages of the Loyalist exile community, which was a distinct circle within British society. They often lived in the same small areas and socialized daily at the same coffeehouses with one another. People belonging to this Loyalist community virtually took over St. James park for their daily promenade; in fact, several comments were made at the time that there was no place in London more American than St. James Park.[26] Margaret ensured she was daily among their numbers while in town. This group was initially composed of individuals who were either trapped in Great Britain at the start of the Revolution or were Loyalists who fled their homes for Great Britain in hopes of protection from angry neighbors. They hoped to exert some influence over British policy toward the American colonies and believed reconciliation was the most desirable outcome.[27] As the war dragged on, however, these hopes of the early community were dashed as they were neither consulted nor considered; they were mostly ignored.[28] As new arrivals flooded the ranks of the Loyalists, they began to separate themselves according to which colony they came from; for example, New Englanders rarely associated with those from the south.[29] However, just as there were elite Loyalists in New Brunswick, there were also elite Loyalists in England who were recognized by each Loyalist community. It was among that group that Margaret James socialized.

With her maiden name, she was also able to associate with prominent Americans and Britons in London for business and pleasure. Among the names of her acquaintances appearing in her correspondence were such prominent families as the Lows (a wealthy New York merchant family), the Pinckneys (a family from South Carolina prominent in politics), and the Carletons (high-ranking British military officials), to name a few. Clearly Margaret was not destitute, just not able to support herself in the manner she desired.

Although Margaret did not have sufficient funds to support an elegant lifestyle, she did not let that stop her. In this respect, she was no different from the rest of the exiled Loyalist community. Most individuals received a pension from the British government; the standard annual allotment was £100.[30] According to Mary Beth Norton, the pension was a "simple, if somewhat cumbersome, charitable operation, intended only to supply them with a minimal temporary support until they could return to their homes."[31] Yet for most exiles, the pension was a compensation, a reward for their loyalty, and as such, frequent protests over the amount and length of time the pension was to continue became a continual sore spot between the Loyalists and the government. The circumstances of most Loyalist women in Britain were dire. Many were forced to pawn their clothes, take in needlework, and rely on the generosity of their community to keep from starving and becoming homeless.[32] Margaret was clearly not in the same situation as those women, yet at the same time she was not content to accept her lot. As a child, Margaret had witnessed her father's economic and social fall from elite circles to a certain extent, and she also witnessed her mother, Sarah Reade, bring her inheritance to bear to save the family from disgrace and ruin.[33] Likewise, her grandmother, Margaret Van Cortlandt, also maintained her status based on her separate estate after her husband's death. The examples of these women no doubt influenced Margaret's decision to maintain herself in the circles to which she was accustomed. No doubt Mr. Martin, as a man from Great Britain and used to English Common Law rather than the Dutch traditions in which Margaret was raised, resented the fact that Margaret, a woman, controlled anything that would eventually go to his wife and therefore to him.[34]

The frequent eruptions between Margaret James and Mr. Martin meant that Margaret James often stayed in London until Mr. Martin apologized and sent for her. In a letter from February of 1800, Margaret wrote to Frederick that she had word that her daughter had given birth to a child, christened Margaretta Sarah, but that she had yet to see the child. Margaret further wrote that she would sail for America to see her ailing mother, but that her own funds were exhausted from keeping up appearances.[35] Even so, Margaret was hopeful that she would soon find herself back in America, among her friends and family in the next few months. The hoped-for visit was not to occur, for Mr. Martin apologized. Margaret felt she had no choice but to abandon her designs on America, and make the 200-mile journey to her daughter in South Wales. The journey required her to leave all her trunks behind in London (with storage fees) and to travel alone by carriage, something respectable women of her class just did not do. Margaret lamented the cost of the journey, the cost of storage for her belongings, and the loss of her friends in London. She also pondered what would happen to her should Mr. Martin have a change of heart during her visit.[36]

Though we do not have Frederick's letters to Margaret, it is clear that both he and the rest of the family in New York were concerned for her, and tried to convince her to move back to America. Not only was Margaret far away from the family, she was out of their immediate protection as well. In England, Margaret was at the mercy of strangers, both their compassion and hostility, just as she was subject to the whims of Mr. Martin. In America, she would benefit from the power of the family name as well as the extended family there. In England she had to conduct business with the agents of the family who tended to look after business interests rather than family interests. Despite these issues, Margaret remained in England in the hope of being an aide to her daughter.

While Margaret wrestled with Mr. Martin, money, and respectability in England, the family in New York faced no less daunting circumstances as they dealt with the estate of James DePeyster, who died in 1799, Sarah Reade's declining health, and the death of Frederick's wife, Helen Hake, in September of 1801. The cause of Helen's death is unknown, but as it occurred more than a year after the birth of her last child, it is unlikely his birth caused her death. Helen's separate estate, established for her by the will of her grandfather, Robert Gilbert Livingston, passed to her sons and was held in trust for them by Frederick until they passed their minority.[37] When Margaret learned of Helen's death in May of 1802, Margaret sent her condolences to her brother and his sons and once again expressed her anguish at not being with the family at this critical juncture.[38]

With the passing of Sarah Reade, the major impetus for Margaret to return to the United States vanished. Though she never completely gave up the idea of returning permanently to New York with her daughter's family in tow, Margaret resigned herself to living in England as long as her daughter lived there, but that meant that she was all the more anxious to ensure that her American property remained hers. Margaret entreated her brother to secure and send, as soon as possible, two boxes of books that she had left with their Aunt and Uncle Charlton, and paintings left with Frederick.[39] Margaret also reminded Frederick to secure her portion of their parents' estate for her:

> . . . some plate that did belong to my dear Father let it be
> ever so trifling I should value it for their Sakes . . . the Tur-
> tleshell Tea Box . . . and my d^r Brother James' Pictures . . .[40]

The reason behind this particular request was the development of yet another rift between Margaret and Mr. Martin in May 1803. When Mr. Martin found out about the American property and that Margaretta had a share in it, he requested his wife's share.[41] When Margaret proved less than enthusiastic about his suggestions, Mr. Martin sent her away. Margaret was once again on her own in London. There, she decided that it would be better for her to comply with Mr. Martin's wishes in order to see her daughter and grandchildren, despite the risk of losing these items to Mr. Martin's needs. Having made her request for the items, Margaret gave Frederick directions for the best way to send the goods to ensure their safe arrival and tax-free importation. She strictly warned Frederick to send everything immediately except in case of war, in which case he was to retain the items until she wrote again.[42]

Aside from the physical items left to Margaret by various family members, there were properties and financial legacies to sort out as well. To speed these matters along, Margaret gave Frederick her Power of Attorney to deal with the sale of lands left to the DePeyster siblings in Bergen County, New Jersey.[43] Frederick informed her that to get the most out of her money, she needed to invest the funds and live off the interest. Further, to get the maximum amount of interest possible, Margaret needed to invest the money in America.[44] Margaret grudgingly agreed, and the Power of Attorney expanded to include all of Margaret's American finances, which involved various settlements from the estates of various family members: her father, mother, grandfather Reade, grandmother DePeyster, Aunt Chambers, and sister Sarah.[45] But although Frederick invested Margaret's money, and told her that she could draw on him for £100 interest due her,[46] he had not actually disclosed to her the amount of her principal.[47]

Margaret's not knowing how much money she really had, the lack of control over her own money, and untimely remittances, lent a certain tension to the siblings' relationship. For Margaret, this situation was extremely frustrating. She grew up with examples of women who controlled their own finances, and now that she had her own fortune she was no doubt anxious to exert her own authority over it. Instead, she was an ocean away from her money and had to rely on remittances from her brother. On top of that, the unstable political situation between Britain and France, and the possibility of war between the two nations must have had her wondering what would happen. If the remittances came to an end, she might be forced into a lower station while her American fortune remained out of reach. To garner Frederick's cooperation in the dispersal of her funds when and how she wanted, Margaret used the few tools available to her: the invocation of familial responsibility, her position as a "feeble" woman, and the possible tarnishing of Frederick's personal honor. Although not in the position of power she preferred, Margaret's handling of the situation reveals her prowess as an independent woman in a man's world.

One of the first challenges Margaret faced in this regard was the new Mrs. Frederick DePeyster. In 1803, at age 45, Frederick DePeyster married advantageously again. This time his wife was 27-year-old

Ann Beekman (1778–1857), daughter of Gerard (Garry) G. Beekman (1746–1822), merchant, and Cornelia Van Cortlandt.[48] Gerard Beekman had been a Patriot during the Revolutionary War, while his father, also Gerard G., had aligned himself with the British. Before the war, the two were in business together. Whether the partnership continued during the war is unknown; however, by the end of the war, Garry had enough money to purchase a large portion of the confiscated Philipse estate at Tarrytown, New York, for £9,040.[49] Although we do not have the marriage bond, there can be no doubt that Anne brought some of her father's wealth into the marriage with her. In other respects, the marriage of Ann and Frederick provided many business opportunities for both families. It seems likely that the Beekmans and the DePeysters utilized each other's business contacts. This is certainly the case for the DePeysters who, thanks to Beekman relatives living in Saint Croix, were finally able to conduct business directly with the West Indies, or at least the neutral, Dutch-controlled islands therein. This is important because the British West Indies were closed to American trade during this time. Additionally, Frederick is often listed as the contact man for Beekman business in advertisements of the day.[50]

Although the marriage proved advantageous to Frederick, for Margaret the marriage was a cause for concern. Margaret had not met Ann and did not trust her. Although the new Mrs. DePeyster attempted to ingratiate herself to Margaret through presents of sweetmeats, they did not have the desired effect. Margaret criticized Frederick for not sending her portion of their mother's belongings quickly enough; she informed him in no uncertain terms that he was to send exactly what was left for her (with a few exceptions she specifically made) and that he was not to allow his new wife to have her pick.[51]

It was not until Margaret met with the recently arrived General and Mrs. Carleton[52] that her opinion of the new Mrs. DePeyster took a turn for the better. The former governor of Canada and his wife knew of Frederick's Ann and "highly recommended" Frederick's choice.[53] Before the recommendation, Margaret was guarded in her approach to Ann. Margaret had no way of knowing whether Ann would talk her husband out of his commitment to safeguarding her estate. The fear was a very real one. Thanks to her inheritances, Margaret possessed a small fortune (despite the fact its exact amount remained unknown to her) and a formidable family name. As a widow she had the ability to act independently, but she also faced significant limitations. Separated from both her family and her fortune, and having signed away her power of attorney to her brother Frederick, Margaret was dependent upon her brother for access to her fortune and for protection. If Frederick suddenly became distracted by his new wife, or convinced that her fortune would better suit them in America, there would be little recourse for Margaret. Margaret always had the option to rescind the Power of Attorney she had given her brother Frederick, but this option could also prove problematic. Frederick was the only person who actually knew the balance of Margaret's fortune. He was also the only person who knew where and with whom those funds were invested. Had he so desired, he could have ceased remittances and drawn the matter out, forcing Margaret to sue him for the remainder. That course would have proved costly as Margaret would then have had to engage an attorney. Even then, the matter could have been drawn out if Frederick "lost" her records. When matters such as these wound through the court systems, it took years to sort out the entanglement of inherited estates, the calculation of interest payments (depending on the investments), the payments made or not made to other heirs, and how the death of another heir might affect further division of the estate. Rescinding the Power of Attorney was an option, but it was an option of last resort, as its outcome was not at all guaranteed. With the recommendation of the Carletons, however, Margaret's demeanor toward Ann became the same as it was for any other member of the DePeyster family.

In March of 1804, Margaret was busy trying to get Frederick to disclose the actual amount of her principal as knowing this would allow her to better balance her accounts and maintain what she considered to be a decent standard of living.[54] Until this time, Margaret felt she had of necessity been "living <u>not quite</u> what a DePeyster or what your sister ought."[55] Margaret also threatened to move the whole of her American fortune over to England if Frederick were not more forthcoming, in order to avoid difficulties that would arise from her being so far from her money.[56] The threat was a clever one, because if Margaret did move all of her money to England, Frederick would no longer be able to use her money to help fund his own enterprises and further increase his wealth. It was a fairly common practice for Frederick to mix all the funds over which he was executor with his own, invest all of them together, and pay out dividends from one common fund. It made bookkeeping far less of a headache, and as long as the investments paid out, there were no problems with the system. If for some reason an investment failed, however, then Frederick and all for whom he invested were out of luck.

Margaret and Frederick kept each other up-to-date on the family, and for the most part, there was little friction in that area. From time to time, Margaret would entreat Frederick to send over one of his sons to be educated in England. She would promise to enter him in the best schools and have him with her at every break, just as she would have with her own child. Frederick politely refused each request, but his denial did not produce any hard feelings or irritation on the part of Margaret, just as earlier failed requests for Abraham's daughter (and Margaret's goddaughter) Augusta to join Margaret in England had not caused hard feelings. Most of the friction between Margaret and Frederick arose from the issue of money and the control of it.

For instance, when their sister Ann (Nancy) died in 1803, she left Margaret £100. Margaret wanted this money immediately and asked Frederick to provide her with an order on his agent in London for the amount.[57] When the order did not come through quickly enough, Margaret convinced an acquaintance, Mr. Moulton, to accept the order in June of 1804. Margaret was not particularly pleased with the exchange when Mr. Moulton demanded interest on her payment.[58] Margaret begged Frederick to deal with the matter immediately, especially because he could have prevented the problem had he sent an order on his agent when she asked. She was sure that Frederick had already paid himself, so why not take care of her. A year later Margaret wrote to her brother again regarding Mr. Moulton. She informed her brother that Mr. Moulton said that he had never received a response from Frederick regarding Margaret's payment and that both of their reputations were now in question.[59] Frederick's reply was quick. He informed her that he had settled the matter with Mr. Moulton in September of 1804, a full year before. Margaret assured her brother that Mr. Moulton had lied to her about everything.[60] Margaret had been taken advantage of by an unscrupulous businessman, and as a single woman, she had very few resources to help solve these problems on her own, but she was not helpless. Margaret brought her best weapon to bear on the situation, her brother Frederick.

By this time, Frederick was a man of some consequence. Through his various investments, business endeavors, and strategic alliances, Frederick built himself a fortune. Although the specifics of his finances are unknown, he had sufficient funds in 1804 to build a country estate in Bloomingdale (near today's Columbia College). That same year, Ann gave birth to their first child, a girl named Joanna Cornelia (Cornelia) (1804–1867).[61] Margaret knew Frederick would come to her assistance to protect not only his sister, but also the DePeyster name. Mr. Moulton had impugned upon Frederick's reputation both in familial and business matters. A man who could not be trusted to care for his vulnerable relations could not be trusted at all. Knowing that his livelihood was on the line, Frederick immediately sent Margaret the particulars of the transaction so that she could confront Mr. Moulton with the facts. To ensure that Margaret would not fall prey to a similar situation again, Frederick established a regular schedule of remittances so that Margaret would know exactly how much she had to live on and for how long.[62] Margaret now had something concrete upon which to plan her expenses.

While Margaret struggled along in England, never quite content with or certain of her situation,[63] Ann gave birth to her second child in 1805, another girl, named Ann Frederica. Margaret sent her congratulations and wondered aloud why none of her brothers had named any of their daughters Margaret, both her and her grandmother's name.[64] Her question was more than reasonable, especially given the naming practices in the family; uncles, fathers, grandfathers, grandmothers, and aunts were all honored in this way. Frederick himself was named after his uncle. Yet the name Margaret, or Margaretta, surfaced only with Margaret's own daughter. By reminding Frederick of the omission, Margaret was reasserting her place in the family and reminding him of his familial obligations. When Frederick's third daughter was born in June of 1806, she was christened Margaret James DePeyster[65] and immediately became Aunt Margaret's "pet." Small gifts, drawings, books, and anything else Margaret could afford, found their way across the Atlantic to the little namesake. Margaret could not have been more pleased with Frederick's gesture, and for a time, threats of relocating her money to England subsided, although a perfect resolution of their business affairs never quite materialized.[66]

The next few years represented a rollercoaster for America, its merchants, and the DePeysters. The Embargo Act was repealed only to be followed quickly by the Non-Intercourse Act, which likewise prohibited trade with nations not willing to acknowledge the right of the United States to carry on trade as a neutral power. As the flow of ships across the ocean slowed, Margaret James once again, and rightly so, became concerned about having access to her estate. Her attempts to liquidate her estate once again caused the siblings to clash.

One such issue over which the siblings squabbled involved the sale of Margaret's half-pew at Trinity Church and some books she left in Frederick's possession when she moved to London. She originally purchased the half-pew for £16, and hoped that Frederick would be able to obtain at least that much for her.[67] In 1808, Frederick sold both the half-pew and the books, but when it came time for Margaret to receive her share, some disagreement arose. Frederick originally agreed to send Margaret six dozen bottles of Madeira wine for the books. Instead he sent only twenty-three bottles of wine and requested a receipt for both the books and pew. Margaret chastised her brother, and insisted that until he secured for her the full amount of wine, she would not send a receipt for the books, and that the matter of the pew was entirely separate from that of the books.[68] Frederick agreed to the original price for the books and set aside the remaining bottles for Margaret. In September, Margaret finally issued a receipt to her brother, £16 for the half-pew.[69]

In the midst of the pew and book incident, Margaret once again made inquiries into her settlement. Margaret wrote in April of 1809 that she still did not know the exact amount of her money in America, and that Frederick should relate that information, in pounds sterling because for Margaret, the new American money system was still something of a mystery.[70] Margaret also requested that Frederick give her the names of all who held her bonds.[71] She protested at the time that she simply wanted to know the balance, and that she had no intention of moving her money to England, but her next letter, dated September 1809, contradicts this. It seems that Margaret was trying to determine how to make her money work harder for her as the current system of remittances was too unreliable and insufficient for maintaining her respectability.[72] She asked Frederick just how long it would take to transfer her money over to England so she would have better access to it and would be able to make sure that she received the most interest from it.[73]

That same year, perhaps in anticipation of finally having control over her own finances, Margaret took rooms on Norton Street, in Portland Place of the Harley-Portland neighborhood, which was, at that time, one of the "principle aristocratic estates" in London.[74] The rooms cost Margaret £90 for the year and included only her rooms. Margaret was forced to pay an additional £7 to her landlady for the use of her maid, an affront to the dignity of the 53-year-old DePeyster.[75]

At the end of September 1809, Margaret asked Frederick to send her a "Muff & Tippet—out of the Aboundance of your riches—if a generous fit of this kind comes over you."[76] Margaret's tone, however, was decidedly altered by the time of her next letter, dated February 1810. In it, she mentioned that she recently met with Mr. McEvers, a very successful New York merchant, who informed her that Frederick "was very rich had a very elegant house—and was very liberal."[77] Mr. McEvers also agreed to "use his influence" with Frederick to ensure that he would send her the muff and tippet as a present. Margaret was certain though, that after hearing his friends boast of Frederick's fine lifestyle and generosity, McEvers's influence would not be necessary, and that Frederick would send the gifts.[78] By March of 1810, Margaret was thanking Frederick for his intention of sending the muff and tippet and for his generous offer of sending them in fur, which was extremely expensive in London that season.[79]

In many respects, the different methods Margaret James employed to persuade her brother to act in the manner she wished were not so different from those employed by the women in William Cooper's life.

As described by Alan Taylor in *William Cooper's Town*, both William's wife and his sister, Letitia Cooper Woodruff, appealed to nonfamily members both to persuade and potentially embarrass William. Letitia would routinely appear at the house of William's influential friend Henry Drinker and beg him to provide her with money (her brother, she explained, would reimburse Mr. Drinker).[80] Taylor states, "she must have recognized that by calling on Henry Drinker she maximized the social pressure on her brother to be generous."[81] No doubt Margaret recognized this as well when she invoked the names of the Carletons and Mr. McEvers to remind Frederick of the good and generous reputation he enjoyed.

Between the letters of September 1809 and March 1810, Frederick had managed once again to convince Margaret to leave her money with him. In agreeing to keep her money in America, however, Margaret had at least one solid term for Frederick to follow: he was never to disclose the amount of her income to her son-in-law, Mr. Martin. Margaret told Frederick that although Mr. Martin knew she received money from America, he did not know the amount, and if he did, she would be "sadly off."[82] Throughout her correspondence leading up to the letter of March 1810, there are subtle hints and full-blown accounts of Mr. Martin's irresponsibility toward his wife and children. Mr. Martin frequently lived beyond his means, badgered his wife and mother-in-law for every cent possible, went without employ, and moved his family around England. Between 1800 and 1805, we know that the Martin family lived in at least three different locations.[83] Margaret considered it imperative to keep her income a secret; if Mr. Martin did not know the true amount, it would be easier for Margaret to say no to his demands.

The majority of the few remaining letters after this point take on more of a newsy quality: how her daughter's family was doing, who Margaret had seen and where she had been, comments on the family in New York, what luck she had locating items for them. Frederick and Margaret seem to have reached a compromise at last. Margaret would live off the interest generated by her money; Frederick would indulge her with periodic gifts, like the fur muff and tippet, to keep her in proper style; and Mr. Martin would be kept in the dark.[84]

This arrangement appears to have worked well until 1814. Margaret James had always disagreed with Mr. Martin over his handling of money, but in 1814 the situation reached the breaking point. At that point, Mr. Martin's bad behavior took a turn for the worse, becoming infamous. By gambling or some other bad habit, Mr. Martin lost a fortune and his children's legacy. The trustees of the children's property had lent Mr. Martin a large portion of the estate without Mrs. Martin's knowledge.[85] Unable to pay "either the principle or interest," the Martins were forced to sell all of their furniture "for a mere song," a third of the original value.[86] In her distress, Margaretta wrote to her mother, confessing all. When Margaret heard of the dreadful news, she immediately sent all she could to her daughter. Margaret begged her brother for understanding, especially as her daughter was once again "in the Family way."[87] With "tears in [her] eyes" Margaret petitioned her brother to call in her bonds so that with her principal she could pay off the majority of the Martin's debt. Margaret knew that by calling in her bonds, she would reduce her income to the point of want, but she stated that she was willing to do so for her only child. She also added that it was within Frederick's power to lessen the financial impact on her. Margaret added that should Frederick have a problem with her scheme, he could transfer her funds to England where she would take full responsibility for her finances.[88]

Although we do not know for sure, it is unlikely that Frederick allowed his sister to deplete her funds to rescue her daughter's family. What is more likely is that Frederick intervened in the situation himself. The existence of Margaret James's will lends credence to the idea. In all probability, Frederick came up with some solution that kept Margaret from a life of poverty, or more accurately, an existence not worthy of a DePeyster, and kept the Martins from much the same.

Shortly after the death of Margaret James in 1815, her daughter's family finally made the move to New York that Margaret had always hoped for but never enjoyed herself. Once there, the Martins contested the will of Margaret James. In her will, Margaret James left all of her fortune in an ironclad trust for her three granddaughters. Neither their mother nor their father was to have access to that money.[89] The trusts established for the girls were guarded by executors, one of whom was

Frederick, with the strict understanding that no loans were allowed to the parents based on the funds within the trust. Margaret believed, with good cause, that if her son-in-law were to have access to the money, it would soon be squandered. However, Margaret did provide for her daughter to receive interest from the trust so that her grandchildren would not be entirely without means of support, should their father again act irresponsibly.[90] Unfortunately for Margaret, because her oldest granddaughter was then past her minority, she petitioned for, and was granted, her share of the inheritance. One presumes that she gave the money to her father to fund his latest endeavor, as stated in her petition. The results of Mr. Martin's endeavor, we do not know. Yet it is clear that through her will Margaret James tried to exert her influence over the next generation in much the same way that her grandmother, mother, and sisters had. In the end, she acted in every manner just as a DePeyster would: she acted to ensure the transmission and preservation of wealth, along with the prestige of the family, to future generations.

For both Margaret and Abraham, finding a way to balance their expectations of what it meant both socially and economically to be a DePeyster was a difficult task. Economically, neither of the two fully realized their ambitions. Socially, the two were better able to hold their ground by calling upon the DePeyster family network. In many cases this meant calling upon their younger brother Frederick, who was able to support himself financially in a manner they all thought befitting a DePeyster. While the call for aid sometimes strained the relationship between the siblings, the constant interaction also served to strengthen the overall ties between the families. Those ties left a legacy of expectations for the upcoming generation of DePeysters. Although the children of these siblings had no memory of the pre-Revolution golden days, they inherited the same sense of prestige and entitlement and the same tenacity to pursue those ideals, that their parents had. The search for wealth to support the DePeyster family name begun here, with Abraham, Margaret, and Frederick, would be a lasting legacy to their children, far more so than their Loyalist past.

Chapter 4

Building a Fortune

*A*fter ten years in New Brunswick, Canada, Frederick DePeyster returned to New York in 1793; he faced no angry mobs, no tar, no feathers. If his past as a Loyalist officer and former refugee made people balk, they did so in a manner that left no record. This unobtrusive return allowed Frederick DePeyster to use his wealth and his social, familial, and business contacts to grow a fortune and a reputation substantial enough to support the colonial weight of his family name. From the 1790s to the 1820s, Frederick used his extensive network of family and friends to increase and solidify the wealth and social standing of the DePeyster family. In doing so, he seamlessly integrated himself into a country whose creation he once opposed and from which he had become an exile.

During Frederick's preliminary visits to New York in 1792, he laid the groundwork for his merchant activities by reestablishing relationships with family and friends. He also began to assume responsibility for the various properties he had inherited from relatives during his youth. While Frederick was still in his minority, it seems that his father, James DePeyster, managed the properties for him, and continued to do so throughout the years Frederick lived in Canada.[1] These properties included lots on Broadway near Cortlandt Street in New York City; land in Bergen County, New Jersey; land in Bedford, New York; and property in Ulster County, New York.[2] These properties would have brought in valuable cash from their leases while Frederick was in cash-poor New Brunswick, and most likely would have eased Frederick's decision and ability to relocate to New York.

Out of all of the states, New York kept its anti-Tory laws on the books the longest. This was in blatant violation of the Treaty of Paris, 1783, which forbade retaliation against civilian Loyalists. Yet for all of New York's bravado where Loyalists were concerned, within a few months of the Loyalist Evacuation in 1783, both state and city became quite willing to forgive a Loyalist his past, so long as he was willing to accept the new government and keep his former alliances quiet. Part of the reason for this was New York's unique occupied position during the American Revolution. As Judith Van Buskirk demonstrates in *Generous Enemies*, so many people in New York City and its environs were forced to work together for mutual survival that the boundary between Patriot and Loyalist was sometimes blurred to the point of obscurity. In short, it was in everyone's best interests to be "forgetful" where appropriate.

Finally, in 1792, New York repealed the last of its anti-Tory laws, bringing the laws of the state in line with the *de facto* attitudes of the people. Nevertheless, Frederick did not attempt a permanent return to New York immediately. He remained in New Brunswick, conducting business and socializing with the elite of that place until 1793, when dramatic changes swept through the British Empire, New Brunswick, and New York affecting the economic systems of those places. That year, when war broke out on the European continent as an outgrowth of the French Revolution, the British government, fearful of being left in short supplies, decided not to enforce the Navigation System in the West Indies, effectively making it a "dead letter."[3] While the British government hoped that New Brunswick would still benefit from the war, the unofficial opening of the British West Indies to American trade, combined with poor harvests in New Brunswick, initially diverted trade from that colony to the United States, and to New York in particular. Frederick DePeyster, watching all of his hoped-for profits funnel away from New Brunswick to New York, must have been less than pleased; he decided to return to New York.

The New York that Frederick returned to was different in many ways from the New York he left, but many features of the city remained the same. The wealthy still clung to the southern tip of the city, and merchants still maintained their families and businesses close to the waterfront, where they would have easy access to the piers, docks, and their merchandise. Upon his return to New York, Frederick took up residence at 24 Broad Street.[4] This location in lower Manhattan was in the heart of New York's merchant community, and was the area where most of the city's wealthy inhabitants resided.[5] By locating himself in the heart of the merchant community, Frederick was declaring not only his profession, but also his intent to succeed. In the tradition of Colonial merchants (including his father and grandfather), Frederick DePeyster no doubt lived in the same building that he conducted business.[6] Frederick wasted no time in utilizing both his Saint John and New York contacts to establish himself in New York. In fact, it seems that Frederick may have laid the groundwork for this shift during visits he made to New York prior to his relocation there. Advertisements from this time reveal that Frederick imported gin, spices, and tea from Amsterdam, and that he sent ships to the Caribbean for Jamaican spirits, sugar, coffee, and Madeira wine.[7] Eventually, Frederick's network extended to ports all around the world: Amsterdam, the West Indies (British and Dutch), New Orleans, Canton (China), and even the more mundane, close-to-home, ports of Providence, Baltimore, Philadelphia, and Campobello.[8]

Frederick's decision to return to the United States, and New York in particular, was clearly a considered decision based on economics. New York held several advantages over Saint John for a merchant. The location of New York was far more developed as a port city than Saint John, which was barely getting its start. New York was able to handle a greater volume of ships than Saint John, which made locating ships for freight transport much less of a headache. New York also had a sufficient quantity of men wealthy enough to invest in different mercantile ventures. Being related to quite a few of those men was an advantage not lost on Frederick. For New York, this unofficial trade with the British West Indies brought with it new prosperity, and helped launch New York's port into the premier position in the United States; Frederick carefully positioned himself to take full advantage of the situation.[9] With the advent of war on the European Continent and the unofficial opening of trade with the British West Indies, ships from New York rushed to fill the needs of the markets they had once dominated.[10] Not to be outdone, the French, who had long allowed restricted trade with the United States, removed all restrictions to trade with their islands in the West Indies.[11] With his base now in New York, Frederick DePeyster was free to trade not only with the British but with the French as well. Problems arose, however, when the British began to stop American ships off the U.S. coast suspected of carrying on trade with the French.[12] Soon thereafter, the French also began to stop American ships in the West Indies suspected of carrying on trade with the British. Conducting business in this environment was risky, but profitable. From 1792 to 1794, New York exports increased by $2,900,000.[13]

Despite the potential profits of trading in the West Indies, this situation proved to be a bane for many New York merchants whose ships were caught in the crossfire of European interests; while it was undoubtedly a bane for Frederick DePeyster as well, he had contingencies. In true merchant-like fashion, Frederick never put all his eggs in one basket. Although he left New Brunswick, Frederick continued to do business there, purchasing and importing goods in New York to sell at New Brunswick. Frederick sold many of the goods he intended for New Brunswick to his brother Abraham, who then sold the items in his store. The brothers had developed a good working relationship before 1792 that continued even after Frederick relocated to New York. As New Brunswick was consistently cash-poor during its early years, Abraham sent fish, primarily salmon and herring, to keep accounts balanced. Frederick then sold the fish in New York or in another port, after he took care to distribute some as gifts to various members of the family. In exchange for the fish, Abraham usually requested flour and Indian corn, which were always in demand in New Brunswick.[14] Although Abraham had debts at this time and complained that they would "for ever keep me Poor, Poor indeed,"[15] they did not prevent the proper flow of business. In this way, Frederick prospered financially despite the squeeze placed on shipping by both the French and the British. Financial success also translated into greater social acceptance, both of which allowed for better integration into American society for this former Loyalist.

With the advent of a European war, opportunity for American merchants in New Brunswick only increased. American merchants shipped their goods to their contacts in New Brunswick, who passed along the goods to their contacts in Britain. American merchants were able to do this by supplying their ships with Canadian papers (to avoid seizure by the British) or by outright smuggling.[16] The geography of the Passamaquoddy Bay lent itself particularly to the latter activity, and locals frequently engaged in what they called "free trade." Locals took advantage of the region's strong currents, which changed with the tides, and could destroy the ships of those unfamiliar with their patterns. Numerous islands throughout the region provided easy shelter for smugglers, who also took advantage of the frequent dense fog to mask their activities. On top of all of this, the border between the United States and Canada was still unclear, providing a ready excuse for a vessel's presence in the wrong territory.[17] As Frederick established himself as a New York merchant, it is clear that his contacts in Canada remained an important element of his success. By utilizing these contacts, most notably his brother Abraham, Frederick firmly established himself in New York when other merchants, lacking these important contacts, were feeling the pinch of British and French ship seizures.

At the time Frederick returned to New York, the very nature of American commerce was undergoing a significant transformation into a new capitalist order of impersonal business. While Frederick continued to succeed in the old personalist merchant economy, he was not shy about embracing the new business order. In this respect, Frederick was no different from many of his contemporaries who put their money to work through diverse investment opportunities.[18] For instance, in 1795, Frederick invested with John Andrew Graham (a Lieutenant-Colonel with the Vermont Militia during the Revolution who went on to be one of Vermont's top-rated criminal attorneys), to whom the state of Vermont had granted exclusive rights for smelting all "gold, silver, lead, brass, & copper ore" for 35 years.[19] Graham had apparently sought the monopoly so that he could sell shares to pay off his debt; he sold at least $10,000 worth of shares.[20]

Another example of Frederick's strategic financial investments and social positioning came in 1796 when Frederick invested in the Western Inland Lock & Navigation Company.[21] The Western Inland Lock & Navigation Company was incorporated in 1792 by the New

York State Legislature.[22] Its purpose was to "develop the route up the Mohawk [River] and beyond to Lake Ontario and, if possible, as far west as the Finger Lakes."[23] At the outset, the Western Company did not consider itself a canal-building operation. As Peter L. Bernstein stated, "the word 'navigation' in these contexts had long meant improving the navigability of the rivers and nothing more than that."[24] Although the Western Company figured it would have to build locks to bypass areas such as "rapids, falls, and long stretches of shallow water," the river itself was to be the primary route.[25] The legislature authorized the company to sell one thousand shares at $25 a share.

The Western Company had the support of the political, social, and economic elite of New York. By investing in the company, Frederick ensured that his name was on the same lists as those elites. Investing in the Western Company also would have provided Frederick with an opportunity to meet those individuals, if he had not already done so, and to further develop his business and social contacts. Before the incorporation of the Western Company, Jeremiah Van Rensselaer, one of the largest landowners in New York, was among its main supporters. The bill of incorporation itself was sponsored jointly in the state legislature by Governor George Clinton and State Senator General Philip Schuyler, heir to the vast Schuyler estate near Albany, hero of the American Revolution, New York state senator, and father-in-law to Alexander Hamilton. Schuyler was then named as president to the Western Company and acted as the company's first chief engineer despite the fact that he had no experience in that area. Then again, not many Americans at that time had engineering experience. Eventually, the company hired William Weston, an English engineer, to fill the position of chief engineer. In 1803, Schuyler went on to serve as a U.S. Senator for the State of New York. Members of the company's board of directors and shareholders were equally distinguished, and included many wealthy merchants and landowners whose acquaintance could be useful to an ambitious man like Frederick DePeyster. Among the investors were the likes of Nicholas Low, a successful merchant and land developer;[26] Robert Troup, judge in the U.S. District Court of New York and member of the New York Assembly;[27] Thomas Eddy, merchant and insurance agent;[28] and the leading New York merchant firm of LeRoy, Bayard & McEvers, just to name a few.[29] We know for certain that Frederick would later utilize his contacts with the firm of LeRoy, Bayard & Co. to secure the position of supercargo for his nephew James DePeyster Ogden in 1812.

For Frederick DePeyster, there also were practical reasons for investing in the Western Company, aside from the status of its peers. Merchants invested with the Western Company in hopes that the improvement of the river would lower the cost of transporting freight and allow for a more timely delivery of goods from upstate New York, such as "meat, flour, furs, lumber, pearl ash (a kind of potash), wheat, butter, lard, salt . . . cotton, linen and glass."[30] No doubt Frederick DePeyster held many of the same expectations. Frederick not only exported many of those goods, he also owned property in upstate New York. If there was easier access to markets for those properties, they would become more profitable for him as well. Frederick would find it easier to locate tenants for those properties, and as those properties became more profitable to the tenants, they likewise would become more profitable to Frederick himself. Frederick continued to invest in the company by buying stock again in March 1797, July 1798, and April 1798.

Although the company was successful in making the Mohawk more navigable by clearing the river of sandbars and debris, and also in opening a water passage between the Mohawk and Wood Creek, the company itself made barely enough money to pay for repairs, and paid out only two dividends in its history, once in 1798 and again in 1813.[31] The Company survived until the state officially purchased its property as part of the Erie Canal project.[32] Despite the financial failure of this company to produce a profit as a private venture, it was important in that it provided a model to the state of New York of what was possible in the realm of waterways, locks and dams, and canals. In short, the Western Company made the building and public financing of the Erie Canal possible.[33]

Frederick continued to invest in transportation throughout his life, including both turnpikes and bridges. Turnpikes were a popular way for states to build roads as it came at very little expense to them and investors enjoyed the idea of earning profits through tolls.[34]

Frederick invested in the Morris Turnpike Company in New Jersey, whose road traversed 62 miles from Elizabethtown Point to the Delaware River.[35] He also invested in the Second Great Turnpike Company, organized by William Cooper,[36] and later in the Third Great Turnpike Company, whose road was plank-covered, but suffered from competition with the Erie Canal.[37] Overall, turnpikes were not the money-makers that investors hoped for, as many individuals simply detoured around the tollgates; what little profits they did make were funneled into road repair and maintenance, not investors' pockets.[38] Bridges, on the other hand, tended to be a more profitable investment as an attempt to bypass the toll gate meant a detour into the river. Frederick invested in the Palatine Bridge, which crossed the Mohawk River in New York. Today, there is a small community in the same spot that carries the name. Remittances from the Palatine Bridge were delivered regularly with the odd exception of ice damage to the bridge. Each of the investments Frederick made would have opened access to his lands in upstate New York and helped to ease the transportation of goods from those places to markets. In this respect, Frederick displays the same desires as many of his contemporaries, like William Cooper, who hoped to open access to the frontier.

In 1796, Frederick DePeyster also invested in the New-York Insurance Company.[39] If not among the elite wealthy of the day, Frederick certainly followed their lead in moneymaking practices. Investing in insurance was a common practice for the wealthy of the day.[40] Investing in insurance—in Frederick's case, marine and fire insurance—was a smart business move. Disasters were going to happen, but as with the insurance industry today, more people buy protection than actually claim its coverage. As ships bearing the American flag fell prey to first the British and then the French during the Quasi-War, more ship owners and merchants were insuring their vessels and cargo, making owning stock in an insurance company a lucrative prospect. It is important to note that even this investment was evidence of the changing American economy and Frederick's willingness to participate in it. Insurance was no longer the community safeguard that it had once been. As insurance companies moved from being mutual ventures to incorporated businesses, actuarial rules guided the allotment of risk and benefit, turning the insurance industry into the profit-driven realm. Thomas Eddy, one of the investors in the Western Company, built a second fortune for himself in this way after failing as a merchant.

From all of his various investments, Frederick DePeyster received dividends from the profits of the ventures, helping to keep himself afloat even if some of his ships went down. The varied and far-ranging investments of Frederick reveal that he was willing to utilize the time-honored traditions of the merchant, which included the willingness to innovate and invest in new and diverse business ventures. It is a pattern that he repeated throughout his life. Again, this pattern was not uncommon, especially in New York, and it was one that the most wealthy residents of New York City employed.[41]

An unusual example of Frederick's diverse activities came in 1799, when John Gray contacted Frederick to request help in the settlement of a property dispute.[42] The reason for his choice is unknown, but he clearly thought Frederick could help in some way. John Gray, of Jamaica, West Indies, was heir to the New Jersey estate called Little Falls.[43] Title to the estate, however, had passed to Colonel Samuel Ogden and his son David B. Ogden, who had purchased the estate from the State of New Jersey in 1780. The Colonel and his son were distantly related to Dr. Jacob Ogden Jr., husband of Mary DePeyster. Both Jacob and the Colonel had the same grandfather, Josiah Ogden, During the Revolutionary War, however, these branches of the family fell on opposite sides of the divide. We do not know what kind of a relationship, if any, existed between these two branches. During the late Revolutionary War, the estate had been confiscated by the for-feiture commission; its owner at the time, James Gray, was a known Loyalist who fled behind British lines and later settled in Montreal. The property was supposed to pass to James's heir, and therefore be safe from confiscation or forfeiture, but this did not happen. John Gray meant to sue the Ogdens for the property because he believed, and had a letter attesting to the fact, that the Ogdens were behind the confiscation of the estate in the first place.[44] John Gray wrote in hopes that Frederick would gather any information pertaining to the situation that could be useful in the suit against the Ogdens.[45] Interestingly, Gray retained Aaron Ogden as his attorney. Aaron Ogden was also distantly related to the Colonel and his son; both Aaron and the Colonel were the great-great grandsons of John Ogden, the first of the Ogdens in America, through different lines. It was Aaron Ogden who would later become famously involved in the landmark legal case, *Gibbons v. Ogden.*

Frederick apparently decided to help John Gray. We do not know why, because any previous relationship between the two is unknown. It could be that Frederick knew James Gray, the original owner, from his Loyalist days and decided to help an old friend. It could be that in helping John Gray, Frederick might in some way increase the value of his property in New Jersey. Another possibility is that John Gray was from Jamaica, and might have provided valuable contacts for Frederick in the West Indies. We simply do not know. Nevertheless, Frederick did decide to help, and the two struck up an association in which Gray seems to have acted as Frederick's land agent in New Jersey, New York, and Canada for a short time afterward, possibly in exchange for Frederick's help. In July 1799, Gray wrote to Frederick that of "our intended prospect" along the Hackensack & Passaic Rivers, "nothing material can be depended upon this season."[46]

Just a month later Gray wrote again, this time from Saint John, New Brunswick, writing that Saint John's ship captains were, "in a most wonderful hurry, and over head and ears in business."[47] This was indeed the case; continued warfare in Europe finally spurred the economy of New Brunswick, creating economic stability in that region for the first time as Britain drew heavily upon the region for its agriculture and timber, and providing opportunity for American merchants. In the separation of New Brunswick from Nova Scotia, four men were particularly influential: Thomas Carleton, Edward Winslow, George Duncan Ludlow, and John Coffin. Although Coffin never became wealthy, he was very influential politically. Coffin served in the New Brunswick Assembly as a representative for King's County for more than twenty years in addition to holding several other government positions. In that same letter, Gray informed Frederick that he delivered his letters to Brigadier Coffin as directed before preparing for a voyage up the Saint John River.[48] Although Gray does not specifically mention it, it is safe to assume he was heading upriver to check on Frederick's properties as other agents did. Gray emphasized the short duration of the trip; he intended to return to Saint John by the 30th of August in order to meet with the governor.[49] That Gray was able to meet with two men of such importance in that place is a testimony to both Frederick DePeyster's continuing level of consequence there and to John Gray's abilities.

For the remainder of the year, John Gray, on business for Frederick DePeyster, made his way from Saint John, to Windsor, and Halifax and back again to Saint John, where he intended to spend the winter. In his letters to Frederick, Gray complains of the difficulty in doing business with New York due to an epidemic of what Gray calls the "Putred [sic] Effluvia."[50] Although not as severe as the yellow fever epidemic of 1798, thanks in part to New York City's Quarantine Act of 1799,[51] it was still bad enough that many vessels refused to dock there, and the wealthy fled for their country estates.[52] Frederick was undoubtedly grateful for his outside investments at this point. Despite the danger and their close proximity to the waterfront, an area where disease usually raged, it appears that the DePeysters stayed in the city; Gray said that the family, which now included four sons and Frederick Augustus,[53] was only "a [short] distance from the malignant air" of the docks and wharves.[54] Gray further recommended that Frederick encourage the city to purify the air by condemning "Front St. Water St. and Pearl St." but to wait until winter to tear up the pavement for those areas because "if you was to attempt removing your paved ground in the summer the foul air would annihilate the states of York & Jersey."[55]

The association between the two men seems to have come to an end in the year 1800, when Gray appears to have abruptly ended his suit for the New Jersey estate of Little Falls (the case was the initial cause for the acquaintanceship).[56] He wrote to Frederick that he understood relations between the United States and Great Britain had taken a bad turn (perhaps in response to the Convention of 1800, which ended hostilities between the United States and France), "and that the Commissioners have left Phil[adelphia] in the outmost disgust."[57] If relations between the two countries grew hostile, the courts of New Jersey would be unfavorable to the idea of returning property to the heir of a Loyalist. Although John Gray was far from happy with the situation, as the land would have provided continued income and not just a one-time payout, he decided to take a settlement offer rather than continue the fight for full restoration of the property. Cases relating to compensation for confiscated Loyalist lands were rarely brought to court because confiscation was a wartime measure. The fact that Gray was able to bring a suit against the purchasers of the estate at all makes it clear that there was more to the case than simple confiscation by the State.[58]

Frederick DePeyster's participation in Gray's suit requires a closer examination because it serves as an important marker in evaluating Frederick's progress in integrating into American society. Reviewing his past, briefly, is important in understanding how far Frederick had come at this point. Frederick was a former Loyalist officer who had left New York at the end of the American Revolution. Frederick settled in New Brunswick, Canada, where he remained for ten years, building a fortune by accumulating land and engaging in merchant activities. In 1793, Frederick, still drawing his military half-pay, returned to New York, the last of the states to repeal its anti-Tory laws (they did so in 1792). Although New York's enforcement of those laws was relatively lax, the obnoxious Loyalist could still draw threats and violence. Frederick quickly set about building his fortune and family reputation through his merchant activities and other investments. By 1799, Frederick had so succeeded at integrating himself into New York society that he was able to assist John Gray in his bid to recover a Loyalist estate, confiscated during the American Revolution, that was in the possession of a prominent Patriot family. He did this without fear of violent retaliation, economic setback, or social backlash. Frederick DePeyster simply took it for granted that he could act in such a manner and he did so. His Loyalist past was simply not an issue.

Although his association with Gray was at an end, Frederick's fortunes do not appear to have been adversely impacted by the event. In 1800 Frederick DePeyster purchased a slave girl named Dinah, between the age of four and five.[59] Dinah was not DePeyster's only slave; he had at least two others, an older woman named Judah and her son, Henry.[60] With an ever-growing household (Frederick and Helen's fifth son and last child was born in 1800), extra help would have been valued. Despite the state's adoption of a plan of gradual emancipation in 1799, ownership of slaves was still a mark of wealth.[61] Although continued ownership of slaves in New York was somewhat unusual after 1799, the DePeysters were by no means an oddity. By 1810, New York City could still count about 1,500 slaves in its households, most of whom were women and children.[62] It should be noted that the majority of households in New York that continued to hold slaves were Dutch households. Thus, in addition to being a marker of wealth, slaveholding was also a mark of cultural heritage. For Frederick DePeyster, it is possible that he was purposefully reminding New York of his family's deep connection and devotion to New York itself rather than to whatever union the state currently belonged.

Another opportunity for Frederick DePeyster to diversify his investments came with the advent of the New York Bread Company. Dating back to its early history, the Common Council in New York City controlled the price of bread through a control known as the assize. New York's bakers had for years petitioned the Council to allow the market to determine the price of bread; in 1800, the Council agreed, so long as the bakers agreed to sell at a reasonable price, not the highest the market would allow. Despite the agreement, the bakers did not lower their prices in 1801 when the price of flour dropped, and the Council brought back the assize.[63] In retaliation, the city's bakers went on strike until the Council allowed them to set their own prices again. The Council gave in, but the fight was far from over. A group of New York's "concerned" gentry, including Frederick DePeyster, came together to form the New York Bread Company. Frederick served as the company's president.[64] The group's stated purpose was to produce bread in large quantities with semiskilled laborers so that the price of bread would remain low; the possibility of profit was no doubt an equally compelling force. This move took the bakers by surprise. Their purpose in agitating for market prices was to control it themselves. The advent of the New York Bread Company and its use of semiskilled laborers caused the bakers to realize the jeopardy in which they had placed their craft.[65] When the bakers began to protest the Company and the damaging effect it would have on their trade, one New Yorker who styled himself "a Bread Eater" wrote a letter to the *Mercantile Advertiser* stating that if the bakers really wanted a free market, as they claimed, they would welcome the addition of the Company, but all the bakers really wanted was to extract "unreasonable profits" from the people of New York.[66] The mass acceptance of the New York Bread Company marked the beginning of a capitalist labor market in New York, and Frederick DePeyster, however unintentionally, helped to bring an end to the age of the skilled artisan.[67]

Meanwhile, Frederick DePeyster continued his trade in Amsterdam gin, spices, tea, Jamaican spirits, West Indian sugar, coffee, and Madeira wine. He also began an association with the firm of Andrews & Campbell around 1804. Based out of Campobello, plaster was the firm's main concern, although they also sent Frederick various other staple items from Passamaquoddy Bay. They sent clear boards, shingles, and staves; they also sent fish, both pickled and smoked (usually alewives). Frederick sent those goods on to Boston, Baltimore, Philadelphia, or Scotland. Frederick also filled orders for Andrews & Campbell in New York, then sent the ships on to Campobello or Saint John, where they were filled with plaster and returned to New York. The fact that the firm was based in Campobello and shipped plaster is an indication that Andrews & Campbell were engaged at least partly in smuggling or "free trade." The British government was attempting to restrict and control the plaster trade. Their efforts resulted in the "Plaster War" of 1820, where local residents took up arms in protest over the matter.[68]

This is significant in that while Britain had suspended the Navigation Acts for the West Indies and had partially suspended them for the importation of foodstuffs into New Brunswick, the majority of the goods exchanged between Frederick DePeyster and Andrews & Campbell, including plaster, were considered contraband by the British Government. The firm of Andrews & Campbell is also interesting in that Israel Andrews "lived in the same household as Thomas Henderson, the British customs officer," and Colin Campbell Jr. was the son of the Passamaquoddy surveyor and head of customs.[69]

While Andrews & Campbell traded in many items, their priority was plaster, or gypsum as it is more commonly known today. Gypsum is a soft rock that is readily extractable in New Brunswick and Nova Scotia. The fact that it was easy to harvest meant that it was often gathered by farmers and other small producers who hoped to supplement their income by selling it to firms like Andrews & Campbell. The plaster itself found a ready market in the United States, where it was used as a chemical fertilizer, particularly in Pennsylvania, Maryland, and Virginia.[70]

Andrews & Campbell quickly found that while plaster was plentiful, and the demand high, it was difficult to find a ship that would transport it. Part of the reason for this was the booming economy of Canada. With the Napoleonic Wars raging in Europe, Britain leaned heavily on its North American holding for food and other staples. Next to those, shipping plaster to New York was far from a priority for many merchants and ship captains. Part of the reason for this was that the product took up a lot of room but was generally not as valuable as other items that might be smuggled, particularly during a war.[71] To help remedy the situation, Andrews & Campbell purchased a third of a ship, the *George*, in 1805.[72] This was a typical pattern for plaster producers.[73] They meant the ship to transport plaster from Windsor to Campobello, and occasionally farther where a larger ship could then transport it as a small part of a larger cargo. Andrews & Campbell also implored Frederick to contract at least two ships from New York to carry plaster for the upcoming summer; they already had one hundred tons of plaster at Campobello awaiting transport.[74] By June, however, Andrews & Campbell still had not located a ship to transport their plaster, so they wrote Frederick and requested his assistance once again. This time, they added that, in addition to sending plaster, they also had a shipment of clear boards and between 800 and 1,000 barrels of smoked and pickled Alewives to send.[75] In July, Andrews and Campbell finally chartered the sloop *Cynthia*, with Captain Price, to carry the plaster and 108 barrels of smoked alewives. They also chartered a schooner by which they would send Frederick more fish if the market in New York was good, and they meant to send the *George* back to New York with a cargo of clear boards when she returned from her present voyage. The men insisted that if Frederick could procure "one or two vessels" they would quickly send the ships back full as they "have now five Hundred tons [of plaster] on hand and [are] daily purchasing more."[76]

As 1805 continued, the plaster finally started moving out for distant ports. With each sale, the partnership requested that Frederick purchase for them pork, ship bread, corn, flour, Indian meal, rye meal,

English cannon powder, iron, and books, because the prices for those articles continued to rise due to increasing scarcity in Saint John and Campobello. They also requested that Frederick have the *George* refitted with new canvas, rope, and interestingly, with "An American Sea Letter," before they sent her on to the West Indies for the winter.[77] By October of that year, the partners had indeed secured "A Compleat Set of fabricated American papers which have proved very useful to Vessels Sailing from this port."[78]

Although their goods were now moving, Andrews & Campbell continued to face the problem of too much cargo and too little ship. When a 300-ton ship the partners hired failed to arrive, they had to scramble to find a 200- to 250-ton ship to carry a portion of the lumber so that the whole load would not remain on the beaches of Campobello over the winter. Accordingly, they finally asked Frederick to buy them a ship (they would eventually pay him back through the sale of plaster) of 180- to 200 tons, "half worn" was fine, so long as the ship was "pretty full built deep in the [hold]."[79] They assured Frederick that they could keep the ship in service year-round, which meant he would receive a steady flow of remittance from the investment.[80]

The correspondence of Andrews and Campbell abruptly ends at the close of 1805. Whether the two actually closed all business relations at this time is unknown. The correspondence ends abruptly; although this could indicate a bad end, it more likely indicates a loss of records, especially as Andrews's name appears again in other correspondence a few years later. Nevertheless, with those men or others, over the next few years, Frederick continued doing brisk business in plaster from Campobello. Problems with ships' registers likewise continued although this time Frederick learned of the problems from business associate Anthony Girard.[81] The two men contracted the schooner *Jane* to sail to Halifax. When the *Jane* arrived there, the collector of the customs house inspected the ship's register and informed the captain, Jered Belding, that the document was "faulty in every respect and the vessel is liable to seizure."[82] The *Jane* was not allowed to load any cargo, so Belding planned to head back to Campobello to have the former owner Israel Andrews (of Andrews & Campbell fame), provide a bill of sale and a new register.[83]

It is important to note that this business was carried on during the years in which trade with the British Empire was restricted by the American government by the Non-Importation Act of 1806, the Embargo Act of 1807, and the Non-Intercourse Act of 1809. Overall, Frederick seems to have had no problem in violating those laws, just as his father had no problem with smuggling during the French and Indian War. He does, however, seem to have paid some sort of lip service to the Acts, perhaps by scaling back his trade with Europe while covertly continuing his trade with New Brunswick. For instance, in 1808, while the Embargo Act was still in force, Frederick DePeyster's business associate Frederick Gebhard wrote to him from Amsterdam, "I expect you will be a complete farmer now, as the Embargo lasted all summer," and went on to muse that Frederick must have retreated to his Bloomingdale estate, where he no doubt spent his time making improvements to the property.[84] Gebhard also mentioned that if Congress would lift the embargo soon, Frederick should send sugar over immediately because the market in Holland was very good for it just then; prices from the West Indies were "exorbitant high," and in any case, "no vessels are at present permitted to enter or to sail, how long this will last is uncertain."[85]

It is important to note that during a time when many merchants suffered under the Non-Importation and Embargo Acts, Frederick DePeyster prospered. While the economy was sluggish, Frederick purchased vessels, in whole or part. He not only purchased a country estate (a clear sign of wealth) but actively made improvements to it. While the family may have spent more time at Bloomingdale, it is quite clear that it was not for want of business in the city. In addition to his Canadian trade, Frederick also became more involved with the so-called cotton triangle. At a time when trade with outside nations was prohibited, the cotton triangle (coastal trade with the southern states) became an important lifeline for many northern merchants. In the cotton triangle, New York merchants brought the southern states into their business sphere by purchasing cotton from the growers in the south, and in return, selling them cheap manufactured goods. The merchants then sold the cotton to manufacturers in the Northeastern states or Liverpool.[86] The specifics and extent of Frederick's involvement in this trade are unknown; however, Frederick often sent the goods he acquired from Canada, both with Abraham and later Andrews & Campbell, on to other markets for sale when New York would not provide the price he wanted for his goods. Likewise, the DePeyster Collection at the New-York Historical Society contains the odd note regarding the consignment of Frederick's goods with merchants in other cities. Additionally, Frederick's son Robert later traveled to South Carolina and Georgia (even a foray into Florida to visit Amelia Island) in an attempt to recoup debts owed to Frederick for past business. Moreover, Frederick later acquired cotton in New Orleans, for sale in both Liverpool and New England. Nevertheless, trading with the American south while trade with outside nations was prohibited developed internal trade and opened new markets for New York merchants, including Frederick DePeyster.[87]

As Jefferson's Embargo settled over the country, New York's economy nosedived. In 1808, international exports dropped by 80 percent, imports by 60 percent. Unemployment raged in the city as shipping came to a crawl.[88] Private charities like the Humane Society (of which Frederick DePeyster was a member) formed to alleviate the plight of the poor and unemployed. Although this was a charitable activity, and Frederick DePeyster may have genuinely felt compassion for his fellow New Yorkers, belonging to charitable associations was also a mark of wealth and status. According to Edward Pessen, "more than 15% of the city's richest men belonged to or were active in five or more" associations.[89] Although we do not know the exact state of Frederick's finances at this time, there is no doubt that he had now gained the acceptance of the social and business elite of New York, cementing the DePeyster name among their numbers for another generation.

In the midst of all of his new investments and activities, Frederick DePeyster did not neglect his older ones that first brought him wealth in Canada. Perhaps at this point, with the downturn in the New York economy, the older investments proved that they were still important. In 1810, Frederick sent Henry Fine to Saint John as his agent in order to secure his New Brunswick property. He advised Fine to oust Timothy Parks from his water lot in Saint John after twenty years of residence there because, in that entire time Parks had not paid anything in rent.[90]

Frederick made it clear that he did not care whether Fine found a new tenant for the property or sold it outright, so long as Parks no longer held residence there. His concern is justified: having lived on the property for so long, Parks could claim title through occupation, and Frederick DePeyster did not want the land to pass from him without some benefit. If Parks refused to leave the property, Frederick advised Fine to file suit with one of two prominent attorneys in Saint John. After seeing to the Saint John water lot, Mr. Fine was to hire a boat, travel up the Saint John River to attend to Frederick's other New Brunswick property, and settle debts owed to Frederick along the way. Mr. Fine was warned that because of the cash-poor environment in the agricultural economy of New Brunswick, some debts might be paid in fish, others in cash, or notes. Frederick admonished Fine to make sure all fish were of good quality and not to leave without some form of payment.[91] For this business, Mr. Fine was to sail up to Maugerville and then to Fredericton and a little beyond.[92]

While Frederick sent Henry Fine to New Brunswick on his business, problems began to crop up for Frederick in another area as a result of the death of William Cooper in December of 1809. Frederick was an investor in William Cooper's high-profile DeKalb development project. Early on, Cooper had registered impressive sales, but his shoddy surveying practices, along with high tenant turnover, soon revealed that he had sacrificed stability and long-term profits for impressive short-term results. At his death, Cooper's heirs anticipated inheriting a large estate that would leave them well provided for; what they received instead was an estate in shambles, much of it tied to the DeKalb project.[93] Cooper's heirs soon discovered that their father's New York partners, including Frederick DePeyster, expected to receive a return on their investment, and meant to receive it.

At first, the New York investors, Frederick included, attempted to work with the heirs to produce dividends. This did not happen.[94] Eventually, Henry Fine made his way to DeKalb, New York to inspect and report on the situation there.[95] It is likely that Frederick was somehow involved in the situation, given the fact that Henry Fine had acted as his agent in New Brunswick. In 1815, the New York investors, frustrated with the management of DeKalb under William Cooper's heirs, convinced the heirs to accept John Fine to manage DeKalb.[96] In short, Frederick DePeyster did not abandon this investment easily, and he worked toward making it profitable for himself and for the other wealthy New York investors.

In 1812, tensions between the United States and Great Britain finally boiled over with a declaration of war by the United States. The situation between the two countries had never been truly peaceful, even following the Treaty of Paris, 1783. Initially, the British refusal to relinquish their claim on the Northwest Territory infuriated the Americans. The situation only grew worse when Britain decided to enforce the Navigation Acts, effectively cutting the United States out of valuable trade with the British West Indies. In the same way that issues of impressment and confiscation brought about the Non-Importation and Embargo Acts, enough Americans grew tired of the disregard for neutral shipping rights and American sovereignty that Congress declared war. The United States, however, was woefully unprepared for war; they lacked both the military and the finances to properly conduct a war. President James Madison turned to staunch supporter and New York merchant Jacob Barker to help with the financial problems by securing loans for the government. Jacob Barker and his activities supporting the war effort are well recorded. Out of his personal finances, Barker lent the U.S. Government $5 million, which was never repaid. Most accounts say the war ruined Barker's finances, but it was the failure of the Life and Fire Insurance Company and his subsequent trial for conspiracy to defraud the public that ended his career in New York. Thereafter, Barker moved to New Orleans and set about rebuilding his fortune.[97]

Within a year of the declaration of war, Britain had succeeded in blockading the American coast. In this difficult situation, Frederick found a new way to continue in his business activities, just as he had through previous obstacles. This time, his opportunity came through Jacob Barker's son Abraham, who had moved to New Orleans just before the declaration of war. In New Orleans, Abraham established a blockade-running operation. The primary contact in New Orleans for the operation was Mayhew Fletcher, from whom Barker, Frederick, and a handful of others obtained sugar, cotton, and flour.[98] Running a British blockade to ship goods to New York was a tricky and dangerous business. The British, who now fought the Americans in addition to their continuing war with Napoléon, were unwilling to allow the Americans any benefit that they could prevent. Despite the risk of confiscation, merchants willing to run blockades could reap great rewards. For Frederick, who had smuggled goods throughout the preceding embargo, those rewards were worth the risk and he and his associates funded illicit voyages in which the shipping manifests were kept purposely vague. For Jacob Barker and Frederick DePeyster, Mayhew Fletcher was the man they trusted to organize and arrange the delivery of the contraband cargo safely.[99]

Fletcher went to great pains to assure Frederick and his other New York clients that the merchandise was of good quality, undamaged by hurricane, and that the sugar and cotton were well concealed beneath the flour in a secret compartment of the *Alfred*'s. Fletcher added that the ship's manifest stated that the cargo consisted solely of flour, that the cargo was loaded prior to the hiring of the crew, and that all except captain and mate believed the ship of flour destined for Lisbon, not New York. Further, the captain was "fully apprized of the Blockade of the Chesapeake & Delaware, intends to give those places a good berth & if boarded . . . will be found in distress."[100]

On June 18, 1813, the *Alfred* was reported as "arrived safe" at Newport. When apprised of that ship's successful voyage, Fletcher let Frederick know that he had another ship, the *Warren*, that they would willingly send on a similar voyage. This time around, however, they would prefer the ship have papers from Halifax and be insured. Fletcher went on to explain that the consensus among merchants in New Orleans was that the British would not enforce the blockade of the Mississippi. No cruisers had yet appeared to do the job, and merchants were hopeful they never would. Failing the Halifax papers, Fletcher informed DePeyster that "some shipments are making via Pensacola to England under the Spanish flag" or through Russian ships willing to carry tobacco and cotton. To help facilitate business, Fletcher attached the current New Orleans price list to his letter.[101] A financial statement issued to Frederick by Abraham Barker at the end of 1813 reveals that Frederick was due $88,599.67 as his share of the *Alfred*'s profits and

$14,740.97 for his share in another ship, the *Adventure*.[102] Frederick was not only making a lot of money during the War of 1812, but he was doing so with men who dominated the economy of New York.

During the war, Frederick made plans to retire to either his farm in Duchess County or his country estate at Bloomingdale, should his home in New York City become threatened by hostilities.[103] He also took the precaution of hiding and burning documents that tied himself and family too closely to the Loyalist past. He later admitted burning documents during this time from Lord Cornwallis and other important personages left over from the Revolutionary War.[104] We do not know why he took these actions. He may have planned to move his family simply to keep them safe during a time of war in a port city. In burning the Revolutionary documents he may have wanted to close the door on his past once and for all. Regardless of his motivations, these actions reveal that Frederick was a careful, calculating man, just as he had been throughout his life as evidenced by his choice of wives, his investments, and the charitable organizations with which he associated himself. For the duration of the war, Frederick remained in his home on Broad Street, continued with his business investments, and proceeded with business as usual; all but his youngest son (Abraham) participated in the war effort.[105]

At the end of the war, changes were once again in store for Frederick DePeyster. On April 14, 1815, the New York State Legislature passed an act to incorporate the National Insurance Company (NIC), which was concerned mainly with marine insurance. One year after that, Frederick DePeyster was elected president of the NIC. While the incident with John Gray revealed the level of Frederick's integration with New York society, being named to the presidency of this type of financial institution reveals the elite social and economic status he had attained, since only individuals of substantial wealth were named to this type of position. Likewise, the men in these positions had to command the trust and respect of the business community; if they did not, the institution would soon find itself without investors or customers. To be president, or even a director, of one of these institutions meant that the individual must own a considerable portion of the company's stock.[106] This was important because it ensured that those in charge would take a personal interest in the company and would be as careful with it as they would with their own finances because the two were intertwined. Frederick continued on as president with the NIC until 1823.

In 1818, not long after being named to the presidency of the NIC, Frederick DePeyster was named as one of the directors of the New York Branch Bank of the Bank of the United States.[107] This was actually the Second Bank of the United States; Congress had allowed the charter for the first Bank to expire in 1811. The Second Bank of the United States was chartered in 1816 in an effort to improve the credit of the United States government, to restore confidence in the banking and monetary system, and harness the postwar economic boom. Its creation was championed by John Jacob Astor and Jacob Barker, among others. As with his position as NIC President, serving as a director for the New York Branch of the Bank of the United States is a marker of the elite social and economic status Frederick DePeyster had attained at that place.

Yet the course of the Second Bank of the United States was anything but smooth, and no doubt gave Frederick more trouble than he anticipated. The bank's first year of operation, 1817, was rough as the bank tried to figure out how to operate in the new economy and somehow straighten out the economic jumble it inherited. In late 1818, the postwar economic boom collapsed. Following the War of 1812, and the end of the Napoleonic Wars in Europe, demand for American goods soared. In 1818, cotton sold for as much as 32 cents a pound, mostly to British textile mills. By 1819, the British turned to cotton from India as a cheaper alternative. The American cotton market collapsed, and cotton sold for about 14 cents a pound that year. The collapse of the price of cotton cascaded into other American markets as foreign demand fell across the board when Europe experienced a bumper harvest. At the same time, cases of extensive fraud and embezzlement surfaced in the Second Bank of the United States.[108] To save itself, the bank constricted credit just when the economy needed it, and pressed local banks to redeem their notes in specie (hard currency), putting even more pressure on the economy. The collision of these events caused panic and recession in the American economy. While the bank scrambled to reform, many Americans called for a repeal of the bank's charter. For Frederick, a director, and for other heavily invested family members, the continuance of the bank was of the utmost importance. While Congress deliberated, the bank's stock in Philadelphia plummeted. Although Congress decided not to repeal the bank's charter, the institution had already lost the public's confidence.[109]

While Frederick served on different financial boards, pursued his DeKalb investment, and widened his participation on the boards of various charitable organizations,[110] he also continued and even expanded his regular merchant activities. In 1818, Frederick still took risks in business and followed the pattern that had first made him successful; he diversified. Frederick invested with a partnership, S. B. & S. Hoffman, who were attempting to make rum in the United States. The idea was that in producing rum domestically, they could sell the liquor cheaper and make a bigger profit than could be had from the sale of the Jamaican variety.[111] Frederick also sent his nephew James DePeyster Ogden to New Orleans to act as his purchasing agent. While there, James Ogden purchased cotton (for sale at Liverpool and in New England), tobacco, and sugar, and he displayed his uncle's talent for turning a profit in difficult economic circumstances by doing so even as the cotton market collapsed in 1819.[112]

Frederick was 61 in 1819, and although he continued to actively carry on with business, his sons began to share a growing concern for their father. Although he continued to be a highly successful merchant in his own right, Frederick's growing list of activities apart from the import-export business caused his sons to worry that one of his many spinning plates would fall and shatter. They sincerely hoped that he would retire from business before these distractions affected his finances and, therefore, the family's elite economic and social position. In response to the growing concerns of his sons, Frederick assured his son James that he would retire from his merchant activities by 1820, and that when he did, his sons would inherit the firm's name DePeyster, Son & Company.[113] After that, he expected them to manage the business on their own, without further financial assistance from him, carrying on the DePeyster tradition themselves and preserving the status of the family into the next generation. In the meantime, Frederick planned to continue as he had before, filling his days with business, social, and humanitarian obligations.[114]

In 1820, the year of Frederick's promised retirement, his status, and therefore that of the DePeyster family, was such that his son, Frederick Jr., was able to arrange a marriage with Mary Justina Watts, daughter of John Watts, one of New York's wealthiest men.[115] At this time in New York, marriage practices continued as they had since the colonial days. The elite married the elite. Their marriages were not random, and they were not necessarily "love" matches. Marriage for the elite, even during this time of democracy and the rise of the common man, were financial arrangements meant to keep wealth and grow it.[116] That Frederick's son was able to marry the daughter of one of New York's wealthiest individuals speaks to the elite economic stature Frederick DePeyster managed to accumulate over his long and varied career.

It seems Frederick made good on his word, turning over the day-to-day operations of his importation business to his sons in 1820. However, Frederick continued to manage his other investments, one of which was the Constantia Iron Company. Frederick made a significant investment in this company, but by 1822 it failed. We do not know how much Frederick invested, but it was enough that the failure of the company spawned a thorough inquiry into the matter and a break with Jacob Barker, former smuggling associate from the War of 1812.[117] The full nature of this business relationship is unknown, as the correspondence between the two is sketchy. The correspondence between the two after this point lasts approximately one year, and is full of hard feelings relating to their financial disagreements. The failure of the Constantia Iron Works did not adversely affect Frederick's finances to the point of interfering with his position on the boards of the various financial and charitable institutions. This is, perhaps, why descriptions of Frederick DePeyster in 1823 as "financially embarrassed and insolvent" and his abrupt resignation from his various appointments, are so surprising.[118] It seems the answer lies in the January 16, 1823, suicide of Oliver G. Kane, Secretary for the NIC. After his death, a note was found in the offices of the company, which read, "My fate may be read in the tragedy of the Gamester."

Following the unusual circumstances of Kane's death, the Board of Directors decided to look into their secretary's papers, and found that many of the company's financial documents had been removed and destroyed. After reconstructing the company's finances, they discovered that Kane had embezzled over $177,000 over a three-year period. Certain stockholders immediately held Frederick DePeyster and the directors financially liable for the losses experienced during their tenure.[119] Although they protested, the case went to court and wound its way through the system until it reached the Chancery Court. The stockholders claimed that Frederick and the directors were negligent in their handling of the finances of the company, allowing Kane to manage all financial accounting without adequate supervision. Frederick and the directors stated emphatically that this was not the case. They brought in presidents and directors from other marine insurance companies to testify that the directors for the NIC had followed industry standards where both Kane and the company's finances were concerned. It should be remembered that the witnesses called in to confirm the position of the NIC's board of directors were men of elite social and financial standing. That Frederick was able to call upon these other boards for confirmation speaks to the network of business and social contacts Frederick had cultivated upon his return to New York. Eventually, the case was settled in favor of Frederick and the directors, but it took until 1833, one year after Frederick's death.[120] Still, this was good news for Frederick's heirs, who would no longer be held responsible for the damages. The case is also significant historically as it helped to clarify the responsibilities of directors to investors.

As a result of the NIC suit, Frederick's cash flow would have been severely restricted, yet it does not appear that he ever declared bankruptcy. He avoided that measure by transferring much of his remaining business and land holdings into his sons' names and by taking out loans. In January of 1824, Frederick took out a loan of $52,800 from the estate of his niece Margaretta Martin; the loan was repaid in full and with interest on January 16, 1827.[121] He also sold property to cover his obligations.[122] After 1823, Frederick no longer conducted business in his own name. He would, from time to time, act as an agent for his son, Frederick Jr., but it seems that for the most part, the elder Frederick lived quietly at his estate in Bloomingdale with his second wife, Ann Beekman, and their children.[123] With the court case finally settled in 1833, both Frederick's name and his fortune were cleared. Because of this, Frederick DePeyster Jr. was ranked among New York's wealthiest individuals in 1845,[124] and Frederick's other sons were accepted as elite members of New York society, socializing with the city's elite, serving on the boards of charitable organizations, and establishing institutions like the New-York Historical Society and the Saint Nicholas Society.

By the time of his death in 1832, Frederick DePeyster attained the goals for which he always strove; increasing the overall wealth and status of his family, and preserving that wealth and status for the next generation. Frederick first attempted to accomplish this feat in New Brunswick, where he moved as a Loyalist officer following the American Revolution. When the economy of that place proved less than conducive to his goals, Frederick returned to New York, where he called on his extensive network of business, social, and familial contacts to establish himself as a successful merchant whose Loyalist past did not matter. Although Frederick employed the old tools of personalism to extend his business opportunities (for instance, with Abraham Barker during the War of 1812), he was not limited to them. Frederick also embraced the new capitalist trends sweeping the American economy by investing in various transportation companies (canals, toll roads, bridges), and then serving as president of an incorporated marine insurance company, which became an important means of growing wealth in the new economy. The key to Frederick's success in navigating the changing economy of the early American republic (and as a result, his success in achieving his own goals) lay in his ability to navigate between the two economic worlds. Those worlds were not always mutually exclusive, and Frederick DePeyster shrewdly navigated between the two, building a fortune and a reputation in less-than-optimal circumstances. As a result of his efforts, the weighty colonial reputation of the DePeyster family continued into the first decades of American nationhood and remained intact for the next generation.

Chapter 5

Preparing the Next Generation

*F*rederick DePeyster's children and wards had privileged childhoods. They received the best education and training available, traveled extensively, moved in the highest social circles, and had more pocket money in one month than some workers made in an entire year. These very opportunities reflect the extent to which Frederick DePeyster, a former officer in the British Loyalist Regiments, had reintegrated into American life.

The DePeyster household at 24 Broad Street must have been a busy place, with customers and employees coming and going in the midst of Frederick's quickly growing family. Frederick and his first wife Helen Hake had five children, all sons, in a short period of time. Four of the children lived into adulthood; James Ferguson (1794–1874), Robert Gilbert Livingston (1795–1873), Frederick Jr. (1796–1882), and Abraham (1798–1836). Frederick's household also included at least three slaves who no doubt helped keep the house and children in order.[1] There was also Frederick Augustus (Augustus or Gus, 1790/2–1868), who was born before Frederick's first marriage and was not publicly acknowledged as Frederick's son. In a will that Frederick wrote in 1812, he simply says, "Frederick Augustus, whom I have brought up," but Frederick was very generous in bequeathing Augustus all of his property in New Brunswick, Canada,[2] which included at least 800 acres of land.[3] This was a substantial grant to make to someone, no matter how favored, who was not a child. Augustus is also listed in the family Bible as Frederick's son, although his mother's name was not recorded.[4] It is equally clear from family correspondence that

Frederick's other children considered Augustus to be their brother, and DePeyster genealogies list Augustus as Frederick's son. The fact that Frederick gave the child the family name also lends credence to Augustus being Frederick's son.

In addition to the earlier mentioned comings and goings, Frederick's household was frequently enlarged by nephews, nieces, and unmarried or widowed sisters. For instance, Frederick's brother Abraham was concerned about the educational opportunities for his oldest child, Catherine Augusta (Augusta), in New Brunswick, Canada, where the family resided, so Abraham made arrangements for Augusta to live with Frederick so she would have access to better education. Although Abraham died in 1798, the arrangement was honored and Augusta joined Frederick's household no later than 1800. She remained with him until her marriage in 1809.[5]

Another addition to Frederick's household was his nephew James DePeyster Ogden, the only son of Frederick's sister Mary Reade (1765–1790) and Dr. Jacob Ogden (1762–1802). Although Jacob lived until 1802, it seems that after his wife's death, Jacob developed a drinking problem and disappeared from "good" society. In 1800, Frederick DePeyster's agent in Canada, John Gray, wrote two letters in which he championed Jacob's return to New York and implored Frederick to have his wife Helen reintroduce Jacob to society there. Gray discussed Jacob's drinking problems, and said he believed the man was sober and was resolved to remain that way.[6] Despite Jacob's good intentions, he did not return to New York and died in 1802. After the death of Mary Reade and the disappearance of Jacob, it was the DePeyster family, specifically Frederick's mother, Sarah Reade, and unwed sister Sarah (Sally) who took in James Ogden. When both grandmother and aunt died in the same year—coincidentally, the same year as Jacob—James Ogden was officially adopted by another of Frederick's sisters, Ann (Nancy) DePeyster.[7] Unfortunately, Ann died in 1803, which brought James Ogden into Frederick's household.

It also seems that Ann Betts DePeyster, widow of Frederick's brother Joseph Reade, lived with Frederick after the death of Sarah Reade. Joseph Reade was somewhat of a black sheep. He married in 1775, just before the American Revolution, and in the midst of his father's embarrassing financial demise. His wife, Ann Betts, was the daughter of a Long Island sheriff, and while respectable, her family was not of the same elite status as that of the DePeysters, financial embarrassment or no. Joseph Reade was the only one of his brothers to marry someone who did not hail from a family whose name carried similar weight to the DePeyster name. Joseph Reade, while also a Loyalist during the Revolution, was the only brother who did not have a commission. During the tumultuous first years of the Loyalist settlement in Canada, Joseph Reade routinely sided with the nonelites while his brothers consistently sided with the elites. We do not know the exact date of Joseph Reade's death; however, his name last appears on record in 1784. It seems that after his death, Ann Betts wasted no time in relocating to Jamaica, Long Island, where both her and her husband's families resided. James and Sarah Reade DePeyster opened their household to their son's widow and his daughter, Ann Reade, providing their granddaughter access to the extensive family network and social connections. Although Ann married in 1794, her mother continued to live with Sarah Reade and then with Frederick until her death in 1807.

In accepting various family members into their households, the DePeysters were not acting unusually for their time or for the elite social strata of New York. This pattern of looking after family members who found themselves in vulnerable situations was common throughout the colonial, Revolutionary, and early republic periods. These same patterns appear with the Livingston family. Throughout the colonial era, the Livingstons built homes and provided small farms for family members who lacked the success to support themselves in a manner that would not embarrass the family reputation. Similarly, during the American Revolution, Livingston family members of both Patriot and Loyalist affiliation flocked to the family seat, Livingston Manor, for protection against combatants and hostile neighbors.[8] William Cooper provides an example of this same pattern in the period of the early republic. Rather than allowing his many siblings to remain destitute, and thus reflect poorly on himself, Cooper tried to aid his relatives by bringing them to Cooperstown or by providing them with farms to support themselves.[9] Although this behavior is not out of the ordinary, it is particularly important to note the fact that the DePeysters followed this pattern as it demonstrates that Frederick had the type of funds to support these additions to his household, and that he had enough of a reputation that it would have been tarnished had he not taken on this type of responsibility. Although failing to take proper care of his family would have darkened Frederick's reputation, the stain of his Loyalist past seems to have been scrubbed away with little effort.

In a short period of time, Frederick, despite being the fourth son, became the *pater familius* for his branch of the DePeyster family. Family members looked to Frederick to not only provide physical care, but also to provide a watchful eye over their financial matters. In the case of Frederick's mother, Sarah Reade, and his sisters Sarah (Sally) and Ann (Nancy), Frederick was named as an executor, a position that could entail years of commitment as properties and debts were sorted out. Just as the women of the previous generations used their wills to show preference or dissatisfaction with their relatives and friends, so, too, did these women; all three left settlements to the children of the deceased Abraham, Joseph Reade, and Mary Reade, all of whom they felt especially deserving due to the deaths of their parents. These settlements provided these younger DePeysters with estates large enough to require management, and the means to establish themselves in a manner worthy of their DePeyster heritage.

In this regard, Frederick played an integral role. In addition to serving as an executor for his mother and siblings, Frederick also accepted financial guardianship for Abraham's children and James Ogden, Mary Reade's son, helping to maintain and grow the wealth of the next generation (Joseph Reade's daughter Ann Reade was married in 1794 to Robert Crommelin and was 27 years old in 1802, so her exclusion was due to her age rather than to any disputes between Frederick and his brother). In the case of James Ogden, Frederick accepted sole guardianship. With Abraham's children, however, Frederick shared guardianship with his brother-in-law William Hammersley.[10] Financial guardianships had certain legal ramifications. If the funds were mishandled, when the ward came of age, the guardian could be held personally liable by the courts. Thus, a person could be guardian over a child whose parents still lived, as was the case with Abraham's children, whose mother still lived, and as was previously seen in chapter 2 with Helen Hake, first wife of Frederick DePeyster.

Although financial security was important to the DePeyster legacy, it was not the only component of that legacy. Refinement and education were also central to establishing the elite character of the DePeyster family and ensuring its continuity to the next generation. In this regard, the DePeysters were no different from many of their contemporaries who wished to establish their superiority in society. With no titles to separate the classes, the wealthy relied on things like manners and education to provide a barrier between the genteel and the common.[11] Therefore, education was a priority for Frederick in the care of his children, nephews, and nieces. We have already seen that Frederick agreed to take in his niece Augusta for schooling, and he did no less for his nephews, William Axtell (Augusta's brother) and James Ogden. The boys were sent to Union Hall Academy in Jamaica, Long Island, where the reputation of Dr. Lewis Ernest Andrew Eigenbrodt attracted children of the elite from all over the United States and the West Indies. Dr. Eigenbrodt was born and educated in Germany. He spoke seven languages fluently and was well versed in math, astronomy, and engineering. He became the principal of Union Hall Academy in January of 1797 and remained there until his death in 1823. As classmates of some of the most influential families, the boys made connections that would serve them throughout their lives both socially and in business. After Union Hall, at least two of Frederick's sons, James and Frederick Jr., attended and graduated from Columbia. A significant accomplishment considering that "only one-tenth of 1 per cent of the population attended any college" at the time, and one that speaks to the value of wealth in creating opportunities for the DePeysters in New York.[12] Frederick thus provided his charges not only with the benefits of education, but also with the blessings of connections to other elite families. No doubt Frederick hoped these valuable connections would allow his charges to establish themselves in the upper echelons of New York society, just as he had.

As part of their education, the sons of Frederick and Helen Hake and their cousins James DePeyster Ogden and William Axtell DePeyster also went on to serve apprenticeships with the leading merchant houses in New York. There were two exceptions to the mercantile apprenticeships: that of Frederick Jr. and Augustus. An apprenticeship was arranged for Frederick Jr. with attorney Peter Augustus Jay, son of John Jay and cousin to the DePeysters. Augustus, on the other hand, was apprenticed to the fleet of John Jacob Astor. Again we see the particular care taken with Augustus. Although sent to sea, he was placed in the fleet of New York's richest man and was placed with Captain Whetten (nephew of Astor's wife) of the famed *Beaver*, flagship of the Astor fleet.[13] These types of apprenticeships were forged on the basis of creating a web of mutual support and could be financially beneficial to all parties involved. Although some apprenticeships were purely paternalistic, most were a combination of paternalism and legal contract in which the family of the apprentice paid for the privilege of having their son (or ward) properly trained.[14] Apprenticeships usually were arranged with masters who had some connection to the family involved. This created another layer of obligation in the apprenticeship process and ensured that the individual would take particular care in the training of the apprentice. That Frederick DePeyster had the funds to pay for multiple apprenticeships at the same time, and had the social connections to arrange those positions with the likes of Peter Augustus Jay, John Jacob Astor, and the firm of LeRoy, Bayard, & McEvers is testimony to the personal wealth Frederick built and the social heights he attained in a very short period of time following his return to the United States from Canada. This feat is even more impressive when one considers that Helen died in 1801, and with his second wife, Ann Beekman, Frederick had five more children before 1812, the very time when Frederick's older sons and nephews were attending college and serving their apprenticeships. It is important to note how Frederick's familial, social, and business contacts, many largely in place upon his return to New York, and the local propensity to forget past loyalties, greatly aided Frederick in his ability to arrange these select apprenticeships.

Where Frederick did not have direct control over the affairs of the extended family, as was the case with his niece Ann Reade Crommelin, daughter of his brother Joseph Reade and Ann Betts, he nevertheless brought his resources to bear in assisting and protecting familial interests where he could. In 1794, Ann Reade married Robert Crommelin. Although Robert may have hailed from a great banking and commercial family, his branch of the Crommelin family does not seem to have been as financially prosperous as the rest.[15] Robert Crommelin listed his profession as that of "grocer," and by 1801, he was financially ruined. The Crommelins were a Dutch family with ties to the Dutch banking house of Crommelin & Son. During the Seven Years War, the Crommelins of both New York and Amsterdam had sponsored and outfitted privateers to operate in the West Indies. The original Robert Crommelin even leased a wharf on the East River near the home of Abraham DePeyster (1696–1767). The Crommelins were discussed in the same terms socially and economically as the DePeysters. They were also related to many of the prominent New York families such as the Verplancks, the Ludlows, the Clarksons, and the Livingstons. According to Bruce Mann, this Robert Crommelin, husband of Ann Reade DePeyster, "obtained an insolvency release" from the state, then went into business with one of Ann Betts's relatives and "slid back into insolvency—this time with Betts in tow."[16] The two planned to use new loans to stall the old creditors and then skip town. Unfortunately for Crommelin, the plan was discovered and he and Betts were again declared insolvent by the state. Although Bruce Mann was unable to identify how Crommelin satisfied his creditors as part of this second bankruptcy, we know from records in the DePeyster Collection at the New-York Historical Society that his creditors were satisfied by the sale of Ann's DePeyster inheritance.[17] In January 1802, Robert and Ann sold off her share in the Tenefly, New Jersey[18] estate of her great-grandmother Margaret DePeyster in order to pay his creditors.[19] Margaret DePeyster died about ten years before Ann's birth, and Ann's portion of the estate came to her through her father. The amount Ann received from this, and the other settlements, which will be discussed, was the same as the portions due James DePeyster Ogden, as the only child of Mary Reade, and the children of Abraham DePeyster together. From the Tenefly estate, the Crommelins received $1,600 from Frederick, not an insubstantial sum.

After the death of aunt Sarah DePeyster in 1802, creditors forced the Crommelins to contest the will. Because Ann's portion was not established as a separate estate for herself, her husband's creditors believed they had the full legal right to pursue this option. Sarah's will was contested on the grounds that she was an unmarried woman. The creditors questioned whether or not Sarah actually had the right to make a will regarding her portion of her father's and her Grandfather Reade's property. If Sarah was denied the right to make a will involving that property, then Ann's portion in those estates would increase, allowing for the creditors to obtain more from the Crommelins. The amount of property in question totaled an estimated $8,700, to be divided into three equal parts between Ann Crommelin, James DePeyster Ogden, and the children of Abraham DePeyster.[20]

Frederick DePeyster, as executor of both Sarah's estate and their father's, approached attorney Samuel Johnes to consult on the matter. It was Johnes's opinion that Sarah did have the right to make a will, but he was less certain about Ann's right to keep her inheritance away from her husband's creditors. Johnes advised that the estate pay Ann her portion to avoid the embarrassment of a trial that would determine the matter legally.[21] Frederick complied with this advice, and in 1804 he duly compensated Ann for her portions in the inherited estates. Ann's settlement from Sarah's estate totaled $4,000, and her portion from the estate of great-grandfather James Reade was $3,800. Frederick also compensated Ann for her share in the property on Broadway from Margaret DePeyster, although that amount is unknown.[22]

Although Frederick could not save Ann's property from confiscation by her husband's creditors, neither did he abandon her family. It seems Frederick continued to play an active role in the Crommelin family, smoothing the road where he could, often acting as a surrogate father to Ann and Robert's children, and protecting family interests. For instance, when the Crommelins' son James Robert wanted to marry in 1819, he asked for Frederick's permission, even though Robert Crommelin still lived.[23]

In taking care of his extended family, Frederick did not neglect to look after his own. In 1812, he made out a will. At 54, Frederick was no longer a young man, and it makes sense that he would want to safeguard his family and their legacy in this way. In his will, Frederick promised $5,000 to each of his children upon reaching adulthood; at the time, he had nine children by his two wives.[24] This clearly indicates that Frederick believed he had at least $45,000 readily available for such purposes. He also provided his second wife, Ann Beekman, with $3,000 annually for the remainder of her widowhood, an indication of the value of his properties in New York.[25] Upon Ann's death, the estate would pass to each of the children equally.

Not only did Frederick ensure the DePeyster legacy to his children in the obvious ways, with their education and wealth in general, but also in the less obvious areas. One such example was Frederick's "Library of Books," which received a special clause in the will. Frederick left his library to his sons, James, Robert, Frederick Jr., and Abraham. The library was not to be divided until all the boys were of age. Although we do not know how many books were in the library, nor do we know the titles, we do know that having a library was a mark of wealth because books in general were quite expensive. Having a library was also a mark of class, signifying education and manners. Another less obvious area appears in the guardians that Frederick chose to care for the maintenance and education of his sons should he die before they came of age. Frederick was careful in his selection of guardians for his children; for the older boys, James (18) and Robert (17), he chose Peter Augustus Jay, while brother-in-law William Hammersley would act for the younger two, Frederick Jr. (16) and Abraham (14). Frederick DePeyster also allotted each son $500 annually, which the guardians would hold and distribute at their own discretion. Frederick strongly urged the guardians to "pay great Attention to complete the education" of his sons.[26]

Although Frederick owned more than 800 acres of land in New Brunswick, Canada, (largely due to his military settlement from the British government following the American Revolution), he left none of it to his sons with Helen Hake. Frederick's New Brunswick property was settled wholly upon Augustus, his illegitimate son, and his only child born in Canada. This generosity toward Augustus undoubtedly demonstrates the care that Frederick took regarding the boy. Nevertheless, it is also revealing that Frederick chose to separate his legitimate sons from his Loyalist past in such a physical way, turning them away from his past much as he already had.[27]

As the United States entered the War of 1812 with Great Britain, the next generation of DePeysters began to enter adulthood. Theirs, however, was not an immediate transition. Thanks to the wealth of Frederick DePeyster, his children and nephews were able to remain in the twilight between childhood and adulthood for an extended period of time, something that would have been impossible for people in lesser financial circumstances. The one exception to this was Augustus DePeyster. Having served his apprenticeship in John Jacob Astor's fleet, he made his way from sailor to mate to captain by 1812. At that time, Augustus (20–22 years old) took command of Astor's privateering vessel the *Chauncey*.[28] At the end of the war, Augustus was given command of Astor's *Seneca*, in which he delivered news of the peace treaty around the Cape of Good Hope, into the Indian Ocean, and all the way to China,[29] a far cry from the meandering course his brothers and cousins took toward becoming serious adults.

James DePeyster joined the army in 1813 at the age of 19, and Robert appears to have joined soon after his brother. While in service, Robert wound up in Washington D.C. shortly before the British burned the Capital. Somehow, Robert found himself in the company of his father's business associate Jacob Barker at the White House on August 24, 1815, and together they persuaded First Lady Dolley Madison to leave the place before the British Army arrived. As she left, Mrs. Madison ordered the two men to either take the portrait of George Washington with them, or destroy it before the British could do so. The two men successfully removed the portrait from the White House and delivered it to a local farmer for safekeeping, where it remained until Barker was able to return the portrait to Mrs. Madison.[30] Frederick Jr. remained enrolled at Columbia for the duration of the war, but joined a militia unit out of Columbia College known as the "College Greens" and helped build the fieldworks at McGowan's Pass near Harlem. Abraham, who was 14 years old at the start of the war, continued with his education, and played no noted role in the war effort. For Frederick's sons, there was no conflict of loyalty; they were simply serving their country.

While this military service may sound like a jump-start into adulthood, it was a false start. More characteristic of the paths Frederick

DePeyster's sons would follow after the war is the one taken by James DePeyster Ogden during the war. Before the war, James Ogden apprenticed for the prestigious firm of LeRoy, Bayard, & McEvers (later just LeRoy, Bayard & Company), which was known worldwide for its savvy business practices and integrity. Although not specifically a banking firm, as with most merchant firms of the day, they did act as bankers. They even served as "American bankers" for the Holland Land Company out of Amsterdam.[31] Although we do not know for certain how James Ogden came by the apprenticeship with Bayard's firm, it is likely that Frederick arranged it just as he had arranged Augustus's placement with Astor's fleet. Ogden began as a clerk (keeping account books and copying correspondence, among other duties) but was soon promoted to the position of "supercargo" for the company. With the promotion, the firm sent James Ogden to Europe with a cargo hold full of goods. As supercargo, it was the young man's duty to escort the cargo, sell it where he could, and hand the merchandise off to more experienced agents when he could not. The position was a sort of stepping-stone toward demonstrating the individual's ability to "enter the commercial world as an independent man."[32] James Ogden was then 22 years old. Because of this promotion to supercargo, when the War of 1812 broke out, James Ogden found himself stranded in Europe.

Throughout the war, James Ogden wrote a number of letters to his uncle Frederick. Although James Ogden would eventually go on to become a businessman of great distinction, he was not one at this time. These letters reveal him as a young man whose illusions of the ease of business were quickly dashed by reality. James Ogden longed for the social world of New York and the comfort of friends and family. Whether he could have returned to the United States in safety or not, James Ogden made no move in that direction, despite having a commission in the New York Militia. Instead, he remained in Europe, followed the developments in the American War, and offered opinions as people often do when following their favorite sports teams. James Ogden also discussed his movements around Europe, supposedly about the business of LeRoy, Bayard & McEvers, as one would discuss a holiday adventure. While his service to the firm was sufficient enough that they would later provide James Ogden with letters of introduction, a seriousness of purpose does not permeate these letters as it would letters from later in his life.

After depositing his original cargo with an agent in Russia, James Ogden took charge of another cargo, which he was supposed to escort back to New York. Before leaving the Baltic Sea, however, James Ogden learned of the United States' declaration of war against Great Britain. No waters seemed safe, and James Ogden knew he would be stuck supervising the property of LeRoy, Bayard & McEvers for longer than anticipated. James Ogden took refuge first in Gottenburg, Sweden,[33] but found the society there depressing. He hoped to either rid himself of his cargo or be released from his duties so that he would be free to head to England and pass the duration of the war with his aunt Margaret James and the Martins. But LeRoy, Bayard & McEvers did not release James Ogden from his responsibilities. As supercargo, as long as there was merchandise to look after, James Ogden was not at liberty to travel at will until his responsibilities were fulfilled. He remained in Sweden as ordered, though it was "miserably dull," he was not completely idle while there. At some point between April 23, 1812, and January 3, 1813, James Ogden made a trip to Landskrona, in the south of Sweden. On his return the temperature dropped so low that Ogden and his companions sledded over the frozen lakes and rivers, and upon their arrival in Gottenburg they discovered the Sound and some port wine frozen over.[34]

Eventually, LeRoy, Bayard & McEvers sent word that James Ogden was to deliver their merchandise to Amsterdam; when this proved untenable, they sent him to Hamburg, Germany.[35] Hamburg was a major business center at this point, and with Napoléon's forces so recently withdrawn, it seemed the perfect market in which to unload the long-held cargo. No sooner had James Ogden arrived, however, than Napoleonic forces laid siege to the city in an attempt to regain control over it. Along with most of the inhabitants of Hamburg, James Ogden fled the city and spent three months in Lubeck, Germany.

Throughout his time in Europe, James Ogden's opinion of the American war with Britain was low. He thought it disgraceful that the Americans were using militia forces and privateers, rather than regular soldiers and the Navy; he also believed the United States was not taking the war as seriously as it should because it was not providing adequate troops or supplies. He went on to state that the government's handling of the war thus far was *vox et praeterea nihil*, "fine words and nothing more."[36] One could easily use Ogden's epitaph against the man himself, for while he railed against the government's execution of the war, he himself longed for nothing more than to spend the duration in England.

Eventually, James Ogden did reach London, where he received the first news of his family in America since his departure in 1812. The letters came by way of his cousin, Augustus DePeyster. Augustus was the captain of the privateer *Chauncey*.[37] James Ogden was delighted to know the family had not forgotten him and had survived the war without adverse consequences. But he could not contain his surprise that Augustus was a privateer: "why why my fine fellow have you not entered the Navy—there was a field of Glory open, the path was luminous & bright."[38] After so thoroughly condemning privateers, Ogden's disappointment at his cousin's choice was complete. On the other hand, the knowledge that cousins James (20) and Robert (19) both joined the regular units of the army must have offered some consolation.

With news of the family in hand, and despite the continuing American War, James Ogden made his way to Devonshire to visit his aunt Margaret James and his cousins the Martins. He was quite impressed with the whole family and stayed longer than he planned. Upon his return to London, Ogden discovered that his employers thought he was still in Gottenburg with their merchandise and that they expected him to take charge of the items again and sell them. For James Ogden the news was a blow. He thought the merchandise was in capable hands and not worth the expense of returning to Sweden, especially because the markets were in a poor state for business.[39] The unexpected arrival of another agent and one of the partners, however, allowed James Ogden to remain in England. With nothing but time on his hands, James Ogden decided to become a tourist, despite the ongoing hostilities between the United States and Great Britain. He spent a month at the resort of Cheltenham, and then proceeded to Worthing and Brighton where he spent his time among the "gentile [sic] & fashionable."[40]

When news came of Napoléon's defeat and exile to Elba, James Ogden made plans to visit Paris. He was bitterly disappointed when, just a few months later, Napoléon Bonaparte escaped from the Island of Elba and made his way back to France, where he again took control of the government and military, plunging Europe back into chaos. England, needing to focus all of its attention and resources on defeating the French, sued for peace with the Americans. In 1815, the Treaty of Ghent officially ended the War of 1812. Renewed hostilities on the Continent forced James Ogden to cancel plans for a trip to Paris. Much to his chagrin, and at long last, he turned his steps back toward America.

After his return from Europe, James DePeyster Ogden continued in his profession as an agent, though whether still in the employ of LeRoy, Bayard & McEvers is unknown, and headed out into greater New York. He visited Albany, Schenectady, Cayuga Lake, and Le Roy. While at Schenectady, James Ogden stopped off to visit the Livingstons, members of the large extended family the DePeysters claimed, and was able to report them in good health.[41] With a careful eye, James Ogden evaluated the countryside surrounding the course he took. Given his route, it seems that James Ogden may have been on retainer at the time for one of the groups proposing to build canals through the area. His evaluation of Le Roy as a place "destined . . . eventually to become, highly valuable & important in every point of view"[42] seems to reinforce this.

Without the elite connections of his uncle, James Ogden would not have been in Europe with a prestigious firm like LeRoy, Bayard & McEvers, and, no doubt, he would not have enjoyed such latitude in his actions. It is also likely that without the fortune James Ogden inherited from his DePeyster relatives, a fortune so carefully managed by his uncle Frederick, his ability to roam around Europe and vacation in England would have been severely restricted. The very fact that James Ogden had that freedom of movement speaks to his wealth and the status of his family and connections, both in New York and beyond. It also demonstrates the care Frederick took in preparing the way for the next generation of DePeysters by managing and growing the wealth and reputation of the family.

In the afterglow of the War of 1812, New York society pulsated with lighthearted vigor, and the DePeysters were active participants in that sphere. They happily attended balls and dinner parties, teas and assemblies. While the DePeyster correspondence discusses these events, it rarely identifies the names of the people holding the events. We know, however, that the DePeysters socialized with the Astors, the Livingstons, the Clarksons, the Bayards, the Munros, the Roosevelts, the Hamiltons, the Jays, and the LeRoys, to name a few. We also know that the DePeysters socialized with Presidents Madison and Monroe to a certain extent. In December of 1815, anticipation for the upcoming New Year's Ball at the Munros' (one of New York's wealthiest families, with some Loyalist skeletons as well) was so high that it led Frederick's Clarkson niece and ward to apply to him for funds, one hundred dollars, to purchase a new dress for the occasion. She also let him know that if he wanted to buy her earrings and a pin, he could accompany her to purchase them.[43] This speaks to the wealth of Frederick, as the average daily wage for a partly skilled laborer in 1815 was about 80 cents, although some earned as much as $1.25 (which could feed a family of six for three days).[44]

In January of 1817, Frederick's son Robert, then 22 years old, bemoaned the fact that he had to leave New York in the midst of the "gay season of the Year" for business in the West Indies. Unfortunately for Robert, the best time to travel to the West Indies was during the winter, or "social" months, when tides and winds favored that direction. On business for his firm Reade & DePeyster, Robert headed to the island of St. Croix where his stepmother, Ann Beekman, had relatives. While there, he conducted some business for his father as well. The Reade of Reade & DePeyster was most likely a cousin through Ann Reade DePeyster, grandmother to Robert and wife of James (Jacobus) DePeyster. Little is known of this partnership, as it is mentioned very little in the DePeyster correspondence, and there are no records of the firm in other collections.[45] Like most merchants, Robert was not above acting as an agent for other firms or individuals should the opportunity arise, as long as that business would not endanger the primary interests of the individual. Despite his absence from New York, Robert continued to inquire after his acquaintances and tease his brothers for their behavior at various events.[46] James Ferguson (James or the Colonel, a childhood nickname),[47] then 23 years old, and Abraham, 19 years old, continued their attendance in society despite their brother's jests.

Frederick Jr., then 21 years old, proved the exception to this rule, however, as he decided his life up to this point had been without much substance. After his graduation from Columbia, Frederick Jr. decided to pursue a legal career; the decision seems to have been a personal one, for there is no indication that he was pushed in this direction by his family. In that same spirit he performed an about-face and decided to forsake company with the "fair sex" as too much distraction.[48] Frederick Jr. first apprenticed with Peter Augustus Jay in New York City, but later retired to Kinderhook, New York, to pursue the study of law at Peter Van Schaack's school of law. Labeled a Loyalist during the Revolution, Van Schaack was banished from the state, his property subjected to confiscation; later, by a special act of the New York legislature, he was forgiven his Loyalist past and allowed to return and resume his legal practice. When ill health forced Van Schaack to retire from regular practice, he began taking in a limited number of students from elite backgrounds. Van Schaack's tutelage of multiple students in this manner constitutes one of the nation's earliest law schools.[49] While in Kinderhook, Van Schaack's disciplined character, devotion to the betterment of society, and honest practice of law so impressed Frederick Jr. that he endeavored to remake himself in the image of his instructor. He filled his letters to his brothers with instructions, old sayings and stories to guide them through their various dilemmas, and for the improvement of their characters. These anecdotes provided endless fodder for his brothers to pick at his "reformed" ways, yet all admired his dedication to his new principles. Frederick Jr. and Van Schaack continued to correspond even after Frederick Jr.'s departure from Kinderhook. Van Schaack's influence, like his correspondence, extended well beyond Frederick Jr.'s tenure at Kinderhook. By the time of his death in 1882, New York papers reported that Frederick DePeyster Jr. was one of the most active citizens in the city, serving on more boards and belonging to more civic institutions than any other person in the city.[50]

During this same period, the DePeyster brothers began traveling both across the United States and to the West Indies. Although some trips were for business, others were for pleasure, and some were a combination of the two. Although travel for the sake of travel was becoming more common at this time (improvements in transportation lowered expense and time involved), the type of trips on which Frederick DePeyster's sons ventured were not the kind available to anyone but the very wealthy.[51] Wherever they went, the young DePeysters were accepted into the elite social circles of that locale and introduced to officials who would be out of reach for ordinary individuals. This immediate acceptance was due to Frederick DePeyster and his constant efforts to advance the family's reputation and standing in society. This reputation now reached well beyond the boundaries of New York.

An example of this may be seen in a visit James Ferguson DePeyster made to Washington D.C. in March of 1817. Like his father, James was a merchant and general importer. The trip to D.C. could very well have been for business with James acting as an agent for his firm, just as Robert had in St. Croix for his. James's letters do not specifically say why he was there although an undated letter, possibly from the same time, indicates that the trip was more for pleasure. If that was the case, James would have relied upon the indulgence of his father or business partner. Whatever the purpose of his visit, it coincided with the inauguration of James Monroe as the fifth president of the United States. James attended the affair, and commented that the ceremony was "very interesting without pomp & in the true Republic style."[52] James Ferguson seemed to have little interest in the swearing-in ceremony of the President, and he likewise displayed little enthusiasm when relating the events that transpired afterward. In a brief few lines, James Ferguson nonchalantly mentions his introduction to the new President and the Madisons. His coverage of attending the inaugural ball with those notables is likewise brief, although this could simply be a result of him being pressed for time due to another engagement. We do not know how James Ferguson DePeyster rated an invitation to Monroe's inauguration or the ball afterward, but it is likely that the invitation was extended to him based on his family name. Mrs. Monroe's son lived in New York City, so the name would not have been unfamiliar.[53]

Nevertheless, it does suggest a high level of comfort in dealing with personages of such elite backgrounds and was no doubt thanks to the position his father attained in New York society.

James Ferguson's real enthusiasm came when he briefly described his visits to the halls of Congress and the Supreme Court. James Ferguson noted that he spent an entire day listening to Congressional debates and was impressed with the speeches of John Gaillard, a Senator from South Carolina, and Henry Clay of Kentucky. James Ferguson, not wanting to carry on a discussion of those speeches through the mail, told his brother he looked forward to discussing everything in person. His description of his visit to the Supreme Court was likewise brief but enthusiastic. James Ferguson noted the justices were venerable, the "attorneys pleading," and that the "bumper of interesting cases" before the Court brought lawyers from "every part of the Union" to the capital.[54]

James Ferguson was not the only brother to travel during this period. Frederick Jr., while on vacation from school, visited Philadelphia in June of 1817, seeing many of the city's brightest attractions, and meeting with people who would be unavailable to the general public. The young man was impressed by the city's attractions, and detailed his visits to a few of the city's new groundbreaking institutions. The Pennsylvania Hospital, although established in 1751, was still the model other states looked to for inspiration in health care. Additionally, Benjamin West had recently donated his painting *Christ Healing the Sick in the Temple* making the hospital an even bigger draw than before. The superintendent of the institution personally guided Frederick Jr. around the hospital, providing sufficient narrative of the hospital's origins to impress the young DePeyster and win him as a fan. The special attention paid to the young man during his visit to Philadelphia was most likely due to his family's name and reputation. Frederick Jr. wrote his father, "it would be injustice to the impressions my visit made barely to say I was pleased."[55] He approved not only of the construction of the building but the efficiency of the place. He was likewise impressed with the housing of Mr. West's painting: "Its construction is great & so adapted as to throw the light most advantageously on the picture."[56] He eagerly looked forward to the prospect of two promised smaller paintings adding to the effect. That the superintendent of the Pennsylvania Hospital personally took the young DePeyster on a tour of the facilities is an indication of the reputation and wealth Frederick DePeyster had accumulated. The DePeyster name was now familiar to those outside of New York and outside of the merchant community. Frederick DePeyster had achieved his goals of conquering New York society and was now expanding his sphere of influence.

While in Philadelphia, Frederick Jr. was also impressed by Philadelphia's Academy of Fine Arts, which housed Tomas Sully's collection. He commented that it was a fine way to spend a morning. The young DePeyster also enjoyed the amiability of Philadelphians and their ability to discuss the fine arts. He lamented the fact that New Yorkers were too bogged down in the "Emporium of Trade" to give much attention to the subject. Frederick Jr. retained hope, however, that as the "London of the W[estern] Hemisphere," New York would become the "patroness of the fine arts" without losing its financial prowess, which was, after all, the basis for much of the DePeyster wealth.[57]

Frederick Jr.'s excitement and enthusiasm for both New York and the United States at large are clearly evident in his descriptions of Philadelphia. He saw the advantages of that city and wished them for his own. His father was already involved in the process of modernizing New York. For many years, the elder Frederick had involved himself with New York's Lying-in Hospital (which provided medical care to pregnant women and was the first of its kind in the country), the New-York Hospital, and the Humane Society. Unlike today's Humane Society, the original in New York was meant to provide relief to New York's poor and unfortunate humans. The Society provided food and fuel to prisoners who were unable to pay for their own in a time when prisons still charged for those luxuries. The Society also passed out money to the poor for the purpose of procuring food; fearing the money was too often diverted to purchase alcohol, rather than food, the Society eventually discontinued handing out cash and instead handed out tickets that could be redeemed for a quart of soup at the soup house. After his visit to Philadelphia, the younger Frederick picked up his father's mantle of concern, and scoured all examples for those that might help his city to move forward as a place of culture and commerce, and a place other cities would wish to emulate. In this respect, Frederick Jr. was no different from many of his social peers, a number of whom undertook philanthropic endeavors in an effort to remake society at large according to their own vision. For example, the Livingstons, who gave up political power as a result of the Revolution, turned to philanthropy in an attempt to exert some of their former influence.

While his cousins traveled at least in some part as tourists, James DePeyster Ogden finally became serious about his career in business. Relying on his uncle's contacts once again, James Ogden asked Frederick to discover whether John Jacob Astor might require an agent aboard his famous *Beaver* when it next sailed. For Frederick DePeyster to determine this was not so difficult because the men, if not good friends, were certainly aware of each other. When Frederick's son Augustus was still quite young, he had arranged for the boy to go to sea on board the ships in Astor's fleet where he would be well cared for. Augustus took to the sailor's trade with ease, quickly rising through the ranks to serve as captain in his own right for Astor. In fact, James Ogden's request of his uncle came at a time when Augustus was captain of the *Beaver*. The job of Captain was no small task, and it speaks volumes to the ability of Augustus. The *Beaver* was the first ship from New York built to reach China in the aftermath of the Revolution. On one voyage alone, the *Beaver*'s cargo brought in $200,000. The captain of this ship had to be responsible, resourceful, and honest. It is possible James Ogden believed that with both Frederick's and Augustus' recommendation he would be a shoo-in for the job. Expecting at least three weeks before the letter reached Frederick, James Ogden assured his uncle he would, at first notice, be able to head for New York to take up the commission if one was available.

James Ogden was probably not hired as agent for the *Beaver*. However, his willingness to travel for work was not dampened by that fact. In November 1816, Ogden again wrote to Frederick, this time from Boston, after a short trip to New Hampshire. From there he proceeded back to New York City and then returned to Le Roy. Later correspondence indicates he probably spent the majority of 1817 in Liverpool, England, before returning to the United States to take up his duties as an agent for the firm of Frederick DePeyster & Son.[58] James DePeyster Ogden was finally following the example of Frederick DePeyster by taking advantage of his family connections to establish himself properly in business.

While James Ogden traveled to Europe, his cousin Robert G. L. DePeyster headed to the island of St. Croix in the West Indies, where he acted as the agent for his firm, Reade & DePeyster. The island of St. Croix was a Dutch possession and had grown in popularity throughout the period immediately following the Revolution when the British cut off trade to their islands. Through the neutral Dutch islands, American merchants were able to obtain sugar and trade their finished goods. The DePeysters had the added advantage of family connections in St. Croix. Sarah Beekman, aunt to Ann Beekman DePeyster, Frederick's second wife, resided there on her estate that they affectionately called the Hob. It is clear that Robert chose St. Croix because of the advantages his familial connections offered him there. In that respect, and at this stage of his career, Robert also appears to have followed the example for success laid out by his father, Frederick Sr.

Robert's primary business concern on St. Croix was to procure sugar, rum, and coconuts, all of good quality, to ship back to New York. His activities were for his own advancement through the firm of Reade & DePeyster; however, Robert was not above utilizing his familial contacts to further his prospects. Likewise, should the family call upon him to act on their behalf, either individually or for DePeyster & Son, Robert would have done so. This activity would not have been considered out of line for merchants of the day, who often acted as agents for other firms when the need arose, though perhaps for a slight fee. In acting in his own interests, Robert had to act as both merchant and agent on his own behalf, hence his extended presence in Saint Croix. A lengthy stay was necessary for him to familiarize himself with the local market and merchants. While there, Robert made contracts with local merchants and ship's captains, supervised the loading of cargo onto ships, and kept abreast of regional concerns; it would not do for privateers from Cartagena to stop his shipments from reaching New York. The city of Cartagena, now in Colombia, declared its independence from Spain on November 11, 1811. From that point on, one of the ways that Cartagena supported itself was through the licensing of privateers. These privateers caused endless headaches for everyone conducting business in the West Indies. Both the British and the Americans tried to prosecute these privateers at different times for their successful disruption of trade. Additionally, rebellions in Puerto Rico could either disrupt business or provide a unique opportunity, depending upon the particular circumstances involved; one had to be familiar with the market, however, to know how to act.[59] Robert's activities in St. Croix exemplify the expectations Frederick DePeyster had for his sons and wards. Although he indulged them with the assistance of his social and business contacts, he wanted them to be self-reliant and self-supporting. After all, Frederick knew from his own experience that the market, and fortune, could turn on a dime. He wanted the next generation of DePeysters to be prepared for such a circumstance.

Robert had planned to leave the island of St. Croix on May 15, 1817, but the sudden arrival of his brother James Ferguson, fresh from his visit to Washington changed his plans. James Ferguson arrived on the island for business; he was to purchase rum and sugar, presumably for DePeyster & Son. The unexpected nature of the voyage, however, suggests he was motivated more by the experience of travel than by business. Again, this ability of the DePeyster sons to travel, for work or pleasure, is evidence of the affluence of Frederick DePeyster. Travel was expensive, regardless of the reasons, yet the DePeysters had the necessary cash on hand to make long trips, even at short notice. James Ferguson's appearance was a surprise for all, but he was not unwelcome, and he quickly became a favorite among St. Croix society.[60]

Shortly after his return from St. Croix, Robert was on the move again, this time to St. Mary, Georgia, in order to collect an unpaid account for his father.[61] Robert thought the business would be conducted quickly and thus planned to make a short tour of it, stopping first in Savannah, then St. Mary, and ending in Charleston. Due to the short duration of the trip, Robert advised his brothers not to write to him, because he did not plan to remain in any one place long enough to receive mail. By December of 1818, however, Robert found his continued presence in St. Mary unavoidable for the foreseeable future.[62] It took Robert until January 1819 to collect $8,000 for his father. He then made plans to return to New York, but delayed his departure until February 25 when the opportunity arose to purchase lumber,[63] the sale of which, Robert hoped, would more than pay for his stay in St. Mary.[64] Again, by taking advantage of this investment opportunity, Robert seems to be following the example for success laid out by his father.

During Robert's absence, the family remained quite busy in their individual pursuits. Frederick Jr. (22) continued in his studies at Kinderhook, far from the "gay amusements" of New York City, where both James (24) and Abraham (20) pursued business activities and busy social lives. Abraham wrote to Frederick Jr. of the different teas and parties he and the "pals" attended, and kept his brother up-to-date on the latest news, including a fire in Boston that consumed the Exchange Building, theaters, and homes, and even the hanging of James Hamilton for murder. In the midst of all this, Abraham finally seems to have embarked seriously on a business career as he coordinated both the repair of ships the family engaged for business and the sailing of various other ships to Guadeloupe and St. Croix, along with managing the day-to-day necessities of the household. It was also during this time that Frederick Jr. provided much amusement to his brothers when he decided to drop the "k" from his name. Whether he did this to appear modern or in an attempt to differentiate himself from his father is unknown. Abraham (21) in particular, enjoyed teasing his brother about the sudden change:

> Dear Frederic—without the K—On the 13th instant an interesting epistle dated the 9th & signed Frederick without the K was handed to me. . . . The *Frederick* with the K has arrived to a bad market[65]

Despite the teasing, the family seemed to accept Frederick Jr.'s new nomenclature without much ado beyond that.

In early February 1819, Robert (24) returned from St. Mary, but stayed in New York only a short while before returning to St. Croix on business. Before Robert's return to the island, Mrs. Beekman died, leaving Robert without a solid business contact on the island. When Mrs. Beekman died, Mrs. Goold (probably a relative although the exact relationship is unknown) became her primary beneficiary and, according to Robert's letters, became the wealthiest widow on St. Croix as a result. Robert remained there through at least June of that year, and by the time he left, Mrs. Sarah Goold was firmly established as the new business contact for DePeyster & Son. Although it was rare for a woman to conduct business in her own name, as a widow and the owner of a plantation, it was an acceptable if somewhat unusual practice. In her business relationship with the DePeysters, they acted as agents for her, taking charge of the goods she sent to New York, even though they were not her only customers. DePeyster & Son also acted as a clearinghouse for her bills of exchange, paying her creditors for goods she purchased from them.

Robert's return to the United States marked the end of one phase in the lives of the DePeysters. Up to this point, all of the activities of this younger generation were carried out under the ever-watchful eye of Frederick DePeyster. The former Loyalist officer who had the nerve and wit to return to New York and prosper so tremendously decided to retire from his merchant activities in 1820 and allow the next generation to take the lead in guiding the family's future. New York proved an ideal environment for returning Loyalists who were willing to forget Revolutionary alliances because so many residents had, of necessity, blurred the lines of loyalty. In New York, the ability to "forget" was a valuable commodity. To establish the DePeyster family's fortune and reputation in the upper echelons of New York society, Frederick brought to bear his shrewd business acumen, his inherited wealth, and extensive familial and social connections. Although these connections proved indispensable to Frederick in securing his position in New York, he did not rely solely on them. Frederick's success was also due to his willingness to adapt to the swiftly changing economic situation. Frederick provided the model for the next generation. He gave them every possible advantage—carefully managed fortunes, education, and apprenticeships—to become successful in their own right and carry on the elite status of the DePeyster name to the next generation. With Frederick's retirement, it was now up to this next generation, who had every advantage and no Loyalist past to negotiate, to demonstrate how well they had learned their lessons.

Chapter 6

Continuing the Tradition

$\mathcal{B}$y 1820, the DePeyster family was firmly ensconced as a leading New York family in every way, and Frederick DePeyster, age 62, was ready to retire from his merchant activities. The responsibility of maintaining the familial wealth and reputation then fell to the next generation of DePeysters, Frederick's sons and nephews. At the same time, this next generation was coming of age well equipped to live up to DePeyster standards. Unhindered by the family's Loyalist past, they all followed the same basic principles whenever possible: use both the family network and social and business connections, marry into prominent families, make the most of the DePeyster name, and manage inherited wealth and property with care. Yet not all experienced the same degree of success. Much as with Frederick's generation, success in living up to DePeyster standards also required shrewd judgment and luck. Those who were willing to innovate and adapt, as Frederick had, were the most successful.

When Frederick DePeyster retired in 1820 he turned his attention to active service in philanthropic organizations such as the New-York Lying-in Hospital and the Humane Society. He also continued to serve as president for the National Insurance Company. What his retirement meant for his sons and nephews, however, was that he now expected them to be self-sufficient, with little further assistance from him. This is not surprising as Frederick himself was independent at a young age and had been so under much more difficult circumstances than those in which the young DePeysters found themselves. Additionally, families during this period generally encouraged independence for young men starting in their teens.[1] Frederick had done his part. He had provided his sons and nephews with the proper education, the right social connections, and a close familial network. These factors, combined with their inherited wealth, would have been the foundation for future wealth. At his retirement, Frederick left his sons one last gift: his firm's name, DePeyster & Son. This was indeed a boon; his sons were then able to take advantage of their father's client list and his business contacts, not to mention the solid reputation Frederick had developed over a lifetime. Although the record is not clear, it is likely that James Ferguson (26) became the primary partner while Abraham (22) traveled for the firm, with the other brothers occasionally filling in where needed. For instance, in 1822, James Ferguson sent Frederick Jr. to St. Croix to ensure the safe delivery of cargo to their brother Robert at that place.[2]

As head of the DePeyster family, Frederick's influence extended beyond his own sons. Before his retirement, Frederick attempted to assist his nephew James DePeyster Ogden one last time by sending him to New Orleans as a purchasing agent for DePeyster & Son. The only child born to Mary Reade DePeyster (sister of Frederick DePeyster) and Dr. Jacob Ogden Jr., James DePeyster Ogden was taken into the DePeyster family fold when his mother died shortly after his birth in 1790. Jacob Ogden did not handle her death well and turned to alcohol as a result. James Ogden went first to live with his DePeyster grandparents and aunts at their home in Jamaica, Long Island. He remained there until 1803 when, after the deaths of his grandparents and aunts, he entered his uncle Frederick's household at Number 24 Broad Street, New York City. Once there, Frederick treated James Ogden as one of his own. Frederick sent James Ogden to the same elite boarding school as his own sons: Union Hall Academy at Jamaica, Long Island, under the tutelage of Lewis Eigenbrodt. Frederick also provided James Ogden with the same merchant apprenticeship opportunities as his sons—placing him with the prominent firm of Van Horne and Clarkson.[3] Clearly, James Ogden was not just a poor orphan relative but a valued member of the family.

Although James Ogden received many advantages because of his uncle Frederick, he was slow to appreciate them. Throughout his early career, particularly the period from 1812 to 1818, James Ogden seemed to take it for granted that he would have positions of responsibility with prestigious firms. Often during this early period, he bemoaned the fact that his responsibilities to his employers kept him from enjoying the company and society of family and friends. By 1819, however, James Ogden seems to have finally realized his fortunate position as a member of the DePeyster family. After that point, James Ogden worked diligently to establish his own legacy as one of New York's merchant elite.

James Ogden routinely signed his name as James DePeyster Ogden (or Jas D.P. Ogden) by 1812, incorporating his mother's family name into his own. Perhaps this was a way to identify with the branch of the family that raised him, or maybe James Ogden was hoping to benefit from the social and business advantages the DePeyster name would have lent him in New York; we can only speculate. As previously discussed, in 1812, James Ogden was acting as supercargo for the prestigious firm of LeRoy, Bayard & McEvers aboard the *America*. The ship sailed from New York at the end of February 1812 and arrived in Gottenburg, Sweden, in April of that year. After staying a month in Sweden, James Ogden proceeded with the cargo to St. Petersburg, Russia (the voyage lasted three weeks), where he transferred the goods to another agent. James Ogden remained at St. Petersburg for six weeks before taking charge of a cargo for his return voyage to New York. Nine days after leaving St. Petersburg, his ship was hailed by a New York vessel, which informed them that the United States had declared war on Great Britain. Greatly alarmed by the news, the captain headed to port in neutral Sweden for protection.[4] As a result of the unexpected declaration, James DePeyster Ogden spent the duration of the War of 1812 in Europe, unhappily shepherding cargo around Europe while trying to avoid Napoleon's armies, and hoping to spend time in England with his aunt Margaret despite the ongoing war with the United States. When finally released from his duties with LeRoy, Bayard & McEvers, James Ogden breathed a sigh of relief. He spent the remainder of the War of 1812 in England, visiting with family and mingling with the fashionable elite at resort spas. His biggest disappointment came when Napoléon escaped Elba and Britain sued for peace with the United

States. Not only were his plans for a leisurely visit to France cancelled by necessity, but he had no further excuse for remaining in Europe, so in 1815 James Ogden finally returned to New York.

Upon his return to the United States, James Ogden worked in upstate New York. While we do not know the exact nature of his responsibilities at that time, his business took him along the future route of the Erie Canal, so it is possible he was working in some capacity for that project. LeRoy, Bayard & McEvers were also large investors in both land and canal projects in upstate New York, so it may be that he remained in their service, although no records confirm this. Nevertheless, his letters throughout this time reveal him as a restless young man of wealth, always looking for a brighter opportunity. At one point, James Ogden even hoped to serve as supercargo aboard John Jacob Astor's famous Canton vessel the *Beaver*, captained by his cousin, Augustus DePeyster. The seeming nonchalance with which James Ogden moved about the globe places him squarely within the norm for his generation. As Joyce Appleby notes, "[p]rospering in the early nineteenth-century economy often required movement—onto new land, towards urban opportunity, into new types of ventures."[5] However, his attitude of irresponsibility set him apart, as most members of his cohort moved with the purpose of bettering their lives and escaping the family farm.

If James Ogden was lackadaisical about his responsibilities as an agent, he was nevertheless attentive to his own concerns during these years. One area in particular to which James paid attention was the management of his inheritance. Beginning with his return to the United States, and continuing until 1836 when his correspondence ends, James Ogden consistently conferred with his uncle Frederick about the price of stocks in the different institutions in which they had both invested like the Bank of the United States or the National Insurance Company; he also noted changes in the personnel of the governing boards of those institutions. James Ogden also followed the debates of Congress that related to business and the attitudes of both the general population and the business community. This type of careful management was key to ensuring that his inherited wealth would do more than just sustain him in a comfortable lifestyle. James Ogden wanted to grow his wealth and ensure his position among New York's elite.[6]

It was, perhaps, James Ogden's dedication to managing his own fortune that induced his uncle Frederick to employ the young man as a purchasing agent for DePeyster & Son in New Orleans in 1819. James DePeyster Ogden was then 28. He was to procure tobacco and cotton for the firm, but he found tobacco had suffered a poor season and was unreasonably expensive. As a result, James Ogden spent the majority of his time in New Orleans learning the intricacies of the cotton market, and he proved an enthusiastic student.[7]

During this time, cotton made up about 39 percent of exports in the United States.[8] Nearly half of that went to Britain; more specifically to Liverpool. While there was a growing textile industry in the United States at this time, they purchased lower quality cotton than did their European competitors; no doubt the profit from selling to the U.S. manufacturers was lower as a result. Of all the cotton that James Ogden procured, the vast majority of it went to Liverpool, while just a few bales went to Baltimore. Since 1817, cotton prices had been falling, and James Ogden was confident that he would be able to obtain good prices in 1819 as well. Indeed, cotton prices in 1819 were at their lowest point since the slide began.[9] Despite this, Ogden's job was not an easy one in the tough economic environment America was entering. As the Depression of 1819 set in, Ogden's job became more difficult. Growers held out for better offers from European agents on their good-quality cotton. At the same time, growers worried over the increasing threat to their "middling" stuffs caused by India cotton.[10]

James Ogden began his journey to New Orleans in November 1818. He first traveled aboard a ship from New York to Philadelphia and then overland to Pittsburgh where he planned to travel via steamboat to New Orleans. The steamboat was still a relative novelty at this time for western travel. It was only in 1811 that the first steamboat appeared on the Mississippi. After that boat made it to New Orleans, proving that the muddy waters could be tamed, more began to slowly appear. According to Joyce Appleby, in 1818, there were twenty steamboats on the Mississippi and Ohio rivers; in just ten years, that number grew to two hundred.[11] At Pittsburgh, James DePeyster Ogden booked passage aboard the *James Ross* to Louisville.[12] The 700-mile journey took the vessel only 103 hours; but for some repairs, James Ogden felt sure it would have arrived in seventy hours.[13] At Louisville, James had hoped to find tobacco ready for immediate sale, but found none on hand because the tobacco crops had yet to reach the market. While many agents made their way up the smaller rivers into the interior of the countryside to buy tobacco directly from the farmers, James Ogden shunned this practice due to the unpredictability of delivery. Once purchased, the tobacco waited in storehouses by the waterway for a rise in the river level sufficient to float it down to Louisville. Should there be a dry season, where the water did not rise, the agent was forced to wait until it did. Ogden reported that some tobacco purchased two years earlier was still waiting for delivery. He decided to wait for purchase until the tobacco that could reach the market did so, either in Louisville or New Orleans.[14] As a result, James Ogden made plans to leave Louisville for New Orleans, and the next day, he left on board the steamboat *Cincinnati*. The usual passage for a steamboat from Louisville to New Orleans was ten days, but the *Cincinnati* ran aground on a sandbar near New Madrid only four days out and could go no farther. The six passengers engaged another boat to take them to Natchez, Mississippi, where they arrived seventeen days later. Despite this delay, when James Ogden finally arrived in New Orleans on January 12, 1819, he was able to say that he was the first of the agents from the East to arrive that year.[15]

For James Ogden, this trip to New Orleans provided a crash course in conducting business in a quickly shifting and unpredictable market. Although James Ogden hoped that his early arrival would give him a competitive edge over other purchasing agents, he was disappointed in the market at New Orleans. He found the cotton market was higher there than at Natchez; he also discovered that New York bills had a lower exchange rate in New Orleans than at Natchez. However, much to James Ogden's frustration, he discovered he was unable to conduct business at Natchez as he wished, and so was forced to do business in New Orleans.

Business at this time was based largely on personal relationships. As a stranger in a new market, James Ogden found the doors to business in Natchez closed in front of him. Letters of introduction from an associate or a well-known merchant house could have thrown the doors open wide. Benefits of such a relationship were the extension of credit and advice on the local market from an insider. Frederick DePeyster made certain that James Ogden carried letters of introduction with him, and that he picked up more along the way in the different cities where he stopped. These letters were meant to facilitate the business he had in New Orleans. Unfortunately for James DePeyster Ogden, the letters he carried did him no good at Natchez, where he found high-quality cotton for sale at a good price. Once in New Orleans, James Ogden wrote anxiously to hurry the arrival of a promised letter from his old firm of LeRoy, Bayard & Co. so that he would be able to conduct business in Natchez before the price of cotton soared as all predicted it would.[16] Although it may seem strange that Ogden's former employer would write a letter of introduction for him now that he worked for another firm, it was actually fairly common practice at the time to keep tabs on former apprentices and promising individuals. One could never tell when those personal ties would prove beneficial to business; merchants were thinking of future business opportunities, and for James Ogden, a good letter was one of the most valuable tools he had to make himself successful and live up to DePeyster expectations.[17]

Once settled in New Orleans, James Ogden kept a close eye on exchange rates, the price of cotton, and the competition for the business of textile manufacturers from merchants of India cotton, both in Liverpool and the United States. As business was also quite personal, he cultivated friendships and acquaintances among the elite circles of New Orleans society. During 1819, James Ogden dined with members of the Louisiana Legislature and all the top merchants there. In this way, with careful planning and purpose, he was able to cultivate business contacts that served him well in later years. When his cousin Robert DePeyster later went to New Orleans on business in 1825, he stated that James Ogden's success in that quarter was due to his social network.

Although 1819 proved a difficult year in the cotton market, James Ogden and the DePeysters managed to break even. By the end of the 1819 cotton season, James Ogden had purchased 507 bales of cotton at an average price of 21 cents per pound when the average market price of cotton that year was 25 cents per pound. He accomplished this feat by purchasing from small growers in small quantities (anywhere from two to six bales at a time) so as to avoid the attention of other buyers.[18] Out of the 507 bales, the majority went to Liverpool, for sale in England, and the rest went to Baltimore, as the market for cotton at New York collapsed. Much to James Ogden's disappointment, the cotton market at Liverpool dropped over the course of the season, and by the time his cotton came to market, prime cotton was selling at £.18; less than he anticipated but more than he needed to break even, James Ogden managed to do so even at a time when many merchants were recording losses, thanks in part to his ability to adapt and innovate in the midst of a difficult situation.[19]

James Ogden eventually established himself as a cotton merchant under the firm name of James DePeyster Ogden & Co. at New York, and also at Liverpool under the name Roskell, Ogden & Co.[20] Throughout the rest of his career James Ogden established a reputation as a savvy, trustworthy businessman. He served as president for the Nautilus Insurance Company (now New York Life) and the New York City Chamber of Commerce among others. James Ogden lived until 1870, when he was 80 years old. Throughout his career, but particularly in this early period, we see that his success was due in part to his ability to utilize the family network, his social and business contacts, and his familial names. Being a careful manager of his inherited wealth also helped him fund his business enterprises. James Ogden was able to adapt to changing situations and innovate when necessary in order to come out ahead of his competitors in difficult situations. In short, James DePeyster Ogden followed the model laid out by his uncle Frederick DePeyster for a lifetime of wealth and success.

Around the same time James DePeyster Ogden established himself in the world of business, Frederick DePeyster's son Robert G. L. DePeyster seemed to lose his footing. After his apprenticeship and service in the army during the War of 1812, this son of a Loyalist officer went into business with one of his Reade cousins to form the firm of Reade & DePeyster. The partnership imported sugar and rum from the island of St. Croix in the West Indies. Robert was the partner who actually traveled to St. Croix to purchase the firm's merchandise, and as a result, he spent a good portion of each year there. It made sense for Robert to take on this responsibility as his stepmother, Ann Beekman, had relatives there. Robert took advantage of these familial connections to establish himself in business in much the same way that James Ogden had used the business contacts of Frederick DePeyster to establish himself. While in St. Croix, Robert stayed with Ann's aunt, Sarah Beekman, at her plantation. Sarah Beekman provided him with personal servants, horses, and a carriage, and most importantly, valuable entrance into the elite social and business circles of St. Croix. In Robert's case, the familial connections proved his most valuable assets in establishing himself in the DePeyster tradition.

Although Robert's endeavors were, for the most part, profitable, a hurricane passed through the West Indies in 1819 and altered his fortunes in St. Croix. Human losses were low, but the hurricane destroyed the crops at St. Croix. The hurricane also destroyed the majority of ships anchored there, a number of which belonged, at least in part, to the DePeysters.[21] Crops recovered slowly, adversely impacting the finances of Reade & DePeyster. By February of 1820, some of the vegetables had grown back, but the fruit was slower to recover. Robert DePeyster (25) returned to the island to put his business there back together again. Despite this unexpected disaster, Robert's social standing in New York was not affected immediately. Nor would we expect it to be. Although this particular business venture did not work out, Robert was still a DePeyster and only 25 years old. Based on his age and familial wealth, there was still plenty of time for Robert to make a fortune in another area. In 1822, Robert was included in the audience of John Searles's painting *Fashionable New Yorkers at the Park Theater*, which featured members of New York's elite.[22] Unfortunately, Robert's financial problems had still not been resolved by 1823. A letter from Abraham to Frederick Jr. implies that unfavorable business speculation had ruined Robert's finances and brought the firm of Reade & DePeyster to bankruptcy.[23] Although the family still maintained a connection to the island through Sarah Goold for some time after this, the loss of a secure financial base sent Robert DePeyster away from St. Croix for good.

When it came time for Robert to rebuild his fortunes, he turned to New Orleans, where his cousin James DePeyster Ogden had previously conducted business and maintained contacts. Robert arrived at New Orleans in November of 1823 with high hopes for a revival of his fortunes. In Robert's view, New Orleans held a prime location for business, with access to the ocean and the backcountry. The daily arrival of steamboats loaded with articles and goods crowded the levees with their cargoes, and impressed Robert, who believed its markets were exceptional.[24] Later correspondence indicates that Robert was not at New Orleans to participate in the sugar market; rather, he was there as a shipping agent, charged with finding space aboard ships for goods purchased by others.

Although Robert was in New Orleans for business reasons, his correspondence to his brothers contains very little detail regarding his activities in this area, giving the impression that he expected to establish himself and succeed with little difficulty or effort. Instead of business, Robert wrote of his impressions of the city, its people, and his acquaintances. Robert thought New Orleans only mildly impressive culturally. The French buildings of the area he thought low and heavy-looking, yet admired their neat and clean appearance. As for order, he thought New Orleans above par, noting its particular quiet after dark.[25]

Upon his arrival, Robert made certain to contact Samuel Steer, old friend of the DePeyster brothers and a member of the Louisiana Legislature. Robert reasonably hoped that by renewing the acquaintance, Steer might be of use in his business and social endeavors. Robert looked forward to January, when the legislature reconvened, so that he might see Steer in action and decide for himself the man's talent in the political arena.[26] In the meantime, Robert set himself to the task of establishing himself in the New Orleans business world.

Just one month after his arrival, however, the markets in New Orleans slowed to a crawl, and Robert felt the relative poverty of the place. When Frederick Jr. inquired whether he might find a good market for his military items, Robert waved him off, telling his brother that items other than whiskey or grog just would not sell at that time.[27] He advised Frederick Jr. to sell the items in New York or not at all, as the commission would surely destroy any hoped-for profits.

With the deflation of business came a general slowdown in the amusements of the city, which seemed to be of greater concern to

Robert. He noted that one of the few things to do in the city at that time was to walk down to the levees and watch the boatmen fight. This New York gentleman was fascinated by the boasts and bravado of the boatmen, and he relished telling his brother of their exploits.[28]

With so few refined amusements to distract him, Robert eagerly awaited the start of the Louisiana legislative season when, he believed, his connections would allow him access to the higher levels of society, not to mention the entertainment provided by the colorful politics of the era. Robert was disappointed to find that his old friend Samuel Steer was not an "active" member of the legislature. He did not give speeches and did not participate in debates.[29] Instead, Steer remained popular due to his work ethic on the committees to which he belonged.[30]

Robert's hopes for diversion by politics also fell flat. When the legislature convened on January 3, Robert was thoroughly unimpressed. "They all appear more devotees of their belly—than of those pursuits calculated to make them fitt for high stations with that character and ability—which the people's interest requires."[31] One of Robert's hopes for the political season was met fully, however. His connection to Steer did indeed provide Robert with entry into the highest social circles. The rage among his new set were the masque balls that were held twice a week. According to Robert, the attendees, in disguise, were at liberty to ask any questions not of an insulting nature. At these events, Robert planned to be a regular attendee.[32] Robert mingled with the upper crust of Louisiana society and even dined with Louisiana governor, Henry Johnson, whom he proclaimed a "pleasant companion" and "well adapted to Republican principals."[33]

Although Robert socialized with the elite of New Orleans, he seemed unable to access these contacts for business purposes, and by February, Robert's pocketbook felt the squeeze of his opulent living. He complained to Frederick Jr. that high prices kept agents from purchasing goods. This prevented him, as a shipping agent, from selling space aboard his ships. Robert complained that even his cousin, James DePeyster Ogden, would not purchase that quarter and therefore could not send any business his way.[34]

His most bitter complaints, however, were reserved for his father Frederick. Robert believed that in response to his dire situation, his father could have pulled some strings and secured some business for him. Instead Robert received only silence.[35] This is not wholly surprising as Robert was then 31, and Frederick, having been retired for six years, likely thought his son should have been capable of providing for himself just as Frederick had provided for himself in more difficult circumstances and with fewer resources. It was also part of the emerging culture of the United States to promote independence in one's male children.[36] Neither is Frederick's reaction surprising given what we know of his earlier treatment of his own brother Abraham back in 1797 when Frederick reminded him of the rules governing merchant activity and policies relating to credit. At a certain point, Frederick expected individuals to take responsibility for their own actions and behave in a manner consistent with the acceptable standards of behavior, especially if they were DePeysters. What is surprising about the situation is Robert's continued insistence that his father assist him.

Frederick was not the only one on whom Robert focused his disappointment. Samuel Steer also fell out of Robert's good graces; but where Robert would forgive his father, he made no such plans to forgive Steer. The old friend had failed to reciprocate Robert's generosity; and at a point where Robert's finances were so thinly stretched, the ungentlemanly behavior was unforgivable. Robert described his old friend in the most scathing terms: "He is in truth a mere puff—a Ball to be tossed about By his friends . . . Puffed up with pride conceit & self importance. . . . a mere sponger & courtier."[37]

Robert's focus on Samuel Steer is interesting. Given their long acquaintance, Robert judged Samuel's behavior against what he expected of himself or someone of the station Robert grew up in. It is possible that Robert may have been more forgiving of his friend's inattention had his own financial situation not been so constrained. As it was, Robert's finances were no doubt forcing him to live, as his aunt Margaret James once said, "not quite what a DePeyster . . . Ought."[38] Suffering that, and then being forced to watch someone he thought unworthy, a "mere puff" who was living above the station for which his *manners* should have marked him was an indignity that Robert found difficult to reconcile himself. In the environment of the early American republic, where the gentry did not exist and all men were equal regardless of their economic rank, manners became a demarcation of class and gentility. Books on etiquette, self-improvement, and manners flew off the shelves and into the eager hands of people wishing to fulfill the American dream by improving their lot in life both economically and socially.[39]

Robert felt his family and friends had abandoned him to the mercies of the world (regardless of what the real situation was), but instead of shrinking, he gathered himself together and determined that he would succeed on his own. Robert decided to train himself in the cotton market, the same area in which his cousin James DePeyster Ogden saw so much success. But cotton was not the easiest market in which to gain entry. It was highly specialized and quite exclusive. There were different qualities of cotton for sale (poor, middling, good), and each quality was affected by a number of factors (color, fiber length and strength, and amount of debris among other things). In order to operate successfully in the market, one had to become a discriminating judge of all types of cotton, and that usually took time and connections. When James Ogden had first attempted the business seven years earlier in 1819, he encountered many difficulties, but his attitude and letters of introduction allowed him a quick education. Robert also had letters of introduction, but came up with very different results. He began by visiting the cotton yards in New Orleans to learn about the different properties of cotton so that he could become a proper judge of the commodity and act as his own agent in the market. Robert's attitude, however, must have been very different from that of James Ogden, because where Ogden found people willing to teach and mentor, Robert found only people trying to take advantage of him. The local dealers seemed to think Robert quite wealthy and repeatedly quoted him higher prices than other agents received. Robert worried that by the time they dropped their prices low enough for him to buy, he would have run himself out of money.[40]

Although he did not wish to give up on commerce as his living, Robert conceded that if he failed in New Orleans, he would have to do just that to try and gain his "independence."[41] He complained bitterly that the "intemperate the ignorant & worthless" succeeded in business while he himself just flailed for survival. It is possible that Robert was just a poor businessman. It is also possible that he found himself attempting to make the kind of money his father had a generation earlier in a profession that was no longer the key to economic riches it once was. At any rate, his lack of success in business, his disappointment in the character of his old friend Samuel Steer, and a bitter break with James DePeyster Ogden, no doubt played a role in his low attitude that spring.

We do not know how long Robert stayed in New Orleans. Family histories and newspaper reports simply state that Robert lived there for "a time." Similarly, we do not know how successful that time in New Orleans was. From the direction his letters point, it could not have been a resounding success. Pierre DePeyster, youngest DePeyster brother and only son of Anne Beekman, eventually moved to New Orleans, and it is unlikely that he would have done so had Robert been thoroughly ruined. On the other hand, Pierre may have looked to his cousin James DePeyster Ogden as a model for success over his brother. We do know that Robert finally married in 1839 to Virginia Shephard of [West] Virginia; he was 44 years old. Robert died in 1873 at the age of 78; he had no children.

While Robert struggled to find success in New Orleans, his brother Abraham attempted to find his as a purchasing agent in Brazil. And it makes sense that he did. Not only was Brazil a longtime rival to the West Indies when it came to sugar, but Brazil also produced tobacco and cotton at good prices—all things the DePeysters traded in.[42] Additionally, Brazil's market was wide open with regard to trade. Beginning in 1642, Portugal signed a series of treaties with Great Britain ceding extraterritorial jurisdiction, freedom of trade with their colonies, and control over customs in exchange for the protection of the British Royal Navy. Perhaps the most significant of these treaties was the Treaty of 1703, which ensured that there would be no industrial development within Brazil.[43] In this position, Brazil was in need of manufactured products that both Great Britain and the United States could provide. The unique position of Great Britain with regard to Brazil ensured that there was a large British community in Salvador, Bahia, the former capital of colonial Brazil (the capital moved to Rio De Janeiro in 1763).

Despite the advantages of trade with Brazil, there were some disadvantages to contend with as well. Northeast Brazil was recovering from a drought in 1816, which depressed the production of crops including sugar and cotton; however, political unrest in the country slowed that recovery and made the availability of both crops and cash unpredictable. The unrest began when João VI declared Brazil to be a kingdom equal to Portugal in 1815. Not long after, the republican spirit began to sweep across the northeast, challenging João rule. With the use of troops, João suppressed the movement. But the violence took its toll, as Abraham would discover.

In August of 1820, Abraham left New York City aboard the *Virginia* as both partial owner and supercargo. Abraham arrived first in Pernambuco and then headed to Salvador before finally landing in Rio De Janeiro. The markets in Brazil were not what he had hoped. Finding them "unusually depressed," Abraham made plans to return to New York before March, by which time he hoped to sell the cargo of the *Virginia*.[44] Whether or not he achieved this goal is unknown, but it is likely that he did as he remained optimistic about Brazil and the opportunities it offered.

It was two years before Abraham was able to return to Salvador, Bahia. He arrived in May of 1822,[45] and as an American, Abraham quickly gained entry into the English-speaking community there; this was a very good thing as he did not speak the local language. This community, composed largely of British subjects along with a small but profitable group of Americans, provided Abraham the connections necessary for conducting business in Bahia. The province, they all believed, had great potential, both for sugar export and as a market for American goods, particularly flour and gunpowder (which was contraband). Although Abraham does not go into great detail, it appears he was an immediate success among the elite of this English-speaking community, for he was given the rare invitation to reside with the American consul there, Woodbridge Odlin of Philadelphia.[46] Although this success may have been due to Abraham's personality, it is likely that the reputation of the DePeyster name played a role in Abraham's acceptance into that small community.

Despite his high hopes for the market in Bahia, Abraham did not arrive at a particularly good moment for economic advancement. Between Abraham's first visit to Brazil in 1820 and his return in 1822, the tense political situation in Brazil had devolved into civil war. The states of Brazil revolted not only against Portugal but also against domination by Rio de Janeiro. Salvador and more specifically Bahia, the state in which Abraham settled himself, experienced particularly fierce fighting.[47] In two separate instances, Salvador came under siege from the countryside.[48] As business slowed and resources became scarce, the merchant community, including Abraham DePeyster, became nervous.

During this time, Portugal hoped that Great Britain would interpret the Brazilian revolt as an attack on Portugal and, in accordance with their treaties, protect Portugal against this threat. Great Britain, in fact, did not care who won the contest for control of Brazil; they believed that whichever side prevailed, their interests would be maintained. If Portugal should win, then Britain's treaties would continue to govern the situation as usual; should Brazil win, they would be so weak that they would sign the same type of treaties Portugal had before them in order to secure their own position.

As a result, Great Britain sent over a war ship to sit in the harbor and protect the British community, which evacuated to the ship. The French followed suit, as did others, until all that was left of the English-speaking community in Salvador was its American contingent. During the second siege, those merchants submitted a petition, addressed to the President of the United States. In it, they requested that the United States send warships to Salvador to protect its citizens. They reminded the President of the importance European nations placed on their trade with Brazil, and Salvador in particular, and that all those nations had at least one ship in harbor to protect their citizens.[49] They requested that the President show as much concern for the interests of his own people. Abraham DePeyster was one of nine merchants to sign the document.[50] This petition to the President demonstrates that while U.S. trade with Brazil was still limited at this time, the merchants in Salvador believed that a trade relationship between the two countries would be beneficial to the United States if it hoped to compete with Great Britain and the other European powers.

Like others in Salvador, Abraham feared that Brazil's struggle for independence would provide its slaves with dangerous ideas about their own independence.[51] The emancipation of Brazil's slave population, Abraham speculated, would retard the progress of the Brazilian markets, for without the slaves to work the fields, crop production would surely fall. Despite those reservations, Abraham retained high hopes for Brazil, and noted he would return again as long as the place provided opportunity. Abraham also feared that the newly freed slave population would, in their resentment, lash out at those who held them in subjugation, making Brazil a dangerous place for whites.[52] In Bahia, at least, these fears were well founded. "Anti-Portuguese disturbances" occurred as "Afro-Brazilian lower classes controlled the streets and were beating Portuguese residents."[53] In relating the situation to his brother, Frederick Jr., in a letter dated April 15, 1824, Abraham described an unsettled state of affairs in which robberies took place on the street in broad daylight with many witnesses around. He also described scenes in which the assailants used knives to threaten their victims and separate them from their valuables. To impress upon his brother the severity of the situation, Abraham added that the victims of these attacks were, in many of the incidents, British and American. One particular incident that he described took place in the English-speaking neighborhood where Abraham lived. The alarm was quickly sounded and the neighborhood descended on the two assailants; the neighbors captured one of the men and beat him so badly "as to be unable to take his 400 lashes." The man, Abraham reported "with pleasure," died the next day.[54] Abraham seemed to think that these incidents of theft and assault were either "overlooked or permitted by the police" but given the instability of the government, it was most likely a matter of whether or not the government *could* do anything about the situation. According to Jeffrey Mosher, "only promises to expel all the Portuguese pacified the Lusophobic crowds" and kept Salvador from anarchy.[55]

Abraham's real grievance with the situation, however, seemed to result from his continued disappointment in business. Just prior to the second siege of Salvador, Abraham invested heavily in tobacco bound for Gibraltar. After the besieging army starved out the poor, as chaos reigned, and the city was ready to fall, the ship contracted to ferry the tobacco was forced to leave its moorings before it was loaded with Abraham's tobacco. His entire investment was lost.[56] Abraham DePeyster left

Salvador shortly after this last letter to his brother was written. It is entirely possible that the financial disaster combined with the continuing political uncertainty finally convinced Abraham to return to New York, but it is impossible to know.

Although Abraham had all of the same advantages as his siblings and cousins, and he proved himself willing to adapt to changing economic situations, he did not seem to prosper as some of the others did. This could be due to the fact that Abraham died at the relatively young age of 38, before he really had the opportunity to establish himself, or it could be that, like his namesake, Abraham was just an "unfortunate man." Regardless, Abraham DePeyster, like his brother Robert, demonstrates that despite having every possible advantage, unbridled success like that demonstrated by their father Frederick could still be elusive.

James Ogden, Robert, and Abraham all tried to build their fortunes on slave-based staple economies. In this, they were all in line with the merchant community of New York. As Sven Beckert noted, it was New York's "intense commitment to cotton that helped it decisively leave Philadelphia, Baltimore, and Boston behind."[57] Merchants especially tied themselves to cotton and other slave-based staples that served as the fuel for the Industrial Revolution. The Industrial Revolution, however, also served to make the world of business ever more volatile, causing merchants to specialize their interests, much as James Ogden had. At the same time, New York's industrialists were increasingly critical of slavery, as they relied more and more on a free-labor system. This increasingly wide divide between merchants and industrialists caused New York to remain decidedly split over the issue of slavery in the years leading up to the Civil War.[58]

While the majority of the young DePeysters went on to enter the world of business, as Frederick had, theirs was not the only path to success. For instance, Frederick Jr. entered into apprenticeships with Peter Augustus Jay (son of John Jay) and Peter Van Schaack (noted colonial attorney and former Loyalist) to learn the law while his brothers and cousins were undergoing apprenticeships with some of the major merchant firms in New York. Although this may have been out of step with his brothers and cousins, it was in line with many other young men of his age. According to Joyce Appleby, due to the low amount of training required for the position, lawyers were "abundant" in this generation.[59] In 1820, at age 24, Frederick Jr. accepted the position of Master in Chancery for the City of New York. Although his choice of profession differed from the choices of other young DePeysters, it could also be seen as a form of innovation and adaption. The economy of America's early republic had already undergone the major transformation to capitalism, and while individuals could still do well as merchants, it was no longer the path to riches that it had once been. Lawyers, however, were increasingly in demand, and as a member of a family and social stratum so heavily tied to the business world, there would be no lack of work (or income) for Frederick Jr.

Just as Frederick Jr. no doubt planned to utilize his extensive familial and social connections to succeed in his legal practice, he followed another time-honored tradition of the wealthy by marrying into the prominent and wealthy Watts family. The same year Frederick Jr. was named Master in Chancery, he married Justina Watts (1801–1821), only daughter of John Watts. The Watts family had roots going back just as far as the DePeysters, and were even wealthier. In 1828, John Watts ranked among New York City's wealthiest two hundred residents.[60] Without the status and wealth of the DePeyster name, Frederick Jr.'s marriage with Justina would have been impossible. After his marriage, Frederick Jr. moved into the home of his father-in-law. Justina Watts died just one month after giving birth to son John Watts DePeyster; Frederick Jr. and his son continued to live in the Watts residence. In what he hoped would become his autobiography, John Watts DePeyster wrote that after his mother's death, he was cared for by a series of nannies and, later, tutors. His grandfather John Watts decided to make the child his sole heir; as a result he indulged the boy and contradicted Frederick Jr.'s orders and plans. Because of the connections of both his father and grandfather, John Watts DePeyster was able to meet and mingle with the elite of American society, including several presidents. Frederick Jr. and his son lived in the Watts home until Frederick Jr. remarried in 1839, this time to Maria Antoinette Kane Hone, the wealthy widow of John Hone.[61]

Soon after Frederick Jr.'s marriage to Justina Watts, John Watts (his sons having preceded him in death) entrusted his son-in-law with the management of the considerable Watts estate. Frederick Jr. was so successful at estate management that he was able to leave his position as Master in Chancery and travel extensively for both work and pleasure, with his son John often accompanying him. Frederick's ability to leave his position also allowed him to participate and hold office in a large number of philanthropic and social organizations. He was a founder and one-time president of the New-York Historical Society, the Nicholas Society, and the Society for the Prevention of Cruelty to Children, among others. Frederick was very much in step with his contemporaries who also looked to these types of organizations to reinforce their elite status as well as their influence in an increasingly diverse city.[62] By the time John Watts DePeyster came of age, the family wealth was such that it was unnecessary for him to have any profession whatsoever. Frederick DePeyster Jr. died in 1882 at the age of 86, having lived up to all of the DePeyster ideals by following the same basic principles as his father, without actually participating in the same profession.

Augustus DePeyster, oldest (and illegitimate) son of Frederick DePeyster, accomplished a similar feat as a ship's captain. It should be noted, however, that there were many similarities between the professions of captain and merchant; the most successful captains thought like merchants. As Jacques M. Downs noted, captains "knew the trade, the ports, the merchants, the ships, the goods and the weather. . . . They weighed and measured cargoes, supervised loading, hired crews and officers, inspected ships and goods, registered marine protests," and they were less likely to be "bamboozled" than outsiders.[63] Although his success was not as meteoric as that of his father or brother, Augustus did become one of the most respected and wealthy captains of his age.

After his apprenticeship to Captain Whetten of the famed *Beaver*, flagship of John Jacob Astor's fleet, Augustus became a captain in his own right for Astor. Captaining privateers and then the *Beaver* in the Canton trade, Augustus remained with Astor until 1828, when he was about 38 years old. It was about this time that John Jacob Astor was himself getting out of the China trade. At that point, Augustus began sailing the packet to Havre, France for Francis DePau.[64] It is unknown how long Augustus sailed for DePau, but it is likely he served in this capacity until 1845, when he agreed to become governor of the Sailors' Snug Harbor on Stanton Island, New York, when he was about 55 years old. The Sailors' Snug Harbor was established in 1801 to serve as a residential retirement and care facility for sailors too worn out by a life at sea to properly care for themselves. Augustus was, apparently, a favorite among the residents of the institution, and long after his disappearance, they regaled visitors with tales of the Captain's exploits while at sea.[65] The exact date of Augustus's death is unknown; however, it is safe to assume he died early in 1868, at about 78 years old, when the newspaper reported his "mysterious disappearance."

With Augustus, the use of those standard DePeyster principles is evident in his success. Although his positions with both John Jacob Astor and Francis DePau were undoubtedly due to his own skill as a sailor and captain, his family name would not have been a hindrance to him in those positions, nor later when he became the governor of Sailors' Snug Harbor. In all likelihood, Augustus took advantage of the DePeyster reputation to bolster his own, already high and well earned, in order to secure business for himself in merchant circles around the world. Augustus also married into the prominent Varick family, a feat that speaks to his own status and wealth. On top of all of this, Augustus proved himself willing to adapt to changing economic conditions and innovate when necessary. We see evidence of this with his willingness to captain a privateering vessel during the War of 1812, engage in the Canton trade, and then captain packet ships as the need arose.

James Ferguson DePeyster, meanwhile, was busy running DePeyster & Son and later his own firms in New York. In 1822, when he was 28 years old, James Ferguson married his cousin Susan Maria Clarkson, daughter of General Matthew Clarkson. Susan died one year later giving birth to daughter Susan Maria Clarkson DePeyster. After the death of his wife, James Ferguson focused on running the family's business and ensuring that his daughter had every advantage she would need to live up to DePeyster standards. He was rewarded when she married Robert Edward Livingston of Clermont, New York. James Ferguson eventually remarried in 1838 at age 39 to Francis Goodhue Ashton and had three more children. It was his son Frederick James DePeyster who was included on Mrs. Astor's original 400 list in 1892.[66]

Little is known of the other DePeyster siblings. Pierre, Frederick's youngest and only son by Ann Beekman, graduated from Columbia in 1833. Sometime after that, he moved to New Orleans where he married and established himself. Of the sisters, Cornelia and Catharine married. Cornelia married Richmond Whitmarsh, a prominent merchant from Rhode Island who formed a partnership with her brother James Ferguson. Catharine married Benjamin Hazard Field, who was wealthy enough to be remembered as a philanthropist, and was involved in many of the same charitable organizations as Frederick Jr. and James Ferguson. In marrying prominent, wealthy individuals, Cornelia and Catharine were following their parents' examples as well as acting within the expectations of their social and economic class. Ann never married, but she lived with her brother James Ferguson until her death in 1840 at 35. It is likely that prior to James remarrying in 1838, Ann was responsible for raising her niece and keeping the house in order. She would have been a valued member of his family, not just a dependent. Like Ann, neither Margaret James nor Mary married. Margaret James lived to be 60 years old, dying in 1866. Mary lived with her sister Catharine and her husband until her death in 1892 at 83. Catharine died sometime before this.

After Frederick DePeyster returned to New York in 1793 from his Loyalist exile in Canada, he so successfully integrated himself into American society that his sons were able to participate in the defense of the United States during the War of 1812. By the time Frederick retired from his merchant activities in 1820, his ever-increasing economic and social status within New York made his Loyalist past even more irrelevant. Certainly Frederick's Loyalist past, both service and exile, was not a bar to the success of his children or wards in the United States. Out of all of Frederick DePeyster's male children and wards, those who were able to innovate and adapt themselves in the changing economy were the most successful. James Ferguson, Frederick Jr., and James DePeyster Ogden (and even Augustus in his own right) were more successful than the others, just as Frederick Sr. was more successful than his siblings. Simply put, they used their inherited strengths to their greatest advantages, they utilized the family network when necessary and appropriate, employed both social and business connections, married into other prominent families, and managed their inheritances with a shrewd eye. There is no evidence of this pattern among the others; theirs was, at best, a maintenance (and sometimes a loss) of wealth while James Ferguson, Frederick Jr., and James Ogden built enough wealth to propel them into the higher levels of society, truly following in the DePeyster tradition.

Conclusion

*W*hen Rip Van Winkle returned to his village on an election day after sleeping away the Revolution in the Catskill mountains, he declared his loyalty to the King and was immediately met with cries of "tory! spy! refugee!" When Rip showed proper ignorance as the basis for his Loyalist leaning, he was accepted back into the village fold without much more ado. Rip Van Winkle's real-life parallel Frederick DePeyster returned to his own "village" of New York City after his own "sleep" in Canadian exile with a more complicated history. Frederick left the United States in the wake of the Revolutionary war not only as a Loyalist in sympathies, but also a veteran of the British Army. His sojourn in Canada, however, allowed the immediate passions of wartime to recede. Like the fictional Rip Van Winkle, Frederick was recognized by his community and welcomed back in 1793. The story of Rip Van Winkle ends with a peaceful and satisfactory old age. So, too, does the story of Frederick DePeyster. By the time of his retirement from business in 1820, he was a respected businessman, a pillar of New York City society, and a devoted philanthropist. These were not easy accomplishments, but they proved to be manageable ones due to his own savvy, established wealth, social network, and most significantly, being in the right location with the right socioeconomic climate.

One reason Frederick DePeyster was able to return to and seamlessly integrate himself into the United States, a nation whose creation he fought against, was the nature of the place to which he returned. New York had a unique position during the American Revolution due to the occupied status of New York City. For survival's sake, the boundary between Loyalist and Patriot was blurred, and "forgetting" those alliances in the postwar period proved to be to the benefit of everyone. Those Loyalists who kept their former alliances quiet, even those who had borne arms for the King, like Frederick DePeyster, were able to blend into that community without raising eyebrows.

Another reason Frederick was able to return and successfully integrate into the very nation against whose creation he had fought was his extensive social network. Prior to the American Revolution, the DePeysters were a prominent family who had married into many of the other prominent families of New York. Despite the Revolution, blood trumped political loyalty, at least in most cases. As a result, Frederick was able to rely upon those familial connections to help reestablish himself among New York's social elite. Additionally, Frederick used his primary contacts to make others, which he in turn employed to further his economic aspirations.

Just as place and connection were important aspects in the successful return of Frederick DePeyster to New York, so, too, was his personal wealth. Frederick was a favorite among his relatives from a young age, and he was remembered in many of their wills. Even before the Revolution began, Frederick had amassed a valuable estate consisting largely of property. When Frederick resettled in New Brunswick, after the war he received a large settlement (800 acres) of land from the British government for his service in the army. He was able to take that land, lease it out, and use the profits to launch himself into business as a merchant. By the time Frederick returned to New York, he had the means to support himself in style. He was a drain on no one's resources and, in fact, was able to provide economic opportunities to others through his Canadian connections. There can be no doubt that Frederick's wealth helped to speed along his acceptance and integration into American society.

These factors, combined with Frederick's personal appeal, helped to make his Loyalist past increasingly less important even as he worked to establish himself and his family among New York's social and economic elite. So successful was Frederick's integration that during the War of 1812 his own sons fought for the United States against Great Britain. Similarly, while Frederick's sons saw themselves as DePeysters first and New Yorkers second, they also saw themselves as Americans and encountered no obstacles related to their father's loyalty during the Revolution. After Frederick DePeyster's retirement from his merchant activities in 1820, the majority of his sons followed his example of innovation and adaptability to establish themselves among the social and economic elite of New York in their own right.

The ease of Frederick DePeyster's return to New York indicates that this type of phenomenon, returning Loyalists, was far more common than previously believed. Historians have long known that Loyalists could stay in or return to the United States successfully but with an actual example of how the process could work, we can surmise, despite the unique circumstances of Frederick DePeyster, that many other Loyalists returned and integrated with similar success, though perhaps with a lower profile.

The challenge now is to identify other returning Loyalists in order to determine their numbers and in which states or communities they clustered. With that information, perhaps the long-held notion of the Loyalist as traitor and enemy to the Republic will be revealed as an historical construct. While Americans undoubtedly chose sides during the Revolutionary War, what I am proposing is that the lines were not black and white, not just for the vicinity of New York City, but for a much larger area. Frederick DePeyster's Loyalist past was well known and yet he did business without any apparent hindrance in almost all of the former colonies. Then, as now, people had more than one identity; just as Frederick was a Loyalist, he was also a New Yorker, a merchant, and a DePeyster. Although the title of Loyalist was trotted out from time to time as a lynchpin of unity, the DePeyster experience reveals that people were generally willing to overlook a Loyalist past in favor of the person they knew.

The trajectory of Frederick DePeyster and his children demonstrate that, particularly in New York, active Loyalist service was not a bar to social and economic success in the United States following the Revolution. The pursuit of national unity among the first generation of Americans likewise assisted Frederick's integration by lauding the individual's ability to conform. Frederick DePeyster's example therefore shows that, given the right circumstances and a little *savoir-faire*, a former Loyalist could not only survive but thrive in the United States.

Appendices

DePeyster Genealogy 1

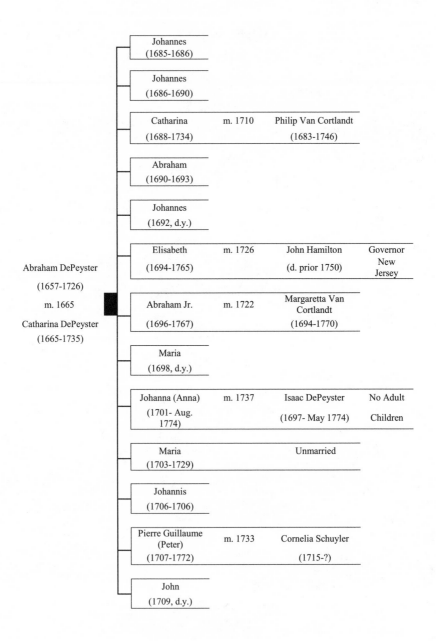

DePeyster Genealogy 2

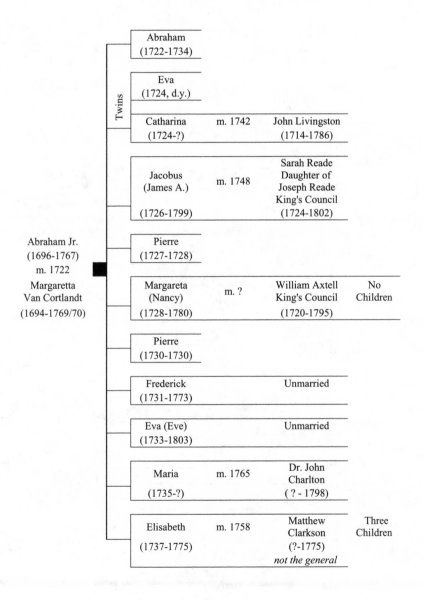

DePeyster Genealogy 3

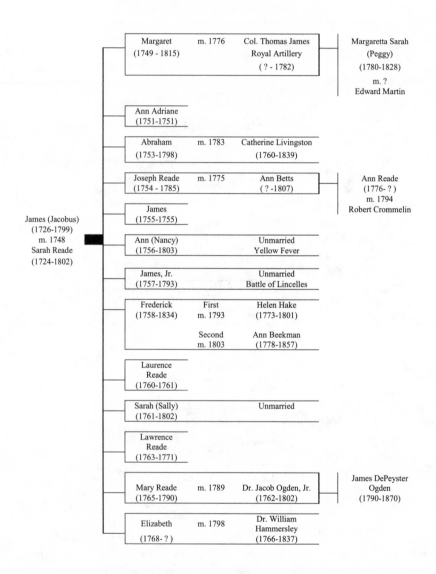

	Margaret (1749 - 1815)	m. 1776	Col. Thomas James Royal Artillery (? - 1782)	Margaretta Sarah (Peggy) (1780-1828) m. ? Edward Martin

Margaret (1749 - 1815) — m. 1776 — Col. Thomas James, Royal Artillery (? - 1782) — Margaretta Sarah (Peggy) (1780-1828) m. ? Edward Martin

Ann Adriane (1751-1751)

Abraham (1753-1798) — m. 1783 — Catherine Livingston (1760-1839)

Joseph Reade (1754 - 1785) — m. 1775 — Ann Betts (? -1807) — Ann Reade (1776- ?) m. 1794 Robert Crommelin

James (1755-1755)

James (Jacobus) (1726-1799) m. 1748 Sarah Reade (1724-1802)

Ann (Nancy) (1756-1803) — Unmarried, Yellow Fever

James, Jr. (1757-1793) — Unmarried, Battle of Lincelles

Frederick (1758-1834) — First m. 1793 — Helen Hake (1773-1801); Second m. 1803 — Ann Beekman (1778-1857)

Laurence Reade (1760-1761)

Sarah (Sally) (1761-1802) — Unmarried

Lawrence Reade (1763-1771)

Mary Reade (1765-1790) — m. 1789 — Dr. Jacob Ogden, Jr. (1762-1802) — James DePeyster Ogden (1790-1870)

Elizabeth (1768- ?) — m. 1798 — Dr. William Hammersley (1766-1837)

Appendix D

DePeyster Genealogy 4

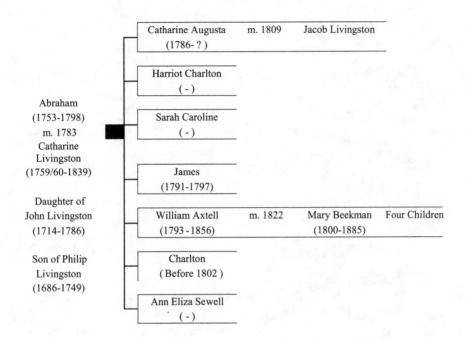

Abraham
(1753-1798)
m. 1783
Catharine
Livingston
(1759/60-1839)

Daughter of
John Livingston
(1714-1786)

Son of Philip
Livingston
(1686-1749)

Catharine Augusta   m. 1809   Jacob Livingston
(1786- ?)

Harriot Charlton
(-)

Sarah Caroline
(-)

James
(1791-1797)

William Axtell   m. 1822   Mary Beekman   Four Children
(1793 - 1856)   (1800-1885)

Charlton
(Before 1802)

Ann Eliza Sewell
(-)

DePeyster Genealogy 5

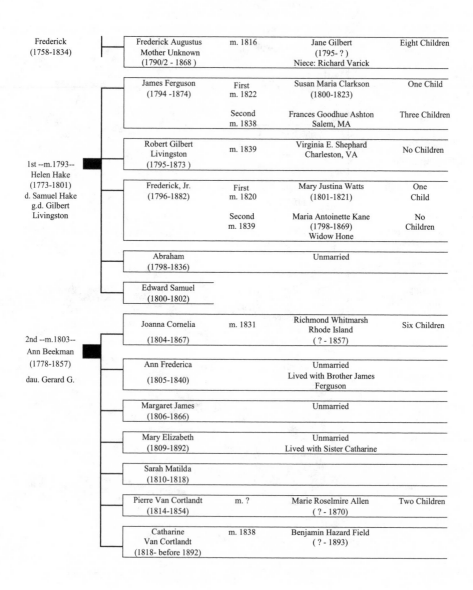

Frederick (1758-1834)	Frederick Augustus Mother Unknown (1790/2 - 1868)	m. 1816	Jane Gilbert (1795- ?) Niece: Richard Varick	Eight Children
	James Ferguson (1794 -1874)	First m. 1822	Susan Maria Clarkson (1800-1823)	One Child
		Second m. 1838	Frances Goodhue Ashton Salem, MA	Three Children
	Robert Gilbert Livingston (1795-1873)	m. 1839	Virginia E. Shephard Charleston, VA	No Children
1st --m.1793-- Helen Hake (1773-1801) d. Samuel Hake g.d. Gilbert Livingston	Frederick, Jr. (1796-1882)	First m. 1820	Mary Justina Watts (1801-1821)	One Child
		Second m. 1839	Maria Antoinette Kane (1798-1869) Widow Hone	No Children
	Abraham (1798-1836)		Unmarried	
	Edward Samuel (1800-1802)			
2nd --m.1803-- Ann Beekman (1778-1857) dau. Gerard G.	Joanna Cornelia (1804-1867)	m. 1831	Richmond Whitmarsh Rhode Island (? - 1857)	Six Children
	Ann Frederica (1805-1840)		Unmarried Lived with Brother James Ferguson	
	Margaret James (1806-1866)		Unmarried	
	Mary Elizabeth (1809-1892)		Unmarried Lived with Sister Catharine	
	Sarah Matilda (1810-1818)			
	Pierre Van Cortlandt (1814-1854)	m. ?	Marie Roselmire Allen (? - 1870)	Two Children
	Catharine Van Cortlandt (1818- before 1892)	m. 1838	Benjamin Hazard Field (? - 1893)	

Notes

Introduction. The Disappearance of the Loyalists

1. The use of the term *Canada* both here and throughout the text refers to today's geographic understanding of Canada, rather than the contemporary understanding of Canada. At the time, Nova Scotia and more specifically, the territory that would become New Brunswick was technically considered "British North America." The Province of New Brunswick did not officially become part of Canada until 1867.

2. Oscar Ziechner, "The Loyalist Problem in New York After the Revolution," *New York History*, vol. 21, 284–302.

3. While the population of Loyalists (or perhaps those who did not oppose the British) was higher in New York than in many states, Loyalists were by no means the majority of the population in the State as demonstrated by Bernard Mason, *The Road to Independence: The Revolutionary Movement in New York, 1773–1777*. Philip Ranlet, *The New York Loyalists*.

4. Judith Van Buskirk, *Generous Enemies: Patriots and Loyalists in Revolutionary New York*.

5. Henry Onderdonk, *Queens County in Olden Times: Being a Supplement to the Several Histories Thereof*, 51.

Chapter 1. The DePeyster Tradition

1. The actual date of Johannes DePeyster's death is unknown. His will is dated 1699 but was not proved until 1725. It is doubtful that Johannes actually lived until that year, so for the purposes of this discourse, the year of the will is used as year for Johannes' death.

2. Johannes was also offered the position of Mayor in 1677 but declined as he believed his command of the English language inadequate to the task. Frank Allaben, *John Watts DePeyster*, 17–18. James Grant Wilson, *The Memorial History of the City of New York*, 1.

3. Cathy Matson, *Merchants & Empire: Trading in Colonial New York*, 134, 137, 144.

4. Descriptions of the DePeyster mansion may be found in a number of different sources, the following are a brief list. Ester Singleton, *Social New York Under the Georges, 1714–1776: Houses, Streets, and Country Homes, Furniture, China, Plate and Manners; Appleton's Journal of Literature, Science, and Art*, vol. 12, July 4 to December 26, 1874. Martha J. Lamb and Mrs. Burton Harrison, *History of the City of New York: Its Origins, Rise and Progress, in Three Volumes*. Wilson, *The Memorial History of the City of New York*, 1893. Charles Knowles Bolton, *The Founders: Portraits of Persons Born Abroad Who Came to the Colonies in North America Before 1701.*

5. Joyce D. Goodfriend, *Before the Melting Pot: Society and Culture in Colonial New York City, 1664–1730*. Alice Morse Earle, *Colonial Days in Old New York*. Deborah A. Rosen, "Women and Property Across Colonial America: A Comparison of Legal Systems in New Mexico and New York," *William and Mary Quarterly*, 355–381. David E. Narrett, "Dutch Customs of Inheritance, Women, and the Law in Colonial New York City," *Authority and Resistance in Early New York*, 27–45.

6. Bolton, *The Founders*, 760. Waldron Phoenix Belknap Jr., *The DePeyster Genealogy*, 6.

7. Matson, *Merchants & Empire*, 354.

8. Ibid., 84.

9. Belknap, *The DePeyster Genealogy*. Lamb and Harrison, *History of the City of New York*. The great-grandson of James DePeyster, John Watts DePeyster, recorded that DePeyster's "extensive maritime fleet" was "swept from the seas by American and French privateers," although he mistakenly attributes the damage to the Revolutionary War. Allaben, *John Watts DePeyster*, 21.

10. Matson, *Merchants & Empire*. Philip L. White, *The Beekmans of New York in Politics and Commerce, 1647–1877*. E. Countryman, "The Uses of Capital in Revolutionary America: The Case of the New York Loyalist Merchants," 3–28. Joseph S. Tiedemann, *Reluctant Revolutionaries: New York City and the Road to Independence, 1763–1776*. Thomas M. Truxes, *Defying Empire: Trading With the Enemy in Colonial New York.*

11. Belknap, *The DePeyster Genealogy*.

12. Tiedemann, *Reluctant Revolutionaries*, 20.

13. Ibid., 22, 23.

14. Some histories list James DePeyster's residence at Dock Street but this is not contradictory. The lower portion of Queen Street was known as Dock Street.

15. Lamb and Harrison, *History of the City of New York*, 628.

16. Ibid.

17. *DePeyster Collection*, New-York Historical Society.

18. Truxes, *Defying Empire*, 10.

19. Ibid., 6.

20. Ibid., 1.

21. The State of New York, *The Colonial Laws of New York From the Year 1664 to the Revolution, Vol. IV*, 1005.

22. Tiedemann, *Reluctant Revolutionaries*, 36.

23. Virginia D. Harrington, *The New York Merchants on the Eve of the Revolution*, 40. Flick, *Loyalism in New York*, 18–19. Despite the fact that the country party supported the elected assembly over the governing council, the family itself did not support separation from Great Britain until after the British takeover of New York City crushed the more radical element of their party, forcing the party into upstate New York where the country party had more support and thus were able to direct the form of government the new state would take and to ensure the continued position of the elite.

24. Tiedemann, *Reluctant Revolutionaries*, 35.

25. Harrington, *The New York Merchants*, 40. Flick, *Loyalism in New York*, 18–19.

26. Flick, *Loyalism in New York*, 18–19. Tiedemann, *Reluctant Revolutionaries*, 35. Cynthia A. Kierner, *Traders and Gentlefolk: The Livingstons of New York, 1675–1790*, 176.

27. Kierner, *Traders and Gentlefolk*; the later chapters of Michael Kammen, *Colonial New York: A History*; Flick, *Loyalism in New York*; Tiedemann, *Reluctant Revolutionaries*; Harrington, *The New York Merchants*.

28. Kammen, *Colonial New York*, 337–375.

29. Ibid., 338. For more information on New York's colonial protests during this time, see also: Richard M. Ketchum, *Divided Loyalties: How the American Revolution Came to New York*. Thomas Jones, *History of New York During the Revolutionary War, and of the Leading Events in the Other Colonies at That Period*. Mason, *The Road to Independence*. Daniel J. Hulsebosch, *Constituting Empire: New York and the Transformation of Constitutionalism in the Atlantic World, 1664–1830*. Tiedemann, *Reluctant Revolutionaries*.

30. Tiedemann, *Reluctant Revolutionaries*, 39. Edwin G. Burrows and Mike Wallace, *Gotham: A History of New York City to 1898*, 202. Ketchum, *Divided Loyalties*, 140–141.

31. For more information on the Stamp Act Riots, see also: Edmund S. Morgan and Helen M. Morgan, *The Stamp Act Crisis: Prologue to Revolution.* F. L. Engelman, "Cadwallader Colden and the New York Stamp Act Riots," 560–578. Benjamin H. Irvin, "Tar, Feathers, and Enemies of American Liberties, 1768–1776," 197–238.

32. Burrows and Wallace, *Gotham*, 198.

33. Major Thomas James as quoted in Tiedemann, *Reluctant Revolutionaries*, 1. Burrows and Wallace, *Gotham*, 199.

34. Tiedemann, *Reluctant Revolutionaries*, 1.

35. Near today's Warren and Chambers Streets. Tiedemann, *Reluctant Revolutionaries*, 1, 45. Burrows and Wallace, *Gotham*, 199.

36. Tiedemann, *Reluctant Revolutionaries*, 45.

37. "G" to Printer, *New York Gazette, or, The Weekly Post Boy*, November 7, 1765, as quoted in Tiedemann, *Reluctant Revolutionaries*, 3. "The Assembly later awarded the major £1,745 to cover the damages, a generous sum." Burrows and Wallace, *Gotham*, 200.

38. For more information on mob activity in New York and the reaction of the elite classes see also: Paul A. Gilje, *The Road to Mobocracy: Popular Disorder in New York City, 1763–1834.* Benjamin L. Carp, *Rebels Rising: Cities and the American Revolution.*

39. Will of Abraham DePeyster, 3 July 1767, from *Abstracts of Wills on File in the Surrogates Office, City of New York, Vol. VII: Collections of the New-York Historical Society for the Year 1898, 104.*

40. *New York City During the American Revolution being a Collection of Original Papers (now first published) From the Manuscripts in the Possession of the Mercantile Library Association of New York City*, chapters 1346, 1354, 1437, 1464, 1490, 1636.

41. This practice of making the individual personally responsible for the debts of his office was common at the time. See Laurel Thatcher Ulrich, *A Midwife's Tale: The Life of Martha Ballard, Based on Her Diary, 1785–1812.*

42. *New York City During the American Revolution*, chapters 1346, 1354, 1437, 1464, 1490, 1636. Tiedemann, *Reluctant Revolutionaries*, 121.

43. It was at this point that the DePeyster mansion was sold to Henry White, member of the King's Council, and one of the founders of the Chamber of Commerce. White was also a Loyalist, and his estate was one of the first confiscated in 1779. The DePeyster mansion was later the residence of Governor Clinton.

44. Tiedemann, *Reluctant Revolutionaries*, 45.

45. *New York City During the American Revolution*, chapters 1354, 1464.

46. Ibid., chapter 1464.

47. For more general examples see David E. Narrett, "Dutch Customs of Inheritance, Women, and the Law in Colonial New York City," William Pencak and Conrad Edick Wright, eds., *Authority and Resistance in Early New York*. For a later example see: Susan Lebsock, *The Free Women of Petersburg: Status and Culture in a Southern Town, 1784–1860*.

48. This phenomenon is described at length in Lebsock, *The Free Women of Petersburg*.

49. Will of Frederick DePeyster, 10 August 1773, from *Abstracts of Wills on File in the Surrogates Office, City of New York, Vol. VIII: Collections of the New-York Historical Society for the Year 1899*, 143.

50. Lyman C. Draper, ed., *King's Mountain and its Heroes: History of the Battle of King's Mountain, October 7th, 1780, and the Events Which led to it*. For more information on the Battle of King's Mountain, see also: Ted Olsen, *Blue Ridge Folklife*. J. David Dameron, *King's Mountain: The Defeat of the Loyalists, October 7, 1780*. Hank Messick, *King's Mountain: The Epic of the Blue Ridge "Mountain Men" in the American Revolution*.

51. Will of Anne Chambers, 11 June 1767, from *Abstracts of Wills on File in the Surrogates Office, City of New York, Vol. VIII: Collections of the New-York Historical Society for the Year 1899*, 168.

52. Will of Ann DePeyster, 14 July 1774, from *Abstracts of Wills on File in the Surrogates Office, City of New York, Vol. VIII: Collections of the New-York Historical Society for the Year 1899*, 193. Ann married her cousin Isaac DePeyster in 1737. The marriage produced no children, and Isaac died just a few months before his wife in 1774.

53. Tiedemann, *Reluctant Revolutionaries*, 119.

54. Burrows and Wallace, *Gotham*, 219. For accounts of Loyalists in New York, see also: Robert A. East and Jacob Judd, eds., *The Loyalist Americans: A Focus on Greater New York*. Flick, *Loyalism in New York*. Ketchum, *Divided Loyalties*. Janice Potter, *The Liberty We Seek: Loyalist Ideology in Colonial New York and Massachusetts*. Ranlet, *The New York Loyalists*. Van Buskirk, *Generous Enemies*. Edward Countryman, "The Uses of Capital in Revolutionary America," 3–28.

55. Tiedemann, *Reluctant Revolutionaries*, 226.

56. Flick, *Loyalism in New York*, 76. Tiedemann, "Queens County," *The Other New York: The American Revolution beyond New York City, 1763–1787*, Joseph S. Tiedemann and Eugene R. Fingerhut, eds., 44. Burrows and Wallace, *Gotham*, 220.

57. Kammen, *Colonial New York*, 367.

58. Ibid., 366. Burrows and Wallace, *Gotham*, 224. For accounts of New York during the Revolution, see also: Daniel J. Hulsebosch, *Constituting Empire: New York and the Transformation of Constitutionalism in the Atlantic World, 1664– 1830.* Thomas Jones, *History of New York During the Revolutionary War, and of the Leading Events in the Other Colonies at That Period.* Ketchum, *Divided Loyalty. New York City During the American Revolution.* Tiedemann and Fingerhut, eds., *The Other New York.* Van Buskirk, *Generous Enemies.* Benjamin L. Carp, "The Night the Yankees Burned Broadway: The New York City Fire of 1776," in *Early American Studies: An Interdisciplinary Journal*, 471–511.

59. Flick, *Loyalism in New York*, 45. For treatment of the Loyalists in New York until the British occupation, see the following: Rick J. Ashton, "The Loyalist Experience in New York." Thomas Jones, *History of New York During the Revolutionary War and of the Leading Events in the Other Colonies at That Period*, ed., Edward Floyd DeLancey. Mason, *The Road to Independence. New York During the American Revolution.* Ranlet, *The New York Loyalists.* Paul H. Smith, *Loyalists and Redcoats: A Study in British Revolutionary Policy.* Van Buskirk, *Generous Enemies*.

60. Burrows and Wallace, *Gotham*, 230.

61. Ibid., 227.

62. Tiedemann, "Queens County," 45.

63. Flick, *Loyalism in New York*, 89.

64. Ibid., 68.

65. Onderdonk, *Queens County in Olden Times*, 51.

66. Flick, *Loyalism in New York*, 95. Burrows and Wallace, *Gotham*, 233.

67. Some of the earliest American histories of the Battle of King's Mountain criticize Abraham's behavior, stating that he didn't even wait for Ferguson's blood to cool before running up the white flag. Others criticize him for trying to trick the Patriots by raising the white flag and then opened fire before learning his lesson and truly surrendering.

68. Melrose apparently has many secret passages, which has given rise to a modern legend surrounding the house. The story is terribly tragic and utterly false. As the story goes, Axtell fell in love with his wife's sister before he and his wife married in Britain. He transported both to New York with him and had the house built with the passages to conceal the sister's presence in the house. While he was away fighting on the frontier, the one slave who knew of the lady's presence died, leaving the lady to suffer a horrible death of starvation before Axtell's return. When he finally arrived, it was to a house full of well-wishers who all witnessed the lady's spirit appear and point an accusing finger at Axtell, whereupon he died. After his funeral, his widow sold the house, moved to England, and their children have ever since been cursed.

69. The Nassau Blues were headquartered at Melrose. Neighbors were not at all enthusiastic for the regiment and often complained of plundering by predatory soldiers. Edwin G. Burrows, "Kings County," in *The Other New York: The American Revolution Beyond New York City, 1763–1787*, eds., Joseph S. Tiedemann and Eugene R. Fingerhut, 31.

70. The story first makes its appearance in: Sabine, Lorenzo. *Biographical Sketches of Loyalists of the American Revolution, With an Historical Essay*, 374. The story is repeated in many of the early Loyalist accounts thereafter almost verbatim, but is not found in more modern histories, which tend to focus less on individuals.

71. Many good histories discuss the attitude of the British toward and their treatment of the Loyalists. The following represent good starting points in this area. Van Buskirk, *Generous Enemies*. Ashton, "The Loyalist Experience in New York." Flick, *Loyalism in New York*. Thomas Jones, *History of New York During the Revolutionary War and of the Leading Events in the Other Colonies at That Period*, ed., Edward Floyd DeLancey. *New York During the American Revolution*. Ranlet, *The New York Loyalists*. Brumwell, *Redcoats*. John Shy, *A People Numerous and Armed: Reflections on the Military Struggle for American Independence*. Christopher Hibbert, *Redcoats & Rebels: The American Revolution Through British Eyes*. Mary Beth Norton, *The British-Americans: The Loyalist Exiles in England, 1774–1789*.

72. Articles 5 and 6 of the Treaty of Paris, 1783.

73. Flick, *Loyalism in New York*, 163. Zeichner, "The Loyalist Problem in New York," 284–302. It should be noted that Zeichner was the first historian who explored the phenomenon of returning/remaining Loyalists and the problems they encountered in the process. I cite Zeichner here because while the issue of returning/remaining Loyalists in New York has recently become the focus of study again with Joseph Tiedemann and Judith Van Buskirk, to name a few, Zeichner presents the immediate 1783 treatment of Loyalists, which was very harsh at that time. Although this eventually changed as the Patriots consolidated their authority (as the text will show and as these later historians indicate), it is this initial period of precedent with which we are concerned at the moment because it was in this time that the DePeysters were in New York and forced to make their decisions.

74. Flick, *Loyalism in New York*, 162. Zeichner, "The Loyalist Problem in New York," 284–302.

75. Wallace Brown, *The Good Americans: The Loyalists in the American Revolution*, 129.

76. David E. Maas, "The Massachusetts Loyalists and the Problem of Amnesty, 1775–1790," Robert M. Calhoon, Timothy M. Barnes, and George A. Rawlyk, eds., *Loyalists and Community in North America*, 65–74. For a fuller

description of Maas's argument see also Maas, *The Return of the Massachusetts Loyalists.*

77. The two executed were John Roberts and Abraham Carlisle. Steven R. Boyd, "Political Choice—Political Justice: The Case of the Pennsylvania Loyalists," *American Political Trials*, 45–56. Claude Halstead Van Tyne, *The Loyalists in the American Revolution.*

78. Zeichner, "The Loyalist Problem in New York," 284–302.

79. Flick, *Loyalism in New York*, 146, 149. Burrows and Wallace, *Gotham*, 257–258.

80. At this time, the State of New York had in its possession 1,500 confiscated estates. Flick, *Loyalism in New York*, 150. Burrows and Wallace, *Gotham*, 258.

81. Robert Kornhiser, "Tory & Patriot: Love in the Revolution," in *Journal of Long Island History*, 36–45.

82. Burrows and Wallace, *Gotham*, 258. Flick, *Loyalism in New York*, 164.

83. Burrows and Wallace, *Gotham*, 258.

Chapter 2. Canadian Exile

1. For more information of the evacuations of Loyalists throughout the Revolutionary War, see also: Benjamin L. Carp, *Rebels Rising: Cities and the American Revolution.* Joseph S. Tiedemann, *Reluctant Revolutionaries: New York City and the Road to Independence, 1763–1776.* Christopher Hibbert, *Redcoats & Rebels: The American Revolution through British Eyes.* J. M. Bumsted, *Understanding the Loyalists.* Ann Gorman Condon, *The Envy of the American States: The Loyalist Dream for New Brunswick.* David Graham Bell, *Early Loyalist Saint John: The Origin of New Brunswick Politics, 1783–1786.* Phyllis R. Blakeley and John N. Grant, eds., *Eleven Exiles: Accounts of Loyalists in the American Revolution.* Robert M. Calhoon, *The Loyalists in Revolutionary America, 1760–1781.* Borden, Morton, and Penn, eds., *The American Tory.* Wallace Brown, *The Good Americans: The Loyalists in the American Revolution.* Alfred Hoyt Bill, *New Jersey and the Revolutionary War.* William Stewart MacNutt, *New Brunswick, A History: 1784–1867.* William H. Nelson, *The American Tory.* Thomas Jefferson Wertenbaker, *Father Knickerbocker Rebels: New York City During the Revolution.* Esther Clark Wright, *The Loyalists of New Brunswick.*

2. Judith Van Buskirk, *Generous Enemies: Patriots and Loyalists in Revolutionary New York.*

3. Ibid., 179. Bell, *Early Loyalist Saint John*, 11–12. Condon, *The Envy of the American States*, 29–38. Wright, *The Loyalists of New Brunswick*, 27–45.

4. Condon, *The Envy of the American States*, 85.

5. Alan Taylor, "The Late Loyalists: Northern Reflections of the Early American Republic," in *Journal of the Early Republic*, 1.

6. Condon, *The Envy of the American States*, 85.

7. Maya Jasanoff, *Liberty's Exiles: American Loyalists in the Revolutionary World*, (New York: Vintage, 2012).

8. Neil MacKinnon, *This Unfriendly Soil: The Loyalist Experience in Nova Scotia, 1783–1791*, 16.

9. Condon, *The Envy of the American States*, 101.

10. Bell, *Early Loyalist Saint John*, 15.

11. Ibid., 16. MacKinnon, *This Unfriendly Soil*, 4, 9.

12. Bell, *Early Loyalist Saint John*, 16.

13. For more information on the military as gentry in New Brunswick, see also: MacKinnon, *This Unfriendly Soil*. Condon, *The Envy of the American States*. Bell, *Early Loyalist Saint John*. Wright, *The Loyalists of New Brunswick*.

14. Van Buskirk, *Generous Enemies*, 179. Bell, *Early Loyalists Saint John*, 11–12. Condon, *The Envy of the American States*, 29–38. Wright, *The Loyalists of New Brunswick*, 27–45.

15. Bell, *Early Loyalist Saint John*, 17.

16. MacKinnon, *This Unfriendly Soil*, 16, 20.

17. The six fleets were the Spring Fleet, the June Fleet, the July Fleet, the August Fleet, the Fall Fleet, and the October Fleet.

18. MacKinnon, *This Unfriendly Soil*, 16.

19. Ibid., 32. This phenomenon of early refugees departing Nova Scotia soon after their arrival is also described in: Van Buskirk, *Generous Enemies*. David E. Maas, *The Return of the Massachusetts Loyalists*. Condon, *The Envy of the American States*. Sharon M. Dubeau, *New Brunswick Loyalists: A Bicentennial Tribute*. Brown, *The Good Americans*. Wright, *The Loyalists of New Brunswick*. Oscar Zeichner, "The Loyalist Problem in New York After the Revolution," in *New York History*, 284–302. G. A. Gilbert, "The Connecticut Loyalists," in *American Historical Review*, 273–291. Kim Marie Klein, "Acquisition of Power: The Membership of the New Brunswick Assembly, 1785–1837." Jasanoff, *Liberty's Exiles*.

20. Condon, *The Envy of the American States*, 72–73. For further descriptions of the St. John River and New Brunswick, see also: Wayne Barrett, *The St. John River Valley*. MacNutt, *New Brunswick*. Wright, *The Loyalists of New Brunswick*. Esther Clark Wright, *The Saint John River*. W. O. Raymond, *The River St. John: Its*

Physical Features, Legends & History, From 1604–1784. Joseph Wilson Lawrence, *Foot-Prints, or, Incidents in the Early History of New Brunswick.*

21. Condon, *The Envy of the American States,* 73.

22. The third settlement was a cluster of villages across the river from Maugerville and the fourth was located on the isthmus that separated northern Nova Scotia from the more populous south. Condon, *The Envy of the American States,* 77.

23. Ibid., 83, 99.

24. Jasanoff, *Liberty's Exiles.*

25. This is a conservative number based on the victulating records of the government ships. This does not include evacuees who hired their own transportation or who did not receive provisions (like slaves or those who walked), and in some cases the victulating records are incomplete. Please see Bell, *Early Loyalist Saint John,* chapter 2. A number more routinely indicated for New Brunswick is 20,000 based on both the military and civilian householders (including family groups) who received land grants up to August 10, 1784. More land grants were made after this time. Alexander Clarence Flick, *Loyalism in New York During the American Revolution,* 191. A number also consistently given for Loyalist evacuees to New Brunswick is 30,000; however, this number seems to be based on the number of people who said they were leaving but did not necessarily do so. For more information on the evacuation of New York, including numbers of Loyalists heading to Canada in general, see also: C. Hood, "An Unusable Past: Urban Elites, New York City's Evacuation Day, and the Transformations of Memory Culture" in *Journal of Social History,* 883–913. Barnet Schecter, *The Battle for New York: The City at the Heart of the American Revolution.* C. Hood, "Prudent Rebels: New York City and the American Revolution," in *Reviews in American History,* 537–544. MacKinnon, *This Unfriendly Soil.* Philip Ranlet, *The New York Loyalists.* Condon, *The Envy of the American States.* Robert M. Calhoon, *The Loyalists in Revolutionary America, 1760–1781.* Brown, *The Good Americans.* William H. Nelson, *The American Tory.* Wright, *The Loyalists of New Brunswick.* Wertenbaker, *Father Knickerbocker Rebels.* W. Stewart Wallace, *The United Empire Loyalists: A Chronicle of the Great Migration.*

26. Condon, *The Envy of the American States,* 39–40.

27. Bell, *Early Loyalist Saint John,* 58–59. For other works that describe this idea of making New Brunswick a model of British respectability, see also: Robert L. Dallison, *The American Revolution and the Founding of New Brunswick, The New Brunswick Military Heritage Series.* Norman Knowles, *Inventing the Loyalists: The Ontario Loyalist Tradition and the Creation of a Usable Past.* J. M. Bumsted, *Understanding the Loyalists.* Condon, *The Envy of the American States.* Wallace

Brown and Hereward Senior, *Victorious in Defeat: The Loyalists in Canada*. Phyllis R. Blakeley and John N. Grant, eds., *Eleven Exiles: Accounts of Loyalists in the American Revolution*. MacNutt, *New Brunswick*. Klein, "Acquisition of Power."

Ann Gorman Condon lists the primary leaders of the elite Loyalists as (in alphabetical order): Isaac Allan (1741–1806), Daniel Bliss (1743–1822), Jonathan Bliss (1742–1822), Amos Botsford (1745–1822), Ward Chipman (1753–1824), John Coffin (1756–1842), William Hazen (1748–1816), George Leonard (1742–1826), Gabriel G. Ludlow (1733–1810), George D. Ludlow (1733–1808), Johnathan Odell (1737–1818), William Paine (1750–1833), James Putnam (1725–1789), Beverly Robinson Jr. (1754–1816), John Saunders (1754–1834), Jonathan Sewell (1728–1796), Joshua Upham (1741–1808), William Wanton (1734–1816), Abijah Willard (1722–1789), and Edward Winslow (1746–1815). Each of these men tirelessly campaigned for their vision of a Loyalist colony and would eventually hold office(s) within the government of New Brunswick.

28. Condon, *The Envy of the American States*, 43. This idea is also echoed throughout Loyalist historiography especially in relation to the Petition of the Fifty-five; see notes 32 and 33.

29. Wright, *The Loyalists of New Brunswick*, 41–42. The other officers who signed the documents were: Lt. Col. Benjamin Thompson, Lt. Col. Gabriel D'Veber, Major Thomas Menzies, Col. Beverly Robinson, Lt. Col. Stephen DeLancey, Col. J. H. Cruger, Lt. Col. Abraham Van Buskirk, Lt. Col. Beverly Robinson Jr., and Lt. Col. William Allen.

30. Condon, *The Envy of the American States*, 42. Wright, *The Loyalists of New Brunswick*, 41–42. Robert Fellows, "The Loyalists and Land Settlement in New Brunswick, 1783–1790: A Study in Colonial Administration," in *Canadian Archivist*, 7.

31. See correspondence of the DePeyster Collection, New-York Historical Society.

32. The official name of the Petition of the Fifty-five is, "Sundry residents of New York to Sir Guy Carleton, 22 July 1783, Headquarters Papers, No. 8500."

33. The justification given in the introduction of the Petition of Fifty-five reads: "Considering our several Characters, and our former Situations in Life we Trust, you will perceive, that our Circumstances will probably be the Contrast to what they have heretofore especially as from our respective Occupations we shall be unable personally to obtain the Means of a Tollerably decent Support unless Your Excellency shall be pleased to Countenance us, by your Recommendations in the following Proposals. . . ." The second article of the Petition discusses the amount of land requested by the Fifty-five: "That this tract or tracts by sufficient to put us on the same Footing with Field officers in His Majesty's

Army with respect to the Number of Acres. . . ." The fifth article describes the benefit to the British Government in granting the Petition: ". . . we wish not to be understood as Soliciting a compensation for the Losses we have Sustained during the War—Because, we are humbly of opinion, that the Settling such a Number of Loyalists, of the most respectable Characters, who have Constantly had great Influence in His Majesty's American Dominions—will be highly Advantageous in diffusing and supporting a Spirit of Attachment to the British Constitution as well as To His Majesty's Royal Person and Family—." P. A. N. S. Vol. 369, doc. 135.

34. Condon, *The Envy of the American States*, 89. For more information on the Petition of the Fifty-five and the counterpetition that followed, see also: Bumsted, *Understanding the Loyalists.* Bell, *Early Loyalist Saint John.* Brown, *The Good Americans.*

35. For more information about these associations, see also: Sandra Riley, *Homeward Bound: A History of the Bahama Islands to 1850 with a Definitive Study of Abaco in the American Loyalist Plantation Period.* Brown and Senior, *Victorious in Defeat.* Condon, *The Envy of the American States.*

36. The counterpetition of the 600 as quoted in *Loyalists and Land Settlement in Nova Scotia, Public Archives of Nova Scotia, Publication No. 4,* Marion Gilroy, ed., 148. Capitalization normalized.

37. Condon, *The Envy of the American States*, 107.

38. Bell, *Early Loyalist Saint John*, 64–65.

39. Sabine is the earliest historian who states emphatically that the marriage took place prior to Abraham's departure for Canada, however, I have been unable to find an actual date for the wedding and most later historians who state that the marriage took place before departing New York reference Sabine. This is not to say that Sabine is incorrect, there is just no corroborating evidence as yet produced to confirm this.

40. Bell, *Early Loyalist Saint John*, 160, 195.

41. Condon, *The Envy of the American States*, 93.

42. Fellows, "The Loyalists and Land Settlement in New Brunswick," 7–8.

43. Ibid.

44. Bell, *Early Loyalist Saint John*, 44.

45. Condon, *The Envy of the American States*, 105–106.

46. Bell, *Early Loyalist Saint John*, 63.

47. Ibid., 195. There is no death certificate or reference to the death of Joseph Reade DePeyster in the DePeyster Collection at the New-York Historical Society. James DePeyster did not keep many papers, and most of what we know of the DePeyster family comes from correspondence, so this is not surprising.

48. Condon, *The Envy of the American States*, 106.

49. Ibid.

50. Ibid., 109. Emphasis original.

51. Ibid., 110–112.

52. Ibid., 116.

53. Ibid., 116, 119, 135.

54. Ibid., 136–137, 140–141.

55. Lawrence, *Foot-Prints*, 55.

56. The town lots that both Abraham and Frederick DePeyster received are actually designated as being located in Parr. Parr lay on the eastern side of the mouth of the St. John River, while Carleton lay on the west; however, these towns were incorporated as Saint John on May 18, 1785. Grantbook Database, Provincial Archives of New Brunswick, Harriet Irving Library, University of New Brunswick, http://www.lib.unb.ca/gddm/data/panb/search.php.

57. Cynthia A. Kierner, *Traders and Gentlefolk: The Livingstons of New York, 1675–1790*, 218.

58. Abraham DePeyster to Frederick DePeyster, 18 August 1793, DePeyster Collection, Captains' Papers, BV, New-York Historical Society, Box 2 (Vols. 2, 3), Folder 17. When discussing recent deaths in St. John, Abraham writes, "I was taken unwell on Saturday with the same complaint, & God Almighty grant, if only for the sake of a wife & five Dear Infants, that I may recover in hopes of providing for those I hold so precious." These five children were Catharine Augusta (Augusta), Harriot Charlton, Sarah Caroline (Caroline), James, and William Axtell. Abraham would have two more children, Charlton and Ann Eliza (Eliza), before his death in 1798. Despite later Loyalist claims of New Brunswick being the healthiest climate in the world, Abraham and family were often ill, compounding rising debt with medical bills.

59. Various Bills and Receipts of Abraham DePeyster. Saint John Free Public Library Primary Source Documents. http://dev.hil.unb.ca/Texts/philo-logic/vvv.html.

60. Bill of sale for two slaves, Munson Jarvis to Abraham DePeyster, July 15, 1797, as reproduced in David Russell Jack, "General John Watts DePeyster," *Acadiensis*, 290. It is likewise unknown whether Frederick owned slaves in New Brunswick, but we know that during the war, Frederick traveled with a slave who was fond of running away, though he often returned for food or when different Patriot companies treated him worse than Frederick did. We do know that upon his return to New York, Frederick's household included slaves. For more information on British policy toward blacks, both free and slave during the Revolution and during the early years of New Brunswick, see also: Bridglal

Pachal, *The Nova Scotia Black Loyalist Experience Through the Centuries.* Simon Schama, *Rough Crossings: Britain, the Slaves, & the American Revolution.* Wallace Brown, *The Black Loyalists in Canada.* John W. Pulls, *Moving On: Black Loyalists in the Afro-Atlantic World.* MacKinnon, *This Unfriendly Soil.* James Walker, *The Black Loyalist: The Search for a Promised Land in Nova Scotia & Sierra Leone, 1783–1870.* Mary Beth Norton, "The Fate of Some Black Loyalists of the American Revolution," in *Journal of Negro History,* 402–426. William Renwick Riddell, "Slavery in the Maritime Provinces," in *Journal of Negro History,* 359–375.

61. Condon, *The Envy of the American States,* 139.

62. Ibid.

63. Ibid., 144–148.

64. Ibid., 158–161.

65. Grantbook Database, http://www.lib.unb.ca/gddm/data/panb/search.php.

66. Ibid. Wright, *The Loyalists of New Brunswick,* 187.

67. Wright, *The Loyalists of New Brunswick,* 188.

68. Lawrence, *Foot-Prints,* 59. Joseph Wilson Lawrence, Alfred Augustus Stockton, and W. O. Raymond, *The Judges of New Brunswick and their Times,* 49–47.

69. According to the Grantbook Database, http://www.lib.unb.ca/gddm/data/panb/search.php, Frederick received 4 acres of island rights in 1789. His earlier land grant in York County in 1787 specifies only that he received land on the Saint John River, which may have included Sugar Island. There was also a practice at the time that allowed for the purchase of additional allotments by groups of people. Any group, however, had to appoint just one person to be named the "grantee." This person would be legally responsible for the allotment. Fellows, "The Loyalists and Land Settlement," 7–8. Frederick received his property both in St. John and York County in 1784 when Governor Carleton began the process of escheat for New Brunswick. If Sugar Island was held in a common grant by the Provincials, it is likely that they received their grant at the same time as Frederick. There is another element here, too; if Sugar Island had been part of the 1787 grant, and not part of some separate earlier grant, Finucane could have viewed the Provincial possession as theft of property.

70. Lawrence, *Foot-Prints,* 59, 60, 63. DePeyster, who was by then living in New York once again, was not at all certain about the finality of the judgment and appealed to Aaron Burr for his legal opinion in the matter. Burr was of the opinion that DePeyster was in no further danger of appeal.

71. Prince William Street would remain a desirable location throughout the early history of Saint John, first for residences and later for business, with the most prominent merchants residing there above their shops. Lawrence, *Foot-Prints*, 55.

72. By 1793 this was no longer the case, and Edward Winslow lamented that, "our gentlemen have all become potato planters and our shoemakers are preparing to legislate." Edward Winslow to Gregory Townsend, Kingsclear, January 17, 1793, in *Winslow Papers, A.D. 1776–1826*, 399.

73. Letters of Abraham DePeyster to Frederick DePeyster, DePeyster Collection, Captains' Papers, BV, New-York Historical Society. Condon, *The Envy of the American States*, 154.

74. Condon, *The Envy of the American States*, 153–156.

75. Frederick DePeyster to G. D. Ludlow, 18 January 1793, DePeyster Collection, Captains' Papers, BV, New-York Historical Society, Box 5 (Vols. 8, 9), Folder 4.

76. Thomas M. Truxes, *Defying Empire: Trading With the Enemy in Colonial New York*. Cathy Matson, *Merchants & Empire: Trading in Colonial New York*. Virginia D. Harrington, *The New York Merchants on the Eve of the Revolution*.

77. Correspondence, DePeyster Collection, Captains' Papers, BV, New-York Historical Society.

78. James DePeyster to Frederick DePeyster, 21 June 1793, DePeyster Collection, Captains' Papers, BV, New-York Historical Society, Box 2 (Vols. 2, 3), Folder 17.

79. Ibid.

80. This was also prior to Britain entering into war with Revolutionary France in 1793. Edwin G. Burrows and Mike Wallace, *Gotham: A History of New York City to 1898*, 281.

81. The names of these individuals and families are repeated throughout the correspondence of the DePeyster family.

82. Waldron Phoenix Belknap Jr., *The DePeyster Genealogy*, 83.

83. Frederick DePeyster to G. D. Ludlow, January 18, 1793. Capitalization normalized.

84. Riley, *Homeward Bound*, 148.

85. *The Royal Commission on the Losses and Services of American Loyalists, 1783–1785*, Hugh Edward Egerton, ed., 155–165.

86. Riley, *Homeward Bound*, 148.

87. Hake was unaware that his name was removed from the petition until after its presentment. The person responsible for the erasure, Joshua H.

Smith, gave no reason for removing Hake's name. Later, when the committee published a letter thanking Hake for his service to the association, one of the signers published a public retraction for his signature on the document; again, the reason is not explained.

88. Parliament established the Loyalist Claims Commission to compensate the Loyalists for loss of property during the Revolutionary War. The Commission rarely compensated individuals for the full amount claimed in their memorials. Those individuals who actually appeared before the Commission in person or through proxy generally saw better results. At first, Loyalists were forced to appear (or send a representative) to London to testify before the Commission. Later, as New Brunswick became more settled in politics and land, the Commission arranged for a seating of the Commission in America. For more information of the Loyalist Claims Commission see also: *The Royal Commission on the Losses and Services of American Loyalists*. E. R. Fingerhut, "Uses and Abuses of the American Loyalists' Claims: A Critique of Quantitative Analyses," in *William and Mary Quarterly*, 245–258. Van Buskirk, *Generous Enemies*. Brown, *The King's Friends*.

89. Riley, *Homeward Bound*, 147.

90. Lieutenant H. M. Gordon to E. Winslow, November 20, 1785, as quoted in *The Royal Commission on the Losses and Services of American Loyalists, 1783–1785*, 212.

91. "From Mr. Hakes malicious and false information with Respect to my property to his daughter, he may Possible, be ever base enough to endeavor to [malign] my character," Frederick DePeyster to G. D. Ludlow, January 18, 1793.

92. Ibid.

93. Will of Frederick DePeyster, May 1812, DePeyster Collection, Captains' Papers, BV, New-York Historical Society, Box 3 (Vols. 4, 5), Folder 1.

94. Once again the practice of naming children after favored or wealthy relatives is repeated with Abraham's children. Catharine, Charlton, James, and particularly William Axtell represent wealthy relations on both the DePeyster and Livingston sides of the family.

Chapter 3. Sibling Relations

1. Abraham DePeyster to Frederick DePeyster, 23 July 1792, DePeyster Collection, Captains' Papers, BV, New-York Historical Society, Box 4 (Vols. 6, 7), Folder 12.

2. Abraham DePeyster to Frederick DePeyster, 18 August 1793, DePeyster Collection, Captains' Papers, BV, New-York Historical Society, Box 2 (Vols. 2, 3), Folder 17.

3. At some point, Augustus was sent to sea in John Jacob Astor's fleet in the ship commanded by Astor's brother-in-law. Exactly when Augustus left the DePeyster household is unknown; references to the event simply state that he took to the sea at a young age. Augustus is further discussed in chapter 5.

4. D. G. Bell, *Early Loyalist Saint John: The Origin of New Brunswick Politics, 1783–1786*, 44.

5. Abraham DePeyster to Frederick DePeyster, 29 August 1797, DePeyster Collection, Captains' Papers, BV, New-York Historical Society, Box 2 (Vols. 2, 3), Folder 18. Capitalization normalized.

6. Abraham DePeyster to Frederick DePeyster, 25 March 1797, DePeyster Collection, Captains' Papers, BV, New-York Historical Society, Box 2 (Vols. 2, 3), Folder 18.

7. Abraham DePeyster to Frederick DePeyster, 7 May 1797, DePeyster Collection, Captains' Papers, BV, New-York Historical Society, Box 5 (Vols. 8, 9), Folder 20.

8. Frederick DePeyster to Abraham DePeyster (draft), 23 May 1797, DePeyster Collection, Captains' Papers, BV, New-York Historical Society, Box 2 (Vols. 2, 3), Folder 12.

9. Ibid. Capitalization normalized.

10. Abraham DePeyster to Frederick DePeyster, 10 June 1797, DePeyster Collection, Captains' Papers, BV, New-York Historical Society, Box 2 (Vols. 2, 3), Folder 19.

11. Ibid.

12. Abraham DePeyster to Frederick DePeyster, 23 July 1797, DePeyster Collection, Captains' Papers, BV, New-York Historical Society, Box 2 (Vols. 2, 3), Folder 19.

13. Abraham DePeyster to Frederick DePeyster, 2 August 1797, DePeyster Collection, Captains' Papers, BV, New-York Historical Society, Box 2 (Vols. 2, 3), Folder 18. It should be noted that Abraham's son, James, does not appear in the DePeyster genealogies, nor in the autobiography of John Watts DePeyster.

14. Ibid.

15. Ibid.

16. Abraham DePeyster to Frederick DePeyster, 3 September 1797, DePeyster Collection, Captains' Papers, BV, New-York Historical Society, Box 2 (Vols. 2, 3), Folder 18.

17. Abraham DePeyster to Frederick DePeyster, 26 September 1797, DePeyster Collection, Captains' Papers, BV, New-York Historical Society, Box 2 (Vols. 2, 3), Folder 18. Capitalization normalized.

18. Abraham DePeyster to Frederick DePeyster, 5 November 1797, DePeyster Collection, Captains' Papers, BV, New-York Historical Society, Box 2 (Vols. 2, 3), Folder 18.

19. Abraham DePeyster to Frederick DePeyster, 14 December 1797, DePeyster Collection, Captains' Papers, BV, New-York Historical Society, Box 2 (Vols. 2, 3), Folder 18.

20. Dr. Hammersley married Frederick's youngest sister Elizabeth in 1798.

21. Deed of Guardianship, Catherine Augusta DePeyster, daughter of Abraham DePeyster to Frederick DePeyster and William Hammersley, 25 October 1802, DePeyster Collection, Captains' Papers, BV, New-York Historical Society, Box 1 (Vol. 1), Folder 13. Deed of Guardianship, Sarah Caroline DePeyster, William Axtell DePeyster, Ann Eliza Sewell DePeyster, Children of Abraham DePeyster to Frederick DePeyster and William Hammersley, 28 October 1802, DePeyster Collection, Captains' Papers, BV, New-York Historical Society, Box 1 (Vol. 1), Folder 14. Deed of Guardianship, for Harriot Charlton DePeyster, daughter of Abraham DePeyster to Frederick DePeyster and William Hammersley, 25 October 1802, DePeyster Collection, Captains' Papers, BV, New-York Historical Society, Box 1 (Vol. 1), Folder 13. At same time, Frederick DePeyster also accepted guardianship over his nephew, James DePeyster Ogden. Deed of Guardianship, James DePeyster Ogden to Frederick DePeyster, 28 October 1802, DePeyster Collection, Captains' Papers, BV, New-York Historical Society, Box 1 (Vol. 1), Folder 14. In her will, Sarah (Sally) DePeyster [Will of Sarah DePeyster, June 15, 1802, Jamaica, Queens Co., New York Will Testators, Vol. B, 1801–1807, pp. 112–113] left the bulk of her estate to be divided equally between the children of her late brother Abraham and her niece, Ann Crommelin (whose father, Joseph Reade was also deceased). Although we do not have the actual will of Sarah Reade DePeyster, we do know about the will because in 1803, Ann Crommelin's husband Robert was bankrupt, and his creditors wanted Ann's inheritance for payment. The record of this dispute survives and it is from that record that I have drawn this information. Contest and Recommendation Regarding the Will of Sarah DePeyster, 31 January 1803, DePeyster Collection, Captains' Papers, BV, New-York Historical Society, Box 4 (Vols. 6, 7), Folder 13. Legacies also came to the children of Abraham DePeyster more distantly through their great-grandfather Joseph Reade, great-uncle Laurence Reade, great-grandmother Margaret DePeyster, and so on. These legacies were left to James DePeyster and his wife Sarah Reade and on the death of both individuals the legacies would be spread evenly among their children. With Abraham predeceasing his mother Sarah Reade, his portion

passed to his children, just as Joseph Reade's share would pass to his daughter Ann Crommelin. Contest and Recommendation Regarding the Will of Sarah DePeyster, 31 January 1803, DePeyster Collection, Captains' Papers, BV, New-York Historical Society, Box 4 (Vols. 6, 7), Folder 13. Will of Laurence Reade (brother of Sarah Reade, wife of James DePeyster) 6 November 1773, 6 September 1774, *Abstracts of Wills on File in the Surrogate's Office, City of New York, Vol. VIII: Collections of the New-York Historical Society for the Year 1899*, 243–244. Will of Margaret DePeyster (mother of James DePeyster, father of Abraham) 22 December 1769, 27 March 1770, *Abstracts of Wills on File in the Surrogate's Office, City of New York, June 2, 1786–February 18, 1796 with letters of Administration, January 5, 1786–December 31, 1795, Volume XIV: Collections of the New-York Historical Society for the Year 1906*, 116.

22. James Alexander Browne, *England's Artillerymen: An Historical Narrative of the Services of the Royal Artillery, From the Formation of the Regiment to the Amalgamation of the Royal and Indian Artilleries in 1862*, 34.

23. Margaret James to Frederick DePeyster, 18 March 1800, DePeyster Collection, Captains' Papers, BV, New-York Historical Society, Box 3 (Vols. 4, 5), Folder 12.

24. Waldron Phoenix Belknap Jr., *The DePeyster Genealogy*, 79. Margaret James to Frederick DePeyster, 27 December 1802?, DePeyster Collection, Captains' Papers, BV, New-York Historical Society, Box 4 (Vols. 6, 7), Folder 22.

25. Evidence of the contentious relationship between Margaret James and Mr. Martin runs throughout her correspondence in the *DePeyster Papers* at the New-York Historical Society. There are 21 letters in all from Margaret James. In most of these is some reference to the difficult relationship; then, also there is the will of Margaret James, which completely excludes Mr. Martin from having any sort of access to the estate, which was reserved for Margaret James's three granddaughters.

26. Mary Beth Norton, *The British-Americans: The Loyalist Community in England, 1744–1789* 63, 66, 67. Lewis Einstein, *Divided Loyalties: Americans in England During the War of Independence*, 206, 207.

27. Norton, *The British-Americans*, 43.

28. The Loyalist community thought that if the government would listen to anyone, it would be Governor Hutchinson, and so all eagerly awaited his arrival. The biggest slap in the face came to this community, however, when, after a meeting with the King, the government announced its plan for dealing harshly with the Thirteen Colonies and announced it had the Governor's support when he had, in fact, recommended exactly the opposite to the Crown.

29. Norton, *The British-Americans*, 68. Einstein, *Divided Loyalties*, 207.

30. The length of the Loyalist pension was never mentioned specifically as it was originally thought to be just a wartime measure that would go away with the American war once the Loyalists were able to return to their former homes. When this did not occur, the British government found that it could not disentangle itself easily from the pension. The government tried to reduce the number of pensioners by relocating Loyalists to Nova Scotia and New Brunswick, but many were reluctant to exchange London and their pension for the frontiers of Canada. One should keep in mind that £100 was a substantial sum. Most workers in Britain at this time did not earn that much money in an entire year. Margaret, for all of her complaints at not being able to maintain a proper lifestyle, was far from poor.

31. Norton, *The British-Americans*, 56. The payment schedule outlined by Dr. Norton was as follows: standard £100, mandamus councilors £200, civil officers £500, those without status or office £40–£80. The amount typically reserved for women is not discussed. Likewise, we do not know how Margaret's status as the widow of a British officer would have affected her ability to apply for the pension or the amount she would receive.

32. Norton, "Eighteenth-Century American Women in Peace and War: The Case of the Loyalists," in *William and Mary Quarterly*, 386–409.

33. Although bankruptcies were not all that uncommon at this time, and only the very wealthy could even afford to declare bankruptcy, that of James DePeyster does seem to have blackened his name with the family in an out-of-the-ordinary way. His bankruptcy seems to have occurred in such a manner that, if not settled quickly, it would have opened the financial situations of various family members to securitization by the government. Perhaps most telling is that although James's children were often remembered in the wills of various family members, most take a moment to single out James DePeyster as not being allowed to act as an executor for the property left his children. In one case, James was to receive "£5 and no more" while other family members received much higher settlements.

34. Margaret James was in a unique position. She hailed from a wealthy family, which normally would provide her with status and security, and being a widow allowed her to act legally in her own name. For more information on women and middle class in the 18th and 19th centuries, see: Amy Louise Erickson, *Women and Property in Early Modern England.* Jon Stobart, Alastair Owns, eds., *Urban Fortunes: Property and Inheritance in the Town, 1700–1900.* Leonore Davidoff, Catherine Hall, *Family Fortunes: Men and Women of the English Middle Class, 1780–1850.* Jonathan Barry, Christopher Brooks, eds., *The Middling*

Sort of People: Culture, Society, and Politics in England, 1550–1800. Susie Steinbach, *Women in England, 1760–1914: A Social History.* Ronald Hoffman, Peter J. Albert, eds., *Women in the Age of the American Revolution.* Leonore Davidoff, *Worlds Between: Historical Perspectives on Gender and Class.* Joan R. Gundersen, *To be Useful to the World: Women in Revolutionary America, 1740–1790.* Rosemary O'Day, *Women's Agency in Early Modern Britain and the American Colonies: Patriarchy, Partnership and Patronage.* Hannah Barker, Elaine Chalus, eds., *Women's History: Britain, 1700–1850. An Introduction.* Tim Harris, ed., *Popular Culture in England, c. 1500–1850.* Amanda Vickery, *The Gentleman's Daughter: Women's Lives in Georgian England.* Maaja A. Stewart, *Domestic Realities and Imperial Fictions: Jane Austen's Novels in Eighteenth-Century Contexts.* K. D. Reynolds, *Aristocratic Women and Political Society in Victorian Britain.* Ben Wilson, *The Making of Victorian Values: Decency and Dissent in Britain, 1789–1837.* Hazel Jones, *Jane Austen and Marriage.* R. J. Morris, *Men, Women and Property in England, 1780–1870: A Social and Economic History of Family Strategies amongst the Leeds Middle Classes.* Margaret is also an interesting case in the combination of Dutch and English traditions, which governed the DePeyster family. Although the family in New York belonged to the Anglican Trinity Church, they maintained their ties to their Dutch heritage through family connections and traditions.

35. Margaret James to Frederick DePeyster, 12 February 1800, DePeyster Collection, Captains' Papers, BV, New-York Historical Society, Box 4 (Vols. 6, 7), Folder 12.

36. Margaret James to Frederick DePeyster, 15 May 1800, DePeyster Collection, Captains' Papers, BV, New-York Historical Society, Box 4 (Vols. 6, 7), Folder 12.

37. The estate passed to James Ferguson 7; Robert Gilbert Livingston 6; Frederick Jr. 5; Abraham 3; and Edward 1. Edward died a year later in 1802 and his portion of the estate was divided equally between the older brothers. Augustus received no part of this estate.

38. Margaret James to Frederick DePeyster, 18 May 1802, DePeyster Collection, Captains' Papers, BV, New-York Historical Society, Box 4 (Vols. 6, 7), Folder 13.

39. Margaret James to Frederick DePeyster, 27 December 1802?, DePeyster Collection, Captains' Papers, BV, New-York Historical Society, Box 4 (Vols. 6, 7), Folder 22.

40. Ibid., emphasis original. It seems odd that there would not be more to the estate of James and Sarah DePeyster than this. However, no mention of money is ever made regarding this estate in the surviving correspondence, and Sarah's will no longer exists. James's will survived but is unrevealing in

that he simply states he left all of his possessions to his wife for the duration of her life, thereafter to be divided among their children.

41. Margaret James to Frederick DePeyster, 24 May 1803, DePeyster Collection, Captains' Papers, BV, New-York Historical Society, Box 4 (Vols. 6, 7), Folder 13.

42. Ibid.

43. Deed, 11 February 1803, recorded 12 May 1804, Bergen Co. Bergen County Deeds (Book S: 167), Bergen County, New Jersey, Recorded 12 September 1803–10 June 1813, recorded at Hackensack. Abstracted by Pat Wardell, 1998. http://files.usgwarchives.net/nj/bergen/land/deed-s.txt ac.

44. The interest rate in Britain at that time was 5 percent; in America it was 7 percent.

45. Margaret James to Frederick DePeyster, 20 March 1804, DePeyster Collection, Captains' Papers, BV, New-York Historical Society, Box 4 (Vols. 6, 7), Folder 13.

46. Margaret James to Frederick DePeyster, 24 May 1803, DePeyster Collection, Captains' Papers, BV, New-York Historical Society, Box 4 (Vols. 6, 7), Folder 13.

47. Margaret James to Frederick DePeyster, 29 June 1803, DePeyster Collection, Captains' Papers, BV, New-York Historical Society, Box 4 (Vols. 6, 7), Folder 13.

48. Frank Allaben, *John Watts DePeyster*, 22.

49. Philip L. White, *The Beekmans of New York in Politics and Commerce, 1647–1877*, 218, 230, 534.

50. For instance, in an advertisement for the sale of Beekman land near Tarrytown, complete with a wharf, a two-story house, cellar, kitchen and storehouse, as well as the sloop *Dreadnought*, Frederick DePeyster and David Beekman were listed as the people to contact with inquiries.

51. Margaret James to Frederick DePeyster, 20 March 1804, *DePeyster Collection*, New-York Historical Society.

52. The General had been the Governor-General Canada from 1786 to 1792, and Lieutenant Governor when the status of New Brunswick was changed. and returned to England that year where, according to Margaret James, he and his wife had "taken a House in Abernal St.—and live quite <u>dashing</u> stile . . ." Margaret James to Frederick DePeyster, 27 April 1804, DePeyster Collection, Captains' Papers, BV, New-York Historical Society, Box 4 (Vols. 6, 7), Folder 13.

53. Margaret James to Frederick DePeyster, 20 March 1804, DePeyster Collection, Captains' Papers, BV, New-York Historical Society, Box 4 (Vols. 6, 7), Folder 13.

54. Margaret James to Frederick DePeyster, 20 March 1804, DePeyster Collection, Captains' Papers, BV, New-York Historical Society, Box 4 (Vols. 6, 7), Folder 13.

55. Ibid. Emphasis original. Capitalization normalized.

56. Ibid.

57. Margaret James to Frederick DePeyster, 27 April 1804, DePeyster Collection, Captains' Papers, BV, New-York Historical Society, Box 4 (Vols. 6, 7), Folder 13.

58. Margaret James to Frederick DePeyster, 30 June 1804, DePeyster Collection, Captains' Papers, BV, New-York Historical Society, Box 4 (Vols. 6, 7), Folder 13.

59. Margaret James to Frederick DePeyster, 7 June 1804, DePeyster Collection, Captains' Papers, BV, New-York Historical Society, Box 4 (Vols. 6, 7), Folder 13.

60. Margaret James to Frederick DePeyster, 23 September 1805, DePeyster Collection, Captains' Papers, BV, New-York Historical Society, Box 4 (Vols. 6, 7), Folder 13.

61. The village of Bloomingdale was located in what is now the Upper West Side of Manhattan, from about 99th Street to 131st Street. Its boundaries included the modern-day campus of Columbia University and Morning Side Park. The old Bloomingdale Road ran the same general course that modern Broadway now follows. All correspondence from the DePeyster family refers to the house at Bloomingdale; also, obituaries for Frederick's various children mention the Bloomingdale estate and its location near the New York Hospital, the old Bloomingdale Asylum, now part of Columbia University.

62. Margaret James to Frederick DePeyster, 23 September 1805, DePeyster Collection, Captains' Papers, BV, New-York Historical Society, Box 4 (Vols. 6, 7), Folder 13.

63. Margaret James to Frederick DePeyster, 20 March 1804, DePeyster Collection, Captains' Papers, BV, New-York Historical Society, Box 4 (Vols. 6, 7), Folder 13.

64. Margaret James to Frederick DePeyster, 15 January 1806, DePeyster Collection, Captains' Papers, BV, New-York Historical Society, Box 4 (Vols. 6, 7), Folder 13.

65. Belknap, *The DePeyster Genealogy*, 84.

66. Correspondence of Margaret James, DePeyster Collection, Captains' Papers, BV, New-York Historical Society.

67. The date when she actually purchased the pew was not mentioned. Margaret James to Frederick DePeyster, 20 March 1804, DePeyster Collection, Captains' Papers, BV, New-York Historical Society, Box 4 (Vols. 6, 7), Folder 13.

68. Margaret James to Frederick DePeyster, 29 April 1809, DePeyster Collection, Captains' Papers, BV, New-York Historical Society, Box 4 (Vols. 6, 7), Folder 14.

69. Margaret James to Frederick DePeyster, September 1809, DePeyster Collection, Captains' Papers, BV, New-York Historical Society, Box 4 (Vols. 6, 7), Folder 14. "Received the Sum of Sixteen Pounds of my Brother Frederick Depeyster for Half a Pew no. 80—Trinity Church—New York—."

70. Margaret James to Frederick DePeyster, 29 April 1809, DePeyster Collection, Captains' Papers, BV, New-York Historical Society, Box 4 (Vols. 6, 7), Folder 14.

71. Ibid.

72. Margaret James to Frederick DePeyster, September 1809, DePeyster Collection, Captains' Papers, BV, New-York Historical Society, Box 4 (Vols. 6, 7), Folder 14.

73. Ibid.

74. Ibid. Paul Whitfield, *London: A Life in Maps*, 58.

75. Margaret James to Frederick DePeyster, September 1809, DePeyster Collection, Captains' Papers, BV, New-York Historical Society, Box 4 (Vols. 6, 7), Folder 14.

76. Ibid. Emphasis original.

77. Margaret James to Frederick DePeyster, February 1810, DePeyster Collection, Captains' Papers, BV, New-York Historical Society, Box 4 (Vols. 6, 7), Folder 14. Capitalization normalized.

78. Ibid.

79. Margaret James to Frederick DePeyster, March 1810, DePeyster Collection, Captains' Papers, BV, New-York Historical Society, Box 2 (Vols. 2, 3), Folder 21.

80. Alan Taylor, *William Cooper's Town: Power and Persuasion on the Frontier of the Early Republic*, 147.

81. Ibid., 148.

82. Margaret James to Frederick DePeyster, March 1810, DePeyster Collection, Captains' Papers, BV, New-York Historical Society, Box 2 (Vols. 2, 3), Folder 21.

83. Correspondence of Margaret James, DePeyster Collection, Captains' Papers, BV, New-York Historical Society.

84. How Margaret James fared during the War of 1812 is unknown.

85. The names of the trustees of this estate are unknown. That information is not present in the DePeyster collection, though Frederick undoubtedly knew their identities at the time. Margaret's letter is dated 10–30 with no given year. Margaret's mention of James DePeyster Ogden, however, places the letter

in 1814, which coincides with his visit to England and precedes her death in 1815. DePeyster Collection, Captains' Papers, BV, New-York Historical Society, Box 2 (Vols. 2, 3), Folder 21.

86. Ibid. The source of this property is unknown. Capitalization normalized.

87. Ibid.

88. Ibid. Emphasis original.

89. Draft of Legal Inquiry Into the Matter of the Last Will and Testament of Margaret James, 17 July 1815, DePeyster Collection, Captains' Papers, BV, New-York Historical Society, Box 5 (Vols. 8, 9), Folder 9.

90. Ibid.

Chapter 4. Building a Fortune

1. James DePeyster to Frederick DePeyster, 21 June 1793, DePeyster Collection, Captains' Papers, BV, New-York Historical Society, Box 2 (Vols. 3, 4), Folder 12. In this letter James writes to his son about a property in New York City on Broad Street that Frederick inherited from his great-aunt Ann, who was married to Issac DePeyster. During the War, James collected rent on this property for Frederick. Now that Frederick was attempting to collect the rents himself, the tenant refused to pay, claiming that he had a deed for the property. James wrote that if the tenant had a deed, "it surely must have been when Adam was placed in Paradise: Astonishing."

2. The exact location of these parcels is not known. The wills that describe the transference of land simply state the general location (county, for instance), not the actual parcel or lot numbers. It should be noted that in *most* instances, but not all, Frederick inherited this property through his uncle and namesake Frederick, who was the original designated heir. Will of Frederick DePeyster, 10 August 1773; 4 November 1773, *Abstracts of Wills on File in the Surrogate's Office, City of New York, Vol. VIII: Collections of the New-York Historical Society for the Year 1899*, 143. Will of Anne Chambers, 11 June 1767; 19 April 1774, *Abstracts of Wills, 1899*, 168–169. Will of Ann (Joanna) DePeyster, 14 July 1774; 7 September 1774, *Abstracts of Wills, 1899*, 193. Will of Laurence Reade, 6 November 1773; 6 September 1774, *Abstracts of Wills, 1899*, 243–244. Will of Margaret DePeyster, 22 December 1769; 27 March 1770, *Abstracts of Wills, 1899*, 116–117.

3. Robert Greenhalgh Albion, *The Rise of the New York Port, 1815–1860*, 7.

4. This was not the former residence of the DePeyster family, which was on Pearl Street. Before the Revolution, that house went up for auction to

satisfy the debts of Abraham DePeyster's estate to the State of New York. After that sale, the family moved to Jamaica, Long Island, permanently.

5. Elizabeth Blackmar, *Manhattan for Rent, 1785–1850*, 77.

6. Although this pattern would start to change as New York gained prominence as a port, in 1793 this was still very much the norm. Blackmar, *Manhattan for Rent*, 78.

7. Advertisement, *Daily Advertiser*, New York, New York, 15 October 1792, Vol. VIII, Issue 2391, page 4. Frederick DePeyster's business records related to his European trade are not contained within the DePeyster Collection at the New-York Historical Society. Whether this is because he destroyed the records or they were lost some other way is unknown. As a result, the finer points of his European business endeavors are unknown. For instance, whether he imported Madeira wine directly from Spain or through Amsterdam is uncertain; we know only that he had a "quantity" of it on hand.

8. Campobello may seem an odd addition to this list, but it was a key point of entry to Passamaquoddy Bay, and therefore, was a center for smuggling goods between the United States and Canada throughout the contentious years of the early republic.

9. Albion, *Rise of the New York Port*, 8.

10. Gordon C. Bjork, "The Weaning of the American Economy: Independence, Market Changes, and Economic Development," *Journal of Economic History*, 551.

11. John H. Coatsworth, "American Trade with European Colonies in the Caribbean and South America, 1790–1812," *William and Mary Quarterly*, 243.

12. Ibid., 250.

13. Albion, *Rise of the New York Port*, 8.

14. Correspondence of Frederick and Abraham DePeyster, DePeyster Collection, Captains' Papers, BV, New-York Historical Society.

15. Abraham DePeyster to Frederick DePeyster, 23 July 1792, DePeyster Collection, Captains' Papers, BV, New-York Historical Society, Box 4 (Vols. 6, 7), Folder 12.

16. We do not know for sure which, if either, activity the DePeysters engaged in at this time; however, during the Embargo Act and the War of 1812, letters related to business in the *DePeyster Collection* at the New-York Historical Society indicate that they engaged in both. Also see Joshua M. Smith, *Borderland Smuggling: Patriots, Loyalists, and Illicit Trade in the Northeast, 1783–1820*, 7.

17. Ibid., 7.

18. Edward Pessen, *Riches, Class, and Power Before the Civil War* (Lexington, MA: Heath, 1973), 68.

19. Despite his service in the Vermont Militia during the Revolution, Graham proclaimed, "I have ever been inclined to regard myself as a citizen of Great Britain as well as of America, and I am persuaded the great majority of my countrymen think in the same manner." In 1796 Graham earned his L.L.D. from the University of Aberdeen. John Andrew Graham, *A Descriptive Sketch of the Present State of Vermont, One of the United States of America*, 5. For a less complimentary view of John Andrew Graham's life see James Benjamin Wilbur, *Ira Allen: Founder of Vermont, 1751–1814 Vol. 2*. Investment Certificate to John Andrew Graham of Vermont, 23 October 1795, DePeyster Collection, Captains' Papers, BV, New-York Historical Society, Box 3 (Vols. 4, 5), Folder 21.

20. Wilbur, *Ira Allen*, 411.

21. Receipt Two Shares Western Inland Lock & Navigation Company, 16 March 1796, 2 March 1797, 9 August 1797, 11 July 1798, and 13 April 1798, DePeyster Collection, Captains' Papers, BV, New-York Historical Society, Box 5 (Vols. 8, 9), Folder 5.

22. Peter L. Bernstein, *Wedding of the Waters: The Erie Canal and the Making of a Great Nation*, 93. Ronald E. Shaw, *Erie Water West: A History of the Erie Canal, 1792–1854*, 15.

23. Ibid.

24. Bernstein, *Wedding of the Waters*, 94.

25. Ibid.

26. Nicholas Low was the younger brother to successful merchant Isaac Low. Nicholas Low would go on to open a hotel in Ballston, New York in 1810, and was among the first in the country to participate in the development of the tourist industry. Both brothers made their fortunes as merchants before the American Revolution. Both also showed early distress at Britain's treatment of the American colonies just before the war. Isaac even served as a representative to the first Continental Congress with John Jay, and then as a member to New York's Provisional Congress in 1775. While Nicholas remained firm in his support of the Colonies, his brother Isaac was accused of consorting with the enemy in 1776 and then remained in New York City during the British occupation. In 1779, Isaac was convicted of treason by the New York Provisional Congress, and all of his property was confiscated. After the war, Isaac was appointed by Sir Guy Carleton to a committee to ensure that evacuating Loyalists were paid any just debts due them. Isaac moved to England where he died in 1791. In England, Isaac, his wife, and his son were among the acquaintances of Frederick DePeyster's sister, Margaret James.

27. Robert Troup was a Patriot during the American Revolution and for a time was a prisoner aboard the prison ship *Jersey*. Afterward, he served as

secretary to General Horatio Gates and then as secretary to the Board of War. In 1800 Robert Troup became the primary land agent for the Pulteney Estate, which also invested in the Western Company. The estate was essentially a land-development firm and acted in much the same way as William Cooper. The Pulteney Estate was owned by three Englishmen: primary partner Sir William Pulteney (who owned 9/12 of the estate), John Hornby (2/12), and Patrick Colquhoun (1/12). Together, the three men purchased a million acres in what would become Steuben County, New York, from Philadelphia financier Robert Morris for about $275,000. The estate's first land agent was Charles Williamson, who discovered the land was not exactly the fertile paradise the owners were led to believe. To complicate matters further, the isolated location of the land and the lack of roads meant that the area was slow to attract settlers. In attempting to sell the land for the Estate, Williamson ran into many of the same problems that had also hindered William Cooper in his attempts to settle the frontier. In the ten years that Williamson served as land agent to the estate, he spent more than $1.3 million attempting to attract settlers to the area by investing in roads, the Western Company, and improvements to the land. Williamson even became a member of the New York Assembly to boost his ability to promote the settlement of the Pulteney Estate. By 1800, however, Williamson had sold only $147,975 in land, and many of those sales were to speculators who were in default. When Robert Troup took over the estate, he brought his military organizational skills to the operation and quickly organized records, ordered new, accurate surveys of the lands, and brought in settlers to the area. James D. Folts, "The 'Alien' Proprietorship: The Pulteney Estate During the Nineteenth Century," *Crooked Lake Review*, http://www.crookedlakereview.com/articles/101_135/129fall2003/129folts.html

28. Thomas Eddy was a Quaker who taught himself how to be a merchant. In 1784, through a series of bad investments he had failed at his chosen trade. In 1790, Eddy entered into the changing world of insurance and built another fortune for himself. Soon thereafter he entered into philanthropic ventures; he helped to establish New York's penitentiary system, served as a governor for the New York Hospital, and helped establish the Bloomingdale insane asylum.

29. Shaw, *Erie Water West*, 16. Bernstein, *Wedding of the Waters, 94.*

30. Bernstein, *Wedding of the Waters*, 99.

31. Bernstein, *Wedding of the Waters*, 95, 98. Shaw, *Erie Water West*, 17, 20.

32. The year of 1820 is provided in Shaw, *Erie Water West*, 20. This seems to contradict Bernstein, *Wedding of the Waters*, 158, in which he provides the year 1811; however, Bernstein provides 1811 as the year that a special commission recommended and the Legislature began to pass a "long series of canal

laws it would enact over the years ahead." Thus, it is possible that there is no contradiction between the two, if it did take the New York Legislature some time to get around to enacting that particular recommendation. The fact that the company paid out dividends in 1813 lends credence to this theory.

33. Bernstein, *Wedding of the Waters*, 98. This idea is also presented, though not specifically stated, in: Shaw, *Erie Water West*. Harvey Chalmers II, *The Birth of the Erie Canal*.

34. George Rogers Taylor, *The Transportation Revolution, 1815–1860*, Vol. IV, 22–31. Taylor, *William Cooper's Town*, 331.

35. Reference Dept., Morris County Library, *Morris Turnpike Company, 1801–1851*, November 2009 (http://mcl.mainlib.org/historic.html).

36. Taylor, *William Cooper's Town*, 331.

37. Robert Campbell to Frederick DePeyster, 14 April 1831, DePeyster Collection, Captains' Papers, BV, New-York Historical Society, Box 2 (Vols. 2, 3), Folder 11.

38. Taylor, *The Transportation Revolution*, 28.

39. List of Subscribers to the New-York Insurance Company, March 1796, DePeyster Collection, Captains' Papers, BV, New-York Historical Society, Box 2 (Vols. 2, 3), Folder 11. Frederick DePeyster is #70 on the list. As doing business became increasingly dicey, insurance became more important to merchants and investors.

40. Pessen, *Riches Class, and Power*, 67.

41. Ibid., 68.

42. John Gray to Frederick DePeyster, 9 February 1799, DePeyster Collection, Captains' Papers, BV, New-York Historical Society, Box 3 (Vols. 4, 5), Folder 20.

43. Ibid. Garret Abeel to John Gray, 14 January 1799, DePeyster Collection, Captains' Papers, BV, New-York Historical Society, Box 3 (Vols. 4, 5), Folder 20.

44. Ibid.

45. John Gray to Frederick DePeyster, 9 February 1799, DePeyster Collection, Captains' Papers, BV, New-York Historical Society, Box 3 (Vols. 4, 5), Folder 20.

46. John Gray to Frederick DePeyster, 9 July 1799, DePeyster Collection, Captains' Papers, BV, New-York Historical Society, Box 3 (Vols. 4, 5), Folder 20. Capitalization normalized.

47. John Gray to Frederick DePeyster, 21 August 1799, DePeyster Collection, Captains' Papers, BV, New-York Historical Society, Box 3 (Vols. 4, 5), Folder 20.

48. Ibid.

49. John Gray to Frederick DePeyster, 21 August 1799, DePeyster Collection, Captains' Papers, BV, New-York Historical Society, Box 3 (Vols. 4, 5), Folder 20.

50. John Gray to Frederick DePeyster, 14 October 1799, DePeyster Collection, Captains' Papers, BV, New-York Historical Society, Box 3 (Vols. 4, 5), Folder 20.

51. Edwin G. Burrows and Mike Wallace, *Gotham: A History of New York City to 1898*, 358.

52. John Gray to Frederick DePeyster, 14 October 1799, DePeyster Collection, Captains' Papers, BV, New-York Historical Society, Box 3 (Vols. 4, 5), Folder 20.

53. Frederick Augustus (Augustus or Gus) was born before Frederick's marriage to Helen Hake. Although he never is referred to as Frederick's son, he is included in the family Bible (his mother's name is not listed) and later family members clearly considered him as such. James Ferguson (1794) was the eldest of Frederick and Helen Hake's children. Then came Robert Gilbert Livingston (Robert G. L.) (1795), Frederick Jr. (Frederic) (1796), and Abraham (1798).

54. John Gray to Frederick DePeyster, 14 October 1799, DePeyster Collection, Captains' Papers, BV, New-York Historical Society, Box 3 (Vols. 4, 5), Folder 20.

55. Ibid. Capitalization normalized. The Legislature did not approve the condemnation of property prone to incubating disease until 1800, by recommendation of the Common Council. Burrows and Wallace, *Gotham*, 363.

56. John Gray to Frederick DePeyster, 18 March 1800, DePeyster Collection, Captains' Papers, BV, New-York Historical Society, Box 3 (Vols. 4, 5), Folder 20.

57. Ibid.

58. Ibid. John Gray wrote to Frederick that he would accept nothing less than full payment for the property plus damages from November 1, 1798, when Gray believed the mismanagement and scheming began.

59. Bill of Sale, Slave Girl Dinah purchased from the estate of Myndert Van Kleeck., 24 May 1800, DePeyster Collection, Captains' Papers, BV, New-York Historical Society, Box 3 (Vols. 4, 5), Folder 12.

60. Deed of Manumission, 2 July 1817, DePeyster Collection, Captains' Papers, BV, New-York Historical Society, Box 7 (Vols. 11, 12), Folder 5. Judah and her son are the only slaves mentioned in this deed. It estimates Judah's age somewhere around 45 and states that she is able to provide for herself and her son.

61. This plan for gradual emancipation stated that all current slaves would remain so for their lifetime. Children born after July 4 were considered free but tied to their mother's master until reaching a certain age—for women 25, and for men 28. Burrows and Wallace, *Gotham*, 349.

62. Ibid. The free black population of New York, meanwhile, climbed to 7,500.

63. Ibid., 335, 356.

64. Map of the New York Bread Company's Facilities, DePeyster Collection, Captains' Papers, BV, New-York Historical Society, Box 3 (Vols. 4, 5), Folder 20. The map shows that the company was built at least partially on land owned by Frederick DePeyster. Burrows and Wallace, *Gotham*, 358.

65. Burrows and Wallace, *Gotham*, 356.

66. Robert Asher, Charles Stephenson, eds., *The New York City Artisan, 1789–1825: A Documentary History*, 158.

67. Burrows and Wallace, *Gotham*, 356. The controversy of the assize and the formation of the New York Bread Company are also described in: Paul A. Gilje and Howard B. Rock, *Keepers of the Revolution: New Yorkers at Work in the Early Republic*. Sidney Irving Pomerantz, *New York, An American City, 1783–1803: A Study of Urban Life*.

68. Correspondence of Andrews & Campbell to Frederick DePeyster, DePeyster Collection, Captains' Papers, BV, New-York Historical Society.

69. Smith, *Borderland Smuggling*, 36, 43.

70. Ibid.

71. Ibid., 42.

72. Colin Campbell Jun. to Frederick DePeyster, 9 February 1805, DePeyster Collection, Captains' Papers, BV, New-York Historical Society, Box 2 (Vols. 2, 3), Folder 6.

73. Smith, *Borderland Smuggling*, 42.

74. Colin Campbell Jun. to Frederick DePeyster, 9 February 1805, DePeyster Collection, Captains' Papers, BV, New-York Historical Society, Box 2 (Vols. 2, 3), Folder 6.

75. Andrews & Campbell to Frederick DePeyster, 5 June 1805, DePeyster Collection, Captains' Papers, BV, New-York Historical Society, Box 2 (Vols. 2, 3), Folder 6.

76. Andrews & Campbell to Frederick DePeyster, 24 July 1805, DePeyster Collection, Captains' Papers, BV, New-York Historical Society, Box 2 (Vols. 2, 3), Folder 6.

77. Andrews & Campbell to Frederick DePeyster, 26 August 1805, DePeyster Collection, Captains' Papers, BV, New-York Historical Society, Box 2 (Vols. 2, 3), Folder 7. This, too, was common practice for smugglers in

Passamaquoddy Bay; again, see Smith, *Borderland Smuggling,* for a full description of smuggling practices in that region.

78. Andrews & Campbell to Frederick DePeyster, 30 October 1805, DePeyster Collection, Captains' Papers, BV, New-York Historical Society, Box 2 (Vols. 2, 3), Folder 6.

79. Andrews & Campbell to Frederick DePeyster, 24 September 1805, DePeyster Collection, Captains' Papers, BV, New-York Historical Society, Box 2 (Vols. 2, 3), Folder 6.

80. Andrews & Campbell to Frederick DePeyster, 2 October 1805, DePeyster Collection, Captains' Papers, BV, New-York Historical Society, Box 2 (Vols. 2, 3), Folder 6.

81. Anthony Girard to Frederick DePeyster, 6 March 1809, DePeyster Collection, Captains' Papers, BV, New-York Historical Society, Box 3 (Vols. 4, 5), Folder 20.

82. Jered Belding to Anthony Girard, 10 February 1809, DePeyster Collection, Captains' Papers, BV, New-York Historical Society, Box 3 (Vols. 4, 5), Folder 20.

83. Ibid.

84. Frederick Gebhard to Frederick DePeyster, 8 November 1808, DePeyster Collection, Captains' Papers, BV, New-York Historical Society, Box 3 (Vols. 4, 5), Folder 20. Capitalization normalized.

85. Ibid.

86. Albion, *Rise of the New York Port,* 95. Burrows and Wallace, *Gotham,* 336.

87. Albion's treatment of the cotton triangle in *The Rise of the New York Port,* if not the first treatment of this trade, certainly is the seminal treatment; all subsequent treatments deal with Albion in some way. For more information on the cotton triangle, see also: David Lewis Cohn, *The Life and Times of King Cotton.*

88. Burrows and Wallace, *Gotham,* 411.

89. Pessen, *Riches Class, and Power,* 258. The idea of helping or improving the poor is also echoed in chapter 14 of Taylor's *William Cooper's Town.*

90. Frederick DePeyster to Henry M. Fine, 6 September 1810, DePeyster Collection, Captains' Papers, BV, New-York Historical Society, Box 3 (Vols. 4, 5), Folder 15.

91. Ibid.

92. Frederick DePeyster to Henry M. Fine, 6 September 1810, DePeyster Collection, Captains' Papers, BV, New-York Historical Society, Box 3 (Vols. 4, 5), Folder 15.

93. Taylor, *William Cooper's Town,* 390.

94. Ibid.

95. Several letters relating to William Cooper's DeKalb project housed in the Stevens-German Library special collection have been transcribed and are now posted online by the DeKalb, New York, Town Historian at http://dekalbnyhistorian.org/CooperLetters/cooperindex.html. Included in this collection are letters to and from William Cooper and his heirs. Also among this collection are letters by Frederick DePeyster, Henry Fine, and John Fine.

96. Taylor, *William Cooper's Town*, 390.

97. For more information see also: R. S. Guernsey, *New York City and its Vicinity During the War of 1812–15: Being a Military, Civic and Financial Local History of That Period, With Incidents and Anecdotes Thereof and A Description of the Forts, Fortifications, Arsenals, Defenses and Camps in and About New York City and Harbor, and Those at Harlem and on East River, and in Brooklyn, and on Long Island and Staten Island and at Sandy Hook and Jersey City, With an Account of the Citizens' Movements, and of the Military and Naval Officers, Regiments, Companies, etc., in Service There*. David Stephen Heidler and Jeanne T. Heidler, eds., *Encyclopedia of the War of 1812*, 36–37. Jacob Barker, *Incidents in the Life of Jacob Barker of New Orleans, Louisiana: With Historical Facts, His Financial Transactions With the Government, and His Course on Important Political Questions, From 1800 to 1855*.

98. Also including merchant George Murray, who had invested in the Western Company and Francis DePau. Murray was a shipping magnate who helped establish the packet ships to Europe. Frederick's son Augustus later would become one of DePau's best captains in the packet fleet as he commanded a line ship that sailed to Le Havre, France. It appears that Barker was the person who introduced Fletcher and Frederick; however, Mayhew Fletcher did correspond directly with Frederick DePeyster. Other investors listed in Account Current with Abraham Barker & Co., 31 December 1813, DePeyster Collection, Captains' Papers, BV, New-York Historical Society, Box 1 (Vol. 1), Folder 16.

99. One of the few books fully devoted to smuggling in the Early Republic is Joshua Smith, *Borderland Smuggling*, which provides an excellent overview of the mechanics of the smuggler's world; what goods were needed where and what paths and measures the smugglers took to get them there.

100. Mayhew Fletcher to Abraham Barker & Co., 10 May 1813, DePeyster Collection, Captains' Papers, BV, New-York Historical Society, Box 3 (Vols. 4, 5), Folder 15.

101. Mayhew Fletcher to Abraham Barker & Co., 19 July 1813, DePeyster Collection, Captains' Papers, BV, New-York Historical Society, Box 3 (Vols. 4, 5), Folder 15. In this letter, Fletcher thanked Barker for informing him of the ship's safe arrival on June 18; hence the discrepancy in the dates.

102. Account Current with Abraham Barker & Co., 31 December 1813, DePeyster Collection, Captains' Papers, BV, New-York Historical Society, Box 1 (Vol. 1), Folder 16. The account does not list Frederick's initial investment, only the amount he was due as a result of the sales.

103. James DePeyster Ogden to Frederick DePeyster, 6 October 1812, DePeyster Collection, Captains' Papers, BV, New-York Historical Society, Box 6 (Vols. 10, 11), Folder 3.

104. It is important to note that the letters specifically from Cornwallis were not addressed to Frederick, but were rather letters Frederick had been storing for the Estate of William Turnbull. Frederick DePeyster to William Turnbull, 23 August 1823. DePeyster Collection, New-York Historical Society, Box 4, Folder 5.

105. In 1812, Frederick's sons were as follows: Augustus, 20–22; James Ferguson, 19; Robert, 17; Frederic, 16; and Abraham, 14.

106. Pessen, *Riches Class, and Power*, 35.

107. James DePeyster Ogden to Frederick DePeyster, 30 November 1818, DePeyster Collection, Captains' Papers, BV, New-York Historical Society, Box 6 (Vols. 10, 11), Folder 3.

108. Taylor, *Transportation Revolution*, 336.

109. Hammond, *Banks and Politics in America*, 259.

110. Frederick served on the boards of the Humane Society, the American Bible Society, the New-York Lying-in Hospital, the Society of the New-York Hospital, and the Free-School Society.

111. S. B. & S. Hoffman to Frederick DePeyster, 9 October 1818, DePeyster Collection, Captains' Papers, BV, New-York Historical Society, Box 4 (Vols. 6, 7), Folder 5. S. B. & S. Hoffman to Frederick DePeyster, 16 October 1818, DePeyster Collection, Captains' Papers, BV, New-York Historical Society, Box 4 (Vols. 6, 7), Folder 5. S. B. & S. Hoffman to Frederick DePeyster, 30 October 1818, DePeyster Collection, Captains' Papers, BV, New-York Historical Society, Box 4 (Vols. 6, 7), Folder 5.

112. Correspondence of James DePeyster Ogden to DePeyster, Son & Company, DePeyster Collection, Captains' Papers, BV, New-York Historical Society.

113. James Ferguson DePeyster to Frederick DePeyster Jr., 20 February 1819, DePeyster Collection, Captains' Papers, BV, New-York Historical Society, Box 3 (Vols. 4, 5), Folder 3.

114. We do not know the extent or amount of Frederick's other sources of income at this point. Whether Frederick destroyed them himself, they were burned by servants, or they were just plain lost, they are no longer are con-

tained within the DePeyster Collections at the New-York Historical Society. Whatever they were, they were sufficient for Frederick to believe that he could retire without harming his financial situation.

115. Pessen, *Riches Class, and Power*, 321.

116. Ibid., 215.

117. W. Bloomfield to Frederick DePeyster, 19 August 1822, DePeyster Collection, Captains' Papers, BV, New-York Historical Society, Box 1 (Vol. 1), Folder 17. This letter provides an accounting of the Constantia Iron Company's finances for the years in which Bloomfield was the company's agent. The letter contains a description as well as a financial accounting of the company's expenses.

118. DePeyster et al. vs. Gould et al. in Henry W. Green, *Reports of Cases Determined in the Court of Chancery of the State of New Jersey Volume II, Containing the Cases From January 1834 to October 1836, Inclusive*, 474–481.

119. The Board of Directors at the time was composed of Isaac Lawrence, Benjamin L. Swan, John Bolton, Jacob P. Giraud, Thomas Lawrence, Joseph Grinnel, Philip Hone, Richard Riker, William Whitlock Jr., James K. Hamilton, James Heard, David Haden, Louis F. Varnet, Cornelius W. Lawrence, Francis H. Nichol, Horace W. Bulkley, Hickson W. Field, and James Lovett.

120. The case, *Scott v. DePeyster et. al.*, is related in full in Charles Edwards, *Report of Chancery Cases Decided in the First Circuit of the State of New York by the Honorable William T. McCoun, Vice-Chancellor, Vol. I*, 513–550.

121. Indenture/Settlement of Frederick DePeyster to the Martin Estate, 1 January 1824/16 January 1827, DePeyster Collection, Captains' Papers, BV, New-York Historical Society, Box 3 (Vols. 4, 5), Folder 5. This is a distinct estate from that of Margaretta James (which went entirely to the children of Margaretta Martin and her husband). The origins of the estate are unclear; however, it appears the estate was established as part of the Martin's marriage settlement.

122. DePeyster et al. vs. Gould et al. in Green, *Cases Determined in the Court of Chancery*, 474–481.

123. Frederick and his wife Ann had seven children together: Joanna Cornelia (1804–1867), Ann Fredrica (1805–1840), Margaret James (1806–1866), Mary Elizabeth (1809–1892), Sarah Matilda (1810–1818), Pierre Van Cortlandt (1814–1854), and Catherine Van Cortlandt (1818–before 1892). Of these children, only Joanna, Pierre, and Catherine married. Joanna married in 1831 to Robert Whitmarsh of North Carolina, and Catherine married in 1838 to Benjamin Hazard Field. The year of Pierre's marriage is unknown, he wed in New Orleans to Marie Roselmire Allen, and remained there.

124. Pessen, *Riches Class, and Power*, 322.

Chapter 5. Preparing the Next Generation

1. Bill of Sale, Slave Girl Dinah purchased from the estate of Myndert Van Kleeck, 24 May 1800, DePeyster Collection, Captains' Papers, BV, New-York Historical Society, Box 3 (Vols. 4, 5), Folder 12. Deed of Manumission, 2 July 1817, DePeyster Collection, Captains' Papers, BV, New-York Historical Society, Box 7 (Vols. 11, 12), Folder 5. Judah and her son are the only slaves mentioned in this deed. It estimates Judah's age somewhere around 45 and states that she is able to provide for herself and her son.

2. Will of Frederick DePeyster, May 1812, DePeyster Collection, Captains' Papers, BV, New-York Historical Society, Box 3 (Vols. 4, 5), Folder 1.

3. Robert Fellows, "The Loyalists and Land Settlement in New Brunswick, 1783–1790: A Study in Colonial Administration," *Canadian Archivist*, 7–8.

4. Waldron Phoenix Belknap Jr., *The DePeyster Genealogy*.

5. The arrangement is alluded to by Abraham, and later mentions of Augusta as part of Frederick's household appear in various letters from Margaret James and Augusta's mother, Catharine. Abraham DePeyster to Frederick DePeyster, 29 November 1796, DePeyster Collection, Captains' Papers, BV, New-York Historical Society, Box 2 (Vols. 2, 3), Folder 18. Margaret James to Frederick DePeyster, 15 May 1800, DePeyster Collection, Captains' Papers, BV, New-York Historical Society, Box 4 (Vols. 6, 7), Folder 12. Catherine Livingston DePeyster to Frederick DePeyster, 20 January 1801, DePeyster Collection, Captains' Papers, BV, New-York Historical Society, Box 4 (Vols. 6, 7), Folder 13. Margaret James to Frederick DePeyster, 27 December, DePeyster Collection, Captains' Papers, BV, New-York Historical Society, Box 4 (Vols. 6, 7), Folder 22.

6. John Gray to Frederick DePeyster, 25 February 1800, DePeyster Collection, Captains' Papers, BV, New-York Historical Society, Box 3 (Vols. 4, 5), Folder 20. John Gray to Frederick DePeyster, 18 March 1800, DePeyster Collection, Captains' Papers, BV, New-York Historical Society, Box 3 (Vols. 4, 5), Folder 20.

7. Will of Ann DePeyster, 14 August 1803, proved 17 November 1803, *New York Will Testators*, vol. 44, 459–461.

8. For more information relating to the Livingston family, see Cynthia A. Kierner, *Traders and Gentlefolk: The Livingstons of New York, 1675–1790*.

9. Please see: Alan Taylor, *William Cooper's Town: Power and Persuasion on the Frontier of the Early American Republic*.

10. Deed of Guardianship, Catherine Augusta DePeyster, daughter of Abraham DePeyster to Frederick DePeyster and William Hammersley, 25 October 1802, DePeyster Collection, Captains' Papers, BV, New-York Historical Soci-

ety, Box 1 (Vol. 1), Folder 13. Deed of Guardianship, Sarah Caroline DePeyster, William Axtell DePeyster, Ann Eliza Sewell DePeyster, Children of Abraham DePeyster to Frederick DePeyster and William Hammersley, 28 October 1802, DePeyster Collection, Captains' Papers, BV, New-York Historical Society, Box 1 (Vol. 1), Folder 14. Deed of Guardianship, for Harriot Charlton DePeyster, daughter of Abraham DePeyster to Frederick DePeyster and William Hammersley, 25 October 1802, DePeyster Collection, Captains' Papers, BV, New-York Historical Society, Box 1 (Vol. 1), Folder 13. At this same time, Frederick DePeyster also accepted guardianship over his nephew, James DePeyster Ogden. Deed of Guardianship, James DePeyster Ogden to Frederick DePeyster 28 October 1802, DePeyster Collection, Captains' Papers, BV, New-York Historical Society, Box 1 (Vol. 1), Folder 14.

11. Taylor, *William Cooper's Town*, 381. Mona Domosh, "Those "Gorgeous Incongruities": Polite Politics and Public Space on the Streets of Nineteenth-Century New York City," *Annals of the Association of American Geographers*, 209–226. David Scobey, "Anatomy of the Promenade: The Politics of Bourgeois Sociability in Nineteenth-Century New York," *Social History*, 203–227. See also: Richard L. Bushman, *The Refinement of America: Persons, Houses, Cities*. Linda Young, *Middle Class Culture in the Nineteenth-Century: America, Australia, and Britain*. David Stephen Heidler and Jeanne T. Heidler, *Daily Life in the Early Republic, 1790–1820*.

12. Pessen, *Riches Class, and Power*, 87.

13. The apprenticeship of Augustus in the Astor fleet is well documented in almost all of the biographies of John Jacob Astor and most studies on clipper ships, New York shipping, the Canton Trade, and so on. For specific references see also: Gerald J. Barry, *The Sailors' Snug Harbor: A History, 1801–2001*, 91. Elizabeth L. Gebhard, *The Life and Ventures of the Original John Jacob Astor*. Arthur D. Howden Smith, *John Jacob Astor: Landlord of New York*. Daniel Henderson, *Yankee Ships in China Seas: Adventures of Pioneer Americans in the Troubled Far East*. Jacques M. Downs, *The Golden Ghetto: The American Commercial Community on the China Coast*. Richard McKay, *South Street: A Maritime History of New York*. John Upton Terrell, *Furs by Astor*. Kenneth Wiggins Porter, *John Jacob Astor, Business Man*.

14. Brian P. Luskey, 'What Is My Prospects?': The Contours of Mercantile Apprenticeship, Ambition, and Advancement in the Early American Economy," *Business History Review*, 665–702.

15. Pessen, *Riches, Class, and Power*, 52.

16. Bruce H. Mann, *Republic of Debtors: Bankruptcy in the Age of American Independence*, 243–244.

17. Ibid.

18. According to the Indenture, Tenefly lay in the Hackensack precinct of Bergen County on the Hudson River. The estate itself consisted of just more than 478 acres.

19. Indenture: Tenefly Settlement, 8 January 1802, DePeyster Collection, Captains' Papers, BV, New-York Historical Society, Box 2 (Vols. 2, 3), Folder 5.

20. Settlement of Sarah DePeyster's Will, 31 January 1803, DePeyster Collection, Captains' Papers, BV, New-York Historical Society, Box 4 (Vols. 6, 7), Folder 13.

21. Ibid.

22. Indenture regarding the Estate of Margaret DePeyster, 22 November 1804, DePeyster Collection, Captains' Papers, BV, New-York Historical Society, Box 2 (Vols. 2, 3), Folder 5.

23. James Robert Crommelin to Frederick DePeyster, 7 February 1819, DePeyster Collection, Captains' Papers, BV, New-York Historical Society, Box 2 (Vols. 2, 3), Folder 9. James Robert Crommelin to Frederick DePeyster, 20 February 1819, DePeyster Collection, Captains' Papers, BV, New-York Historical Society, Box 2 (Vols. 2, 3), Folder 9. Some sources and genealogies give the year of Robert Crommelin's death as 1815, yet it is clear that James Robert believed his father to be very much alive in 1819, writing on February 20, "I trust that my good Father may yet extend his mercy to me."

24. In addition to the $5,000 allotment, Frederick also left various "gifts" to his sons. James, Robert, and Frederick each would receive one of his gold watches. The four sons also were to share Frederick's collection of guns, swords, and pistols. Daughter Margaret, then 6, also received special mention in receiving household property that belonged to Frederick's grandmother, Margaret Van Cortlandt DePeyster. His silver plate was likewise to be divided among all of his children after the death or remarriage of his wife, should she outlive him. Ann Beekman, however, had use of the plate until that time. The plate contained more than three-dozen spoons, which were specifically willed to his four sons along with some other specific pieces. The rest of the plate was referred to for the purpose of division as "the residue of my plate." The plate also was inscribed with the initials "FHDP." It is very likely that the initials were in honor of himself and his first wife Helen.

25. Will of Frederick DePeyster, May 1812, DePeyster Collection, Captains' Papers, BV, New-York Historical Society, Box 3 (Vols. 4, 5), Folder 1.

26. Will of Frederick DePeyster, May 1812, DePeyster Collection, Captains' Papers, BV, New-York Historical Society, Box 3 (Vols. 4, 5), Folder 1.

27. Ibid.

28. James DePeyster Ogden to Captain Augustus DePeyster, 24 May 1814, DePeyster Collection, Captains' Papers, BV, New-York Historical Society, Box 6 (Vols. 10, 11), Folder 4.

29. Gerald J. Barry, *The Sailors' Snug Harbor: A History, 1801–2001*, 91. Elizabeth L. Gebhard, *The Life and Ventures of the Original John Jacob Astor.* Arthur D. Howden Smith, *John Jacob Astor: Landlord of New York.* Daniel Henderson, *Yankee Ships in China Seas: Adventures of Pioneer Americans in the Troubled Far East.* Jacques M. Downs, *The Golden Ghetto: The American Commercial Community on the China Coast.* Richard McKay, *South Street: A Maritime History of New York.* John Upton Terrell, *Furs by Astor.* Kenneth Wiggins Porter, *John Jacob Astor, Business Man.*

30. This account is widely retold, but some recent accounts can be found in Anthony S. Pitch, *The Burning of Washington: The British Invasion of 1814*, and Jon Latimer, *1812: War With America.*

31. Both LeRoy, Bayard & McEvers and the Holland Land Company invested heavily in land speculation in upstate New York. And while LeRoy, Bayard & McEvers invested in the Western Company, the Holland Land Company did not though they are often reported as having done so due to their ties with the merchant firm. In addition to their trade in Amsterdam, England, and Hamburg, LeRoy, Bayard & McEvers also engaged in trade with the West Indies and Russia.

32. Luskey, "What Is My Prospects?" 665–702.

33. James DePeyster Ogden to Frederick DePeyster, 23 April 1812, DePeyster Collection, Captains' Papers, BV, New-York Historical Society, Box 6 (Vols. 10, 11), Folder 3. Gottenburg is the old Anglicized spelling of that city's name Göteborg, which is more commonly used today. Göteborg was the largest port city in Scandinavia and was home to the Swedish East India Company. During the Napoleonic Wars, the city also became a major center of trade. In his letters, James DePeyster Ogden alternates between Gottenburg, Gottenburgh, and Gothenburg. Throughout this work the spelling Gottenburg is used.

34. James DePeyster Ogden to Frederick DePeyster, 3 January 1813, DePeyster Collection, Captains' Papers, BV, New-York Historical Society, Box 6 (Vols. 10, 11), Folder 3.

35. James DePeyster Ogden to Frederick DePeyster, 5 May 1813, DePeyster Collection, Captains' Papers, BV, New-York Historical Society, Box 6 (Vols. 10, 11), Folder 3.

36. James DePeyster Ogden to Frederick DePeyster, 3 January 1813, DePeyster Collection, Captains' Papers, BV, New-York Historical Society, Box 6 (Vols. 10, 11), Folder 3.

37. James DePeyster Ogden to Frederick Augustus DePeyster, 24 May 1814, DePeyster Collection, Captains' Papers, BV, New-York Historical Society, Box 6 (Vols. 10, 11), Folder 4.

38. James DePeyster Ogden to Frederick Augustus DePeyster, 10 June 1814, DePeyster Collection, Captains' Papers, BV, New-York Historical Society, Box 6 (Vols. 10, 11), Folder 4.

39. Ibid.

40. James DePeyster Ogden to Frederick DePeyster, 12 September 1814, DePeyster Collection, Captains' Papers, BV, New-York Historical Society, Box 6 (Vols. 10, 11), Folder 4. Ogden went on at length about the qualities of the British: "The company at those places are more stiff & reserved than with us—not so lively—nor such promoters of form & messerment—but in deportment manners & dress—genteel & elegant—I trust I shall have the pleasure of talking over with you at some future day many an interesting anecdote that has occurred to me, on my visit thro England—I am pleased with the country—Englishmen have their predjudices—who is without them? England had its vices—who are free from them? Britons have their faults—they would not be men if they had not them . . . were I foolish enough (when removed from the fairness of Columbia,) to choose a wife inn the land of the stranger, I would select her from the beuties [sic] the Old England adorn!!!"

41. These Livingstons may have been Frederick's niece, Augusta, and her husband, Jacob Livingston, whom she married in 1809.

42. James DePeyster Ogden to Frederick DePeyster, 24 April 1816, DePeyster Collection, Captains' Papers, BV, New-York Historical Society, Box 6 (Vols. 10, 11), Folder 4. In the end, Le Roy was not part of the canal system in New York.

43. C. Clarkson to Frederick DePeyster, 21 December 1815, DePeyster Collection, Captains' Papers, BV, New-York Historical Society, Box 2 (Vols. 2, 3), Folder 8. It should be understood that Frederick was not a custodial guardian of Miss Clarkson, but rather a financial guardian. Both C. Clarkson and her brother Charlton Clarkson, whom Frederick would later send to St. Croix, were related to Frederick DePeyster through his aunt Elisabeth, who married Matthew Clarkson (not the famous General, though they are related) in 1758. The two were the grandchildren of Elisabeth and Matthew. Although the relationship is actually something like second cousins, the young lady addressed Frederick as "Uncle" and signed herself as his niece.

44. Wages obtained from *Nile's Register, 1815,* as quoted in Edward Channing, *A History of the United States, Volume V: The Period of Transition, 1815–1848,* 96, 97.

45. Robert Gilbert Livingston DePeyster to Frederick DePeyster Jr., 20 January 1817, DePeyster Collection, Captains' Papers, BV, New-York Historical Society, Box 3 (Vols. 4, 5), Folder 1.

46. Robert Gilbert Livingston DePeyster to Frederick DePeyster Jr., 2 February 1817, DePeyster Collection, Captains' Papers, BV, New-York Historical Society, Box 3 (Vols. 4, 5), Folder 1.

47. James Ferguson later married Susan Maria Clarkson, seventh child of General Matthew Clarkson.

48. Robert Gilbert Livingston DePeyster to Frederick DePeyster Jr., 2 February 1817, DePeyster Collection, Captains' Papers, BV, New-York Historical Society, Box 3 (Vols. 4, 5), Folder 1.

49. William A. Benton, "Peter Van Schaack: The Conscience of a Loyalist," *The Loyalist Americans: A Focus on Greater New York*, Robert A. East and Jacob Judd, eds., 54. Based on Paul M. Hamlin's *Legal Education in Colonial New York*, Benton asserts that Van Schaack's school actually constituted the first law school in the United States. The city of Kinderhook still claims this title. Some dispute this, insisting that Van Schaack's school was in fact the second.

50. Waldron Phoenix Belknap Jr., *The DePeyster Genealogy*, 24.

51. The development of travel for the sake of pleasure is described in Richard H. Gassan, *The Birth of American Tourism: New York, the Hudson Valley, and American Culture, 1790–1830*. The book follows the advent of tourism through health spas in the Sarasota Springs area in upstate New York. There is a curious comment in the book that in 1800, young men at the spas were behaving wildly, "including the New York attorney general, a Mr. De Peyster, scion of a prominent and wealthy New York family." The footnote continues, "This was probably Frederic De Peyster, a lawyer from New York City, father of the General Frederic De Peyster." It is unlikely, however, that Gassan hit on the right DePeyster. According to this text, the young DePeyster behaving badly would have to be Frederick DePeyster of Loyalist fame. However, he was a merchant, never a lawyer. Also at the time, Frederick would have been 42 years old, hardly a young man. It is equally unlikely that the text could refer to Frederick Jr. (who was a lawyer and served in the Court of Chancery), as at the time he was only 4 years old. More than likely, this reference describes a DePeyster cousin, but without the first name it is difficult to identify which one. See pages 22, 170.

52. James Ferguson DePeyster to Frederick DePeyster Jr., March 1817, DePeyster Collection, Captains' Papers, BV, New-York Historical Society, Box 3 (Vols. 4, 5), Folder 2.

53. Ibid.

54. Ibid.

55. Frederick DePeyster Jr. to Frederick DePeyster, 17 June 1817, DePeyster Collection, Captains' Papers, BV, New-York Historical Society, Box 3 (Vols. 4, 5), Folder 1.

56. Ibid.

57. Ibid.

58. It is unknown exactly when the firm of Frederick DePeyster & Son was established or how long it operated as the records pertaining to the firm are not extant. Likewise, the records do not indicate who the "Son" was. At this early period it may have been James because we do not know when he formed his first firm. It does seem that Abraham, at a later point, was the son involved as his brothers had gone out on their own.

59. Robert Gilbert Livingston DePeyster to Frederick DePeyster Jr., 2 February 1817, DePeyster Collection, Captains' Papers, BV, New-York Historical Society, Box 3 (Vols. 4, 5), Folder 1.

60. Sarah Beekman to Ann DePeyster, 14 May 1817, DePeyster Collection, Captains' Papers, BV, New-York Historical Society, Box 1 (Vol. 1), Folder 16.

61. Robert Gilbert Livingston DePeyster to Frederick DePeyster Jr., 30 October 1818, DePeyster Collection, Captains' Papers, BV, New-York Historical Society, Box 3 (Vols. 4, 5), Folder 2.

62. Robert Gilbert Livingston DePeyster to Abraham DePeyster, 1 December 1818, DePeyster Collection, Captains' Papers, BV, New-York Historical Society, Box 3 (Vols. 4, 5), Folder 2.

63. Robert Gilbert Livingston DePeyster to Abraham DePeyster, 14 February 1819, DePeyster Collection, Captains' Papers, BV, New-York Historical Society, Box 3 (Vols. 4, 5), Folder 2. Robert Gilbert Livingston DePeyster to Frederick Jr. DePeyster, 28 March 1819, DePeyster Collection, Captains' Papers, BV, New-York Historical Society, Box 3 (Vols. 4, 5), Folder 3.

64. Robert Gilbert Livingston DePeyster to Abraham DePeyster, 14 February 1819, DePeyster Collection, Captains' Papers, BV, New-York Historical Society, Box 3 (Vols. 4, 5), Folder 2.

65. Abraham DePeyster to Frederick DePeyster Jr., 18 February 1819, DePeyster Collection, Captains' Papers, BV, New-York Historical Society, Box 3 (Vols. 4, 5), Folder 2.

Chapter 6. Continuing the Tradition

1. Joyce Appleby, *Inheriting the Revolution: The First Generation of Americans*, 20.

2. Reade & DePeyster to Frederick DePeyster Jr., 8 April 1822, DePeyster Collection, Captains' Papers, BV, New-York Historical Society, Box 3 (Vols. 4, 5), Folder 4.

3. The DePeyster Collection in the New-York Historical Society does not indicate the firm under whom James first apprenticed. Scoville's *The Old Merchants of New York* states that the apprenticeship took place with the firm of Van Horne and Clarkson. Although Scoville's history is highly entertaining and filled with many interesting gossipy tidbits, it must be taken with a grain of salt as the work contains numerous errors throughout. For instance, Scoville states that James DePeyster Ogden served as U.S. Consul to Liverpool; while there is no doubt that James Ogden was a well-known merchant who lived and worked out of Liverpool a great deal of the time, he never served as Consul. An Ogden did serve as Consul to Liverpool from 1829 to 1840, but this was Francis B., not James DePeyster. In the case of James Ogden's apprenticeship, however, Scoville might be correct; the junior partner in the firm of Van Horne and Clarkson was David M. Clarkson, a DePeyster family relative. Joseph Scoville (Pseud. Walter Barrett), *The Old Merchants of New York City*, 93.

4. James DePeyster Ogden to Frederick DePeyster, 6 October 1812, DePeyster Collection, Captains' Papers, BV, New-York Historical Society, Box 6 (Vols. 10, 11), Folder 3.

5. Appleby, *Inheriting the Revolution*, 89, 138.

6. As Appleby notes, "popular lore had it that American wealth was never successfully passed down through three generations." In the DePeyster case, familial wealth had waxed and waned over the different generations. Frederick DePeyster's father James had lost his fortune during the French and Indian War, but familial wealth in the form of inheritances from uncles, aunts, and grandparents provided the base for Frederick DePeyster to grow his own fortune and establish himself among the elite of New York. James Ogden, no doubt well aware of the tenuous nature of fortune and wealth, meant to preserve his own inherited fortune. Appleby, *Inheriting the Revolution*, 139.

7. It is unknown why the DePeysters got involved with the cotton trade, or even if this was their first foray in the cotton market. Perhaps they became involved as a result of Frederick's involvement in the "cotton triangle" during the period of Embargo and Non-Importation Acts. Ogden's letters from his time in New Orleans indicate that he was probably working for other firms as well, as agents often did, although this is not mentioned specifically in these letters. This makes sense as Ogden's letters are business correspondence.

8. North, *Economic Growth of the United States, 1790–1860*, 75.

9. Lewis Charles Gray, *History of Agriculture in the Southern United States to 1860, Volume II*, 692.

10. Gray, *History of Agriculture*, 693, 697.

11. James DePeyster Ogden to Frederick DePeyster & Son, 7 December 1818, DePeyster Collection, Captains' Papers, BV, New-York Historical Society, Box 6 (Vols. 10, 11), Folder 5. Appleby, *Inheriting the Revolution*, 66.

12. James DePeyster Ogden to Frederick DePeyster & Son, 7 December 1818, DePeyster Collection, Captains' Papers, BV, New-York Historical Society, Box 6 (Vols. 10, 11), Folder 5.

13. James DePeyster Ogden to Frederick DePeyster & Son, 14 December 1818, DePeyster Collection, Captains' Papers, BV, New-York Historical Society, Box 6 (Vols. 10, 11), Folder 5.

14. Ibid.

15. James DePeyster Ogden to Frederick DePeyster & Son, 13 January 1819, DePeyster Collection, Captains' Papers, BV, New-York Historical Society, Box 6 (Vols. 10, 11), Folder 5.

16. Ibid.

17. Brian P. Luskey, " 'What is My Prospects?': The Contours of Mercantile Apprenticeship, Ambition, and Advancement in the Early American Economy," 665–702.

18. James DePeyster Ogden to Frederick DePeyster & Son, 27 February 1819, DePeyster Collection, Captains' Papers, BV, New-York Historical Society, Box 6 (Vols. 10, 11), Folder 5.

19. James DePeyster Ogden to Frederick DePeyster & Son, 28 April 1819, DePeyster Collection, Captains' Papers, BV, New-York Historical Society, Box 6 (Vols. 10, 11), Folder 7. Although the British did not officially decimalize their currency at this time, the numbers given are presented as they were recorded in the letters cited.

20. W. Abbott, "Sketch of James DePeyster Ogden," *New York Genealogical & Biographic Record*, 150.

21. Sarah Goold to Frederick DePeyster, 2 February 1820, DePeyster Collection, Captains' Papers, BV, New-York Historical Society, Box 3 (Vols. 4, 5), Folder 21.

22. Edward Pessen, *Riches, Class and Power Before the Civil War*, (Lexington, MA: D. C. Heath and Co., 1973), 20–21.

23. Abraham DePeyster to Frederick DePeyster Jr., 19 September 1823, DePeyster Collection, Captains' Papers, BV, New-York Historical Society, Box 3 (Vols. 4, 5), Folder 4.

24. Ibid.

25. Robert DePeyster to Frederick DePeyster Jr., 29 November 1825, DePeyster Collection, Captains' Papers, BV, New-York Historical Society, Box 3 (Vols. 4, 5), Folder 4.

26. Ibid.

27. Robert DePeyster to Frederick DePeyster Jr., 21 December 1825, DePeyster Collection, Captains' Papers, BV, New-York Historical Society, Box 3 (Vols. 4, 5), Folder 4.

28. Ibid. Robert was convinced that these men, generally from Kentucky or Alabama, were a wholly different race of men and that their boasts of being "¼ horse, ¼ aligator & ½ Steamboat" were not far from truth. The boatmen's fighting style, likewise, captivated Robert. He watched the men "fight like savages Knife, gouge, pull hair, kick and prove that they possess a different character."

29. Robert DePeyster to Frederick DePeyster Jr., 30 December 1825, DePeyster Collection, Captains' Papers, BV, New-York Historical Society, Box 3 (Vols. 4, 5), Folder 4.

30. Robert DePeyster to Frederick DePeyster Jr., 14 January 1826, DePeyster Collection, Captains' Papers, BV, New-York Historical Society, Box 3 (Vols. 4, 5), Folder 4.

31. Robert DePeyster to Frederick DePeyster Jr., 6 January 1826, DePeyster Collection, Captains' Papers, BV, New-York Historical Society, Box 3 (Vols. 4, 5), Folder 4.

32. Ibid.

33. Robert DePeyster to Frederick DePeyster Jr., 30 December 1825, DePeyster Collection, Captains' Papers, BV, New-York Historical Society, Box 3 (Vols. 4, 5), Folder 4.

34. Robert DePeyster to Frederick DePeyster Jr., 12 February 1826, DePeyster Collection, Captains' Papers, BV, New-York Historical Society, Box 3 (Vols. 4, 5), Folder 6.

35. Ibid.

36. Appleby, *Inheriting the Revolution*, 20.

37. Robert DePeyster to Frederick DePeyster Jr., 1 March 1826, DePeyster Collection, Captains' Papers, BV, New-York Historical Society, Box 3 (Vols. 4, 5), Folder 4.

38. Margaret James to Frederick DePeyster, 20 March 1804, DePeyster Collection, Captains' Papers, BV, New-York Historical Society, Box 4 (Vols. 6, 7), Folder 13. Emphasis original.

39. For more on the importance of manners, see also: Appleby, *Inheriting the Revolution*, chapter 5. Richard L. Bushman, *The Refinement of America: Persons, Houses, Cities*. Gordon S. Wood, *The Radicalism of the American Revolution*.

40. Robert DePeyster to Frederick DePeyster Jr., 23 March 1826, DePeyster Collection, Captains' Papers, BV, New-York Historical Society, Box 3 (Vols. 4, 5), Folder 4.

41. Ibid. From the tenor of Robert's article, by "independence" he simply means wealth—money enough to live how he wants, do what he wants, when he wants.

42. Roderick J. Barman. *Brazil: The Forging of a Nation, 1798–1852*, 46.

43. Celso Furtado, *The Economic Growth of Brazil: A Survey From Colonial to Modern Times*. Ricardo W. de Aguiar and Eric Chevler Drysdale, translators, (Sacramento: University of California Press, 1963), 36.

44. Abraham DePeyster to Frederick DePeyster Jr., 26 November 1820, DePeyster Collection, Captains' Papers, BV, New-York Historical Society, Box 3 (Vols. 4, 5), Folder 2.

45. Jeffrey C. Mosher, *Political Struggle, Ideology, and State Building: Pernambuco and the Construction of Brazil, 1817–1850*, 54. It is unclear if Abraham was there on behalf of DePeyster & Son, or his own interests. Certainly there was at least some overlap between family and self-interest. When Abraham returned to Salvador in May of 1822, it was Robert who was sending out the ships from New York.

46. Abraham DePeyster to Frederick DePeyster Jr., 25 May 1822, DePeyster Collection, Captains' Papers, BV, New-York Historical Society, Box 3 (Vols. 4, 5), Folder 4. Odlin was appointed to his post by President Monroe and served until his death in 1840.

47. Mosher, *Political Struggle, Ideology, and State Building*, 2. For a detailed account of the conflict in Bahia during this period, see Barman, *Brazil*, 46–90.

48. Woodbridge Odlin to John Quincy Adams, 25 February 1822, *Despatches From the American Consul at St. Salvador, Bahia, Brazil, 1808–1849*. Government Documents T432, Roll 2. Abraham DePeyster to Frederick DePeyster Jr., 1 February 1823, DePeyster Collection, Captains' Papers, BV, New-York Historical Society, Box 3 (Vols. 4, 5), Folder 4.

49. Brazil was one of the largest markets for British exports, and as such, they had a vested interest in the future of Brazil. Britain eventually helped to broker the peace between Portugal and Brazil in 1825. Mosher, *Political Struggle, Ideology, and State Building*, 79.

50. Petition of the American Merchants at Salvador, Bahia, 13 September 1822. *Despatches From the American Consul at St. Salvador, Bahia, Brazil, 1808–1849*. Government Documents T432, Roll 2.

51. Abraham DePeyster to Frederick DePeyster Jr., 1 February 1823, DePeyster Collection, Captains' Papers, BV, New-York Historical Society, Box 3 (Vols. 4, 5), Folder 4. Mosher, *Political Struggle, Ideology, and State Building*, 60.

52. Abraham DePeyster to Frederick DePeyster Jr., 1 February 1823, DePeyster Collection, Captains' Papers, BV, New-York Historical Society, Box 3 (Vols. 4, 5), Folder 4.

53. Mosher, *Political Struggle, Ideology, and State Building*, 64.

54. Abraham DePeyster to Frederick DePeyster Jr., 15 April 1824, DePeyster Collection, Captains' Papers, BV, New-York Historical Society, Box 3 (Vols. 4, 5), Folder 4.

55. Mosher, *Political Struggle, Ideology, and State Building*, 64.

56. Abraham DePeyster to Frederick DePeyster Jr., 15 April 1824, DePeyster Collection, Captains' Papers, BV, New-York Historical Society, Box 3 (Vols. 4, 5), Folder 4.

57. Sven Beckert, *The Monied Metropolis: New York City and the Consolidation of the American Bourgeoisie, 1850–1896*, 20.

58. Ibid., 22, 77.

59. Appleby, *Inheriting the Revolution*, 109. This idea is also present in Beckert, *Monied Metropolis*, 36.

60. Pessen, *Riches, Class, and Power*, 321.

61. John Hone was the son of the prominent and wealthy merchant John Hone. John Hone, the younger, opened an auction house with his brother Philip. The business was a success, but in 1826 Philip decided to run for political office and became mayor of New York City. Philip sold his share of the auction house to John, who then changed the name from Philip and John Hone to John Hone and Sons. John and Antoinette had five children together, at least three of whom were sons: Henry, John Jr., and Isaac. They had at least one daughter, Emily, but the identity of the fifth child is unknown. John Hone died in Rome in 1829. Frederick Jr. and Antoinette had no children together. Barret, *Old Merchants of New York, Vol. II*, 95–98. Hone v. DePeyster, 4 October 1887, as presented in *The Northeastern Reporter, Vol. 13, Containing all the Current Decisions of the Supreme Courts of Massachusetts, Ohio, Indiana, Illinois and the Court of Appeals of New York, October 14-December 23, 1887*, (St. Paul, MN: West Publishing Co., 1888), 778.

62. Beckert, *Monied Metropolis*, 56.

63. Jacques M. Downs, *The Golden Ghetto: The American Commercial Community at Canton and the Shaping of American China Policy, 1784–1844*, 234.

64. The sailings of Augustus DePeyster are noted throughout the newspapers in the years he served as captain for DePau. His association with DePau is also noted in Robert Greenhalgh Albion, *Square-Riggers on Schedule: The New York Sailing Packets to England, France, and the Cotton Ports*, 314, 334. Richard

C. McKay, *South Street: A Maritime History of New York*. It is curious, however, that McKay lists Augustus as two separate individuals, both "Captain Augustus DePeyster" and "Captain F. A. DePeyster."

65. Gerald J. Barry, *The Sailors' Snug Harbor: A History, 1801–2001*, 91, 95. Barrett, *The Old Merchants of New York City, Vol. II*, 212.

66. Original List of Mrs. Astor's Guests to her Ball in February 1892 as Given by Mr. Ward McAllister to the New York Times, as reproduced at http://www.raken.com/american_wealth/encyclopedia/Mrs_Astors_400.asp.

Bibliography

Primary

Abstracts of Wills on File in the Surrogates Office, City of New York, Vol. VII: Collections of the New-York Historical Society for the Year 1898. New York: New-York Historical Society, 1898.

Abstracts of Wills on File in the Surrogates Office, City of New York, Vol. VIII: Collections of the New-York Historical Society for the Year 1899. New York: New-York Historical Society, 1899.

Abstracts of Wills on File in the Surrogate's Office, City of New York, June 2, 1786–February 18, 1796 with letters of Administration, January 5, 1786–December 31, 1795, Volume XIV: Collections of the New-York Historical Society for the Year 1906. New York: New-York Historical Society, 1906.

Despatches From the American Consul at St. Salvador, Bahia, Brazil, 1808–1849. Government Documents T432

Loyalists and Land Settlement in Nova Scotia, Public Archives of Nova Scotia, Publication No. 4. Marion Gilroy, ed. Baltimore: Clearfield Company Inc., 1937, Fourth Printing, 2002.

New York City During the American Revolution being a Collection of Original Papers (now first published). From the Manuscripts in the Possession of the Mercantile Library Association of New York City. New York: Privately Printed, 1861.

New-York Historical Society, New York: *DePeyster Family Papers, 1741–1836; John Leake Papers, 1753–1835; Watts Family Papers, 1692–1839.*

The Northeastern Reporter, vol. 13. Containing all the Current Decisions of the Supreme Courts of Massachusetts, Ohio, Indiana, Illinois and the Court of Appeals of New York, October 14–December 23, 1887. St. Paul, MN: West Publishing Co., 1888.

The Royal Commission on the Losses and Services of American Loyalists, 1783–1785. Hugh Edward Egerton, ed. New York: Arno Press & *New York Times*, 1969.

State of New York. *The Colonial Laws of New York From the Year 1664 to the Revolution, Including the Charters to the Duke of York, the Commissions and Instructions to the Colonial Governors, the Duke's Laws, the Laws of the Dongan and Leisler Assemblies, the Charters of Albany and New York and the Acts of the Colonial Legislatures From 1691 to 1775, Inclusive.* Albany, NY: James B. Lyon, State Printer, 1894.

Consulted Archives

American Antiquarian Society, Worcester, Massachusetts.
Fairfield Historical Society, Fairfield, Connecticut.
Library of Congress, Manuscripts Division, Washington, District of Columbia.
Maryland Historical Society.
New York Public Library, New York City, New York.

Books

Albion, Robert Greenhalgh. *Square-Riggers on Schedule: The New York Sailing Packets to England, France, and the Cotton Ports.* Princeton, NJ: Princeton University Press, 1938.

———. *The Rise of the New York Port, 1815–1860.* New York: Charles Scribner's Sons, 1939.

Allaben, Frank. *John Watts DePeyster.* New York: Frank Allaben Genealogical Company, 1908.

Appleby, Joyce. *Inheriting the Revolution: The First Generation of Americans.* Cambridge, MA: Belknap Press of Harvard University, 2000.

Appleton's Journal of Literature, Science, and Art, vol. 12, July 4 to December 26, 1874. New York: D. Appleton & Co., 1874.

Asher, Robert, and Charles Stephenson, eds. *The New York City Artisan, 1789–1825: A Documentary History.* Albany: State University of New York Press, 1989.

Barickman, B. J. *A Bahian Counterpoint: Sugar, Tobacco, Cassava, and Slavery in the Reconcavo, 1780–1860.* Stanford, CA: Stanford University Press, 1998.

Barker, Hannah, and Elaine Chalus, eds. *Women's History: Britain, 1700–1850. An Introduction.* New York: Routledge, 2005.

Barker, Jacob. *Incidents in the Life of Jacob Barker of New Orleans, Louisiana: With Historical Facts, His Financial Transactions With the Government, and His Course on Important Political Questions, From 1800 to 1855*. Whitefish, MT: Kessinger Publishing Co., 1855, reprint 2007.

Barman, Roderick J. *Brazil: The Forging of a Nation, 1798–1852*. Stanford, CA: Stanford University Press, 1988.

Barrett, Walter (pseud. Joseph Scoville). *The Old Merchants of New York City*, vol. 2. New York: Thomas R. Knox & Co., 1885.

Barrett, Wayne. *The St. John River Valley*. Toronto: Oxford University Press, 1981.

Barry, Gerald J. *The Sailors' Snug Harbor: A History, 1801–2001*. Bronx, NY: Fordham University Press, 2000.

Barry, Jonathan, and Christopher Brooks, eds. *The Middling Sort of People: Culture, Society, and Politics in England, 1550–1800*. New York: St. Martin's Press, 1994.

Bayly, C. A. *Imperial Meridian: The British Empire and the World, 1780–1830*. London: Longman Press, 1989.

Beckert, Sven. *The Monied Metropolis: New York City and the Consolidation of the American Bourgeoisie, 1850–1896*. New York: Cambridge University Press, 1993.

Belknap, Waldron Phoenix Jr. *The DePeyster Genealogy*. Boston: Privately Printed, 1956.

Bell, David Graham. *Early Loyalist Saint John: The Origin of New Brunswick Politics, 1783–1786*. Fredericton, New Brunswick: New Ireland Press, 1983.

Bernstein, Peter L. *Wedding of the Waters: The Erie Canal and the Making of a Great Nation*. New York: Norton, 2005.

Bill, Alfred Hoyt. *New Jersey and the Revolutionary War*. Princeton, NJ: The New Jersey Historical Society and D. Van Nostrand, 1964.

Blackmar, Elizabeth. *Manhattan for Rent, 1785–1850*. Ithaca, NY: Cornell University Press, 1989.

Blakeley, Phyllis R., and John N. Grant, eds. *Eleven Exiles: Accounts of Loyalists in the American Revolution*. Toronto: Dundurn Press, 1982.

Bolton, Charles Knowles. *The Founders: Portraits of Persons Born Abroad Who Came to the Colonies in North America Before 1701*. Whitefish, MT: Kessinger, 2006.

Borden, Morton, and Penn, eds. *The American Tory*. Englewood Cliffs, NJ: Prentice Hall, 1972.

Brown, Wallace. *The King's Friends: The Composition and Motives of the American Loyalists*. Providence, RI: Brown University Press, 1965.

———. *The Good Americans: The Loyalists in the American Revolution*. New York: Morrow, 1969.

————. *The Black Loyalists in Canada*. Toronto: United Empire Loyalists Association of Canada, 1990.

————, and Hereward Senior. *Victorious in Defeat: The Loyalists in Canada*. Toronto: Methuen, 1984.

Browne, James Alexander. *England's Artillerymen: An Historical Narrative of the Services of the Royal Artillery, From the Formation of the Regiment to the Amalgamation of the Royal and Indian Artilleries in 1862*. London: Hall, Smart and Allen, 1865.

Brumwell, Stephen. *Redcoats: The British Soldier and War in the Americas, 1755–1763*. Cambridge: Cambridge University Press, 2002.

Bumsted, J. M. *Understanding the Loyalists*. Sackville, New Brunswick: Centre for Canadian Studies, Mount Allison University, 1986.

Burrows, Edwin G., and Mike Wallace. *Gotham: A History of New York City to 1898*. New York: Oxford University Press, 2000.

Bushman, Richard L. *The Refinement of America: Persons, Houses, Cities*. New York: Vintage Books, 1992.

Calhoon, Robert M. *The Loyalists in Revolutionary America, 1760–1781*. New York: Harcourt Brace Jovanovich, 1973.

Calhoon, Robert M., Timothy M. Barnes, and George A. Rawlyk, eds. *Loyalists and Community in North America*. Westport, CT: Greenwood Press, 1994.

————, Timothy M. Barnes, Donald C. Lord, Janice Potter, and Robert M. Weir. *The Loyalist Perception and Other Essays*. Columbia: University of South Carolina Press, 1989.

Carp, Benjamin L. *Rebels Rising: Cities and the American Revolution*. New York: Oxford University Press, 2007.

Chalmers II, Harvey. *The Birth of the Erie Canal*. New York: Bookman, 1960.

Channing, Edward. *A History of the United States, Volume V: The Period of Transition, 1815–1848*. New York: Macmillan, 1921.

Cohn, David Lewis. *The Life and Times of King Cotton*. New York: Oxford University Press, 1956.

Condon, Ann Gorman. *The Envy of the American States: The Loyalist Dream for New Brunswick*. Fredericton, New Brunswick: New Ireland Press, 1984.

Dallison, Robert L. *The American Revolution and the Founding of New Brunswick*. The New Brunswick Military Heritage Series, vol. 2. Fredericton, New Brunswick: Goose Lane Editions and the New Brunswick Military Heritage Project, 2003.

Dameron, J. David. *King's Mountain: The Defeat of the Loyalists, October 7, 1780*. Cambridge, MA: Da Capo Press, 2003.

Davidoff, Leonore. *Worlds Between: Historical Perspectives on Gender and Class*. New York: Routledge, 1995.

————, and Catherine Hall. *Family Fortunes: Men and Women of the English Middle Class, 1780–1850.* Chicago: University of Chicago Press, 1987.

Dorson, Richard M., ed. *America Rebels: Narratives of the Patriots.* New York: Pantheon Books, 1953.

Downs, Jacques M. *The Golden Ghetto: The American Commercial Community on the China Coast.* Bethlehem, PA: Lehigh University Press, 1997.

Draper, Lyman C., ed. *King's Mountain and its Heroes: History of the Battle of King's Mountain, October 7th, 1780, and the Events Which Led to It.* Cincinnati, OH: Thomson, 1881. Reprint: Marietta, GA: Continental Book, 1954.

Dubeau, Sharon M. *New Brunswick Loyalists: A Bicentennial Tribute.* Agincourt, Ontario: Generation Press, 1983.

Earle, Alice Morse. *Colonial Days in Old New York.* New York: Empire State Book Co., 1938.

East, Robert A., and Jacob Judd, eds. *The Loyalist Americans: A Focus on Greater New York.* Tarrytown, NY: Sleepy Hollow Restorations, 1975.

Edwards, Charles. *Report of Chancery Cases Decided in the First Circuit of the State of New York by the Honorable William T. McCoun, Vice-Chancellor,* vol. I. New York: Gould Banks & Co., 1833.

Einstein, Lewis. *Divided Loyalties: Americans in England During the War of Independence.* New York: Russell & Russell, 1933, reprint 1970.

Erickson, Louise. *Women and Property in Early Modern England.* London: Routledge, 1993.

Flick, Alexander Clarence. *Loyalism in New York During the American Revolution.* New York: Arno Press & *New York Times,* 1969.

Gassan, Richard H. *The Birth of American Tourism: New York, the Hudson Valley, and American Culture, 1790–1830.* Amherst: University of Massachusetts Press, 2008.

Gebhard, Elizabeth L. *The Life and Ventures of the Original John Jacob Astor.* New York: Brian Printing Co., 1915.

Gilje, Paul A. *The Road to Mobacracy: Popular Disorder in New York City, 1763–1834.* Chapel Hill: University of North Carolina Press, 1987.

————, and Howard B. Rock, eds. *Keepers of the Revolution: New Yorkers at Work in the Early Republic.* Ithaca, NY: Cornell University Press, 1992.

Goodfriend, Joyce D. *Before the Melting Pot: Society and Culture in Colonial New York City, 1664–1730.* Princeton, NJ: Princeton University Press, 1992.

Gould, Eliga H. *The Persistence of Empire: British Political Culture in the Age of the American Revolution.* Chapel Hill: University of North Carolina Press for the Omohundro Institute of Early American History & Culture, 2000.

————, and Peter S. Onuf, eds. *Empire and Nation: The American Revolution in the Atlantic World.* Baltimore: Johns Hopkins University Press, 2005.

Graham, John Andrew. *A Descriptive Sketch of the Present State of Vermont, One of the United States of America.* London: Henry Fry, 1797.

Gray, Lewis Charles. *History of Agriculture in the Southern United States to 1860, Volume II.* Gloucester, MA: Smith, 1958.

Green, Henry W. *Reports of Cases Determined in the Court of Chancery of the State of New Jersey Volume II, Containing the Cases From January 1834 to October 1836, Inclusive.* Elizabethtown, NJ: Edward Sanderson, Printer, 1846.

Grossberg, Michael. *Governing the Hearth: Law and the Family in Nineteenth-Century America.* Chapel Hill: University of North Carolina Press, 1985.

Guernsey, R. S. *New York City and its Vicinity During the War of 1812–15: Being a Military, Civic and Financial Local History of That Period, With Incidents and Anecdotes Thereof and A Description of the Forts, Fortifications, Arsenals, Defenses and Camps in and About New York City and Harbor, and Those at Harlem and on East River, and in Brooklyn, and on Long Island and Staten Island and at Sandy Hook and Jersey City, With an Account of the Citizens' Movements, and of the Military and Naval Officers, Regiments, Companies, etc., in Service There.* New York: Charles L. Woodward, 1895.

Gundersen, Joan R. *To be Useful to the World: Women in Revolutionary America, 1740–1790.* New York: Twayne, Simon & Schuster-Macmillan, 1996.

Hammond, Bray. *Banks and Politics in America: From the Revolution to the Civil War.* Princeton, NJ: Princeton University Press, 1957.

Harrington, Virginia D. *The New York Merchants on the Eve of the Revolution.* New York: Columbia University Press, 1935.

Harris, Tim, ed. *Popular Culture in England, c. 1500–1850.* New York: St. Martin's Press, 1995.

Heidler, David Stephen, and Jeanne T. Heidler. *Daily Life in the Early Republic, 1790–1820.* Westport, CT: Greenwood Press, 2004.

———, eds. *Encyclopedia of the War of 1812.* Santa Barbra, CA: ABC-CLIO, 2004.

Henderson, Daniel. *Yankee Ships in China Seas: Adventures of Pioneer Americans in the Troubled Far East.* New York: Hastings House, 1946.

Henretta, James A., Michael Kammen, and Stanley N. Katz, eds. *The Transformation of Early American History: Society, Authority and Ideology.* New York: Knopf, 1991.

Hibbert, Christopher. *Redcoats & Rebels: The American Revolution Through British Eyes.* New York: Norton, 1990.

Hoffman, Ronald, and Peter J. Albert, eds. *Women in the Age of the American Revolution.* Charlottesville: United States Capital Historical Society–University of Virginia Press, 1989.

Hoffman, Ronald, Michal Sobel, Fredrika J. Teute, eds. *Through a Glass Darkly: Reflections on Personal Identity in Early America.* Chapel Hill: Omohundro Institute of Early American History and Culture & University of North Carolina Press, 1997.

Hulsebosch, Daniel J. *Constituting Empire: New York and the Transformation of Constitutionalism in the Atlantic World, 1664–1830.* Chapel Hill: University of North Carolina Press, 2005.

Jones, Hazel. *Jane Austen and Marriage.* London: Continuum, 2009.

Jones, H. G. *Historical Consciousness in the Early Republic: The Origins of State Historical Societies, Museums, and Collections, 1791–1861.* Chapel Hill: University of North Carolina Press, 1995.

Jones, Thomas. *History of New York During the Revolutionary War, and of the Leading Events in the Other Colonies at That Period.* Edited by Edward Floyd DeLancey. New York: New-York Historical Society, 1879.

Kammen, Michael. *Colonial New York: A History.* New York: Charles Scribner's Sons, 1975.

Ketchum, Richard M. *Divided Loyalties: How the American Revolution Came to New York.* New York: Holt, 2002.

Kierner, Cynthia A. *Traders and Gentlefolk: The Livingstons of New York, 1675–1790.* Ithaca, NY: Cornell University Press, 1992.

Knowles, Norman. *Inventing the Loyalists: The Ontario Loyalist Tradition and the Creation of a Usable Past.* Toronto: University of Toronto Press, 1997.

Kraay, Hendrik. *Race, State, and Armed Forces in Independence-Era Brazil: Bahia, 1790s–1840s.* Stanford, CA: Stanford University Press, 2001.

Lamb, Martha J., and Mrs. Burton Harrison. *History of the City of New York: Its Origins, Rise and Progress, in Three Volumes.* New York: A.S. Barnes & Co., 1877, 1880, 1896.

Latimer, John. *1812: War With America.* Cambridge, MA: Belknap Press of Harvard University Press, 2007.

Lawrence, Joseph Wilson. *Foot-Prints, or, Incidents in the Early History of New Brunswick.* Saint John, New Brunswick: J. & A. McMillian, 1883.

————, Alfred Augustus Stockton, and W. O. Raymond. *The Judges of New Brunswick and their Times.* Fredericton, New Brunswick: Acadiensis Press, 1905, reprint 1907.

Lebsock, Susan. *The Free Women of Petersburg: Status and Culture in a Southern Town, 1784–1860.* New York: Norton, 1985.

Lloyd, T. O. *The British Empire, 1558–1983.* Oxford, England: Oxford University Press, 1984.

Maas, David E. *The Return of the Massachusetts Loyalists.* New York: Garland, 1989.

MacKinnon, Neil. *This Unfriendly Soil: The Loyalist Experience in Nova Scotia, 1783–1791.* Montreal: McGill-Queen's University Press, 1986.

MacNutt, William Stewart. *New Brunswick, A History: 1784–1867.* Toronto: Macmillan, 1963.

Maier, Pauline. *American Scripture: Making the Declaration of Independence.* New York: Vintage Press, 1997.

Mancke, Elizabeth. *The Fault Lines of Empire: Political Differentiation in Massachusetts and Nova Scotia, CA. 1760–1830.* New York: Routledge, 2005.

Mann, Bruce H. *Republic of Debtors: Bankruptcy in the Age of American Independence.* Cambridge, MA: Harvard University Press, 2002.

Mason, Bernard. *The Road to Independence: The Revolutionary Movement in New York, 1773–1777.* Lexington: University of Kentucky Press, 1966.

Matson, Cathy. *Merchants & Empire: Trading in Colonial New York.* Baltimore: Johns Hopkins University Press, 1998.

Mattoso, Katia. *Bahia: Século XIX: Uma Provincia no Império.* Rio de Janeiro: Editora Nova Fronteira, 1992.

McKay, Richard. *South Street: A Maritime History of New York.* New York: G. P. Putnam's Sons, 1934.

Messick, Hank. *King's Mountain: The Epic of the Blue Ridge "Mountain Men" in the American Revolution.* Boston: Little, Brown, 1967.

Mitnick, Barbara J. *New Jersey in the American Revolution.* New Brunswick, NJ: Rivergate Books and the Rutgers University Press, 2005.

Morgan, Edmund S., and Helen M. Morgan. *The Stamp Act Crisis: Prologue to Revolution.* Chapel Hill: University of North Carolina Press, 1953.

Morris, R. J. *Men, Women and Property in England, 1780–1870: A Social and Economic History of Family Strategies amongst the Leeds Middle Classes.* Cambridge: Cambridge University Press, 2005.

Mosher, Jeffrey C. *Political Struggle, Ideology, and State Building: Pernambuco and the Construction of Brazil, 1817–1850.* Lincoln: University of Nebraska Press, 2000.

Mott, Hopper Striker. *The New York of Yesterday: A Descriptive Narrative of Old Bloomingdale.* New York: G. P. Putnam's Son, The Knickerbocker Press, 1908.

Nelson, William H. *The American Tory.* Oxford, England: Oxford University Press, 1961.

North, Douglass C. *The Economic Growth of the United States, 1790–1860.* Englewood Cliffs, NJ: Prentice Hall, 1961.

Norton, Mary Beth. *The British-Americans: The Loyalist Exiles in England, 1774–1789.* Boston: Little, Brown, 1972.

O'Day, Rosemary. *Women's Agency in Early Modern Britain and the American Colonies: Patriarchy, Partnership and Patronage.* New York: Pearson Longman, 2007.

Olsen, Ted. *Blue Ridge Folklife.* Jackson: University Press of Mississippi, 1998.

Onderdonk, Henry. *Queens County in Olden Times: Being a Supplement to the Several Histories Thereof.* Jamaica, NY: C. Welling Publisher, 1865.

Pachal, Bridglal. *The Nova Scotia Black Loyalist Experience Through the Centuries.* Halifax: Nimbus, 2007.

Pasley, Jeffrey et al. *The Tyranny of Printers: Newspaper Politics in the Early American Republic.* Charlottesville: University of Virginia, 2001.

———. *Beyond the Founders: New Approaches to the Political History of the Early Republic.* Chapel Hill: University of North Carolina, 2004.

Pencak, William, and Conrad Edick Wright, eds. *Authority and Resistance in Early New York.* New York: The New-York Historical Society, 1988.

Pitch, Anthony, S. *The Burning of Washington: The British Invasion of 1814.* Annapolis, MD: Naval Institute Press, 1998.

Pomerantz, Sidney Irving. *New York, An American City, 1783–1803: A Study of Urban Life.* New York: Columbia University Press, 1938.

Porter, Kenneth Wiggins. *John Jacob Astor, Business Man.* New York: Russell and Russell, 1966.

Potter, Janice. *The Liberty We Seek: Loyalist Ideology in Colonial New York and Massachusetts.* Cambridge, MA: Harvard University Press, 1983.

———. *While the Women Only Wept: Loyalist Refugee Women.* Montreal, Quebec: McGill-Queen's University Press, 1993.

Pulls, John W. *Moving On: Black Loyalists in the Afro-Atlantic World.* New York: Garland, 1999.

Purcell, Sarah. *Sealed with Blood: War, Sacrifice, and Memory in Revolutionary America.* Philadelphia: University of Pennsylvania, 2003.

Quincy, Josiah. *The History of the Boston Athenaeum with Biographical Notices of its Deceased Founders.* Cambridge, MA: Metcalf & Co., 1851.

Ranlet, Philip. *The New York Loyalists.* Knoxville: University of Tennessee Press, 1986.

Raymond, W. O. *The River St. John: Its Physical Features, Legends & History, From 1604–1784.* St. John, New Brunswick: Bowes, 1910.

———, ed. *Winslow Papers, A.D. 1776–1826.* Boston: Gregg Press, 1972.

Reis, João José. *Slave Rebellion in Brazil: The Muslim Uprising of 1835 in Bahia.* Arthur Brakel, translator. Baltimore: Johns Hopkins University Press, 1995.

Resch, John Phillips. *Suffering Soldiers: Revolutionary War Veterans, Moral Sentiment and Political Culture in the Early Republic.* Boston: University of Massachusetts, 2000.

Reynolds, K. D. *Aristocratic Women and Political Society in Victorian Britain*. Oxford: Clarendon Press, 1998.

Riley, Sandra. *Homeward Bound: A History of the Bahama Islands to 1850 with a Definitive Study of Abaco in the American Loyalist Plantation Period*. 2nd ed. St. Petersburg, FL: Kennedy, 1985.

Sabine, Lorenzo. *Biographical Sketches of Loyalists of the American Revolution, With an Historical Essay*. Boston: Little Brown & Co., 1864.

Schama, Simon. *Rough Crossings: Britain, the Slaves, & the American Revolution*. Toronto: Viking Canada, 2005.

Schecter, Barnet. *The Battle for New York: The City at the Heart of the American Revolution*. New York: Walker, 2002.

Shaw, Ronald E. *Erie Water West: A History Of the Erie Canal, 1792, 1854*. Lexington: University of Kentucky Press, 1990.

Shy, John. *A People Numerous and Armed: Reflections on the Military Struggle for American Independence*. New York: Oxford University Press, 1976.

Sieburt, Wilbur H. *The Legacy of the American Revolution to the British West Indies and the Bahamas: A Chapter out of the History of the American Loyalists*. Boston: Gregg Press, 1972.

Singleton, Ester. *Social New York Under the Georges, 1714–1776: Houses, Streets, and Country Homes, Furniture, China, Plate and Manners*. New York: D. Appleton & Co., 1902.

Smith, Arthur D. Howden. *John Jacob Astor: Landlord of New York*. New York: Cosimo Books, 2005.

Smith, Joshua M. *Borderland Smuggling: Patriots, Loyalists, and Illicit Trade in the Northeast, 1783–1820*. Gainesville: University Press of Florida, 2006.

Smith, Paul H. *Loyalists and Redcoats: A Study in British Revolutionary Policy*. Chapel Hill: University of North Carolina Press, 1964.

Steinbach, Susie. *Women in England, 1760–1914: A Social History*. New York: Palgrave-Macmillan, 2004.

Stewart, Maaja A. *Domestic Realities and Imperial Fictions: Jane Austen's Novels in Eighteenth-Century Contexts*. Athens: University of Georgia Press, 1993.

Stobart, Jon, and Alastair Owns, eds. *Urban Fortunes: Property and Inheritance in the Town, 1700–1900*. Aldershot, England: Ashgate, 2000.

Taylor, Alan. *William Cooper's Town: Power and Persuasion on the Frontier of the Early Republic*. New York: Vintage Books, 1995, reprint 1996.

Taylor, George Rogers. *The Transportation Revolution, 1815–1860, Volume IV*. White Plains, NY: Sharpe, 1951.

Terrell, John Upton. *Furs by Astor*. New York: Morrow, 1963.

Tiedemann, Joseph S. *Reluctant Revolutionaries: New York City and the Road to Independence, 1763–1776*. Ithaca, NY: Cornell University Press, 1997.

————, and Eugene R. Fingerhut, eds. *The Other New York: The American Revolution Beyond New York City, 1763–1787*. Albany: State University of New York Press, 2005.

Truxes, Thomas M. *Defying Empire: Trading With the Enemy in Colonial New York*. New Haven, CT: Yale University Press, 2008.

Ulrich, Laurel Thatcher. *A Midwife's Tale: The Life of Martha Ballard, Based on Her Diary, 1785–1812*. New York: Vintage Books, 1991.

Van Buskirk, Judith L. *Generous Enemies: Patriots and Loyalists in Revolutionary New York*. Philadelphia: University of Pennsylvania Press, 2002.

Van Tyne, Claude Halstead. *The Loyalists in the American Revolution*. New York: Peter Smith, 1929.

Vickery, Amanda. *The Gentleman's Daughter: Women's Lives in Georgian England*. New Haven, CT: Yale University Press, 1998.

Waldstreicher, David. *In the Midst of Perpetual Fetes: The Making of American Nationalism 1776–1820*. Chapel Hill: University of North Carolina Press, 1997.

Walker, James. *The Black Loyalist: The Search for a Promised Land in Nova Scotia & Sierra Leone, 1783–1870*. London: Longman, 1976.

Wallace, W. Stewart. *The United Empire Loyalists: A Chronicle of the Great Migration*. Toronto: Brook & Company, 1922.

Wertenbaker, Thomas Jefferson. *Father Knickerbocker Rebels: New York City During the Revolution*. New York: Charles Scribner's Sons, 1948.

White, Philip L. *The Beekmans of New York in Politics and Commerce, 1647–1877*. Baltimore: Waverly Press, for the New-York Historical Society, 1956.

Whitfield, Paul. *London: A Life in Maps*. London: British Library, 2006.

Wilbur, James Benjamin. *Ira Allen: Founder of Vermont, 1751–1814*, vol. 2. Boston: Houghton Mifflin Company, 1928.

Wilson, Ben. *The Making of Victorian Values: Decency and Dissent in Britain, 1789–1837*. New York: Penguin Press, 2007.

Wilson, James Grant. *The Memorial History of the City of New York: Biographical*. New York: New York History Company, 1892.

Wood, Gordon S. *The Creation of the American Republic, 1776–1787*. Williamsburg, VA: University of North Carolina Press for Omohundro Institute of Early American History and Culture, 1969.

————. *The Radicalism of the American Revolution*. New York: Knopf, 1992.

Wright, Esther Clark. *The Loyalists of New Brunswick*. Yarmouth, Nova Scotia: Sentinel, 1955, Fifth Printing, 1985.

————. *The Saint John River*. Toronto: McClelland & Stewart, 1949.

Wright, J. Leitch Jr. *Florida in the American Revolution*. Gainesville: University of Florida Press, 1975.

Young, Linda. *Middle Class Culture in the Nineteenth-Century: America, Australia, and Britain.* New York: Palgrave Macmillan, 2003.

Zakim, M. *Ready Made Democracy.* Chicago: University of Chicago Press, 2004.

Articles

Abbott, W. "Sketch of James DePeyster Ogden." *New York Genealogical & Biographic Record* XXII, no. 3 (July 1891), 150–151.

Allan, A. A. "Patriots and Loyalists: The Choice of Political Allegiances by the Members of Maryland's Proprietary Elite." *Journal of Southern History* 38, no. 2 (1972): 283–292.

Bailyn, Bernard. "Thomas Hutchinson in Context: The Ordeal Revisited." *Proceedings of the American Antiquarian Society, A Journal of American History and Culture Through 1876* 114, part 2 (2006): 281–299.

Barkley, Murray. "The Loyalist Tradition in New Brunswick." *Acadiensis* IV, no. 2 (Spring 1975): 3–45.

Beddard, R. "The Guildhall Declaration of 11 December 1688 and the Counter-Revolution of the Loyalists." *Historical Journal* 11, no. 3 (1968): 403–420.

Bjork, Gordon C. "The Weaning of the American Economy: Independence, Market Changes, and Economic Development." *Journal of Economic History* 24, no. 4 (December 1964): 541–560.

Boyd, Steven R. "Political Choice—Political Justice: The Case of the Pennsylvania Loyalists." *American Political Trials.* Edited by Michal R. Belknap. Westport, CT: Greenwood Press, 1994.

Brown, R. D. "The Confiscation and Disposition of Loyalists' Estates in Suffolk County, Massachusetts." *William and Mary Quarterly* 21, no. 4 (1964): 534–550.

Carp, B. L. "Nations of American Rebels: Understanding Nationalism in Revolutionary North America and the Civil War South." *Civil War History* 48, no. 1 (2002): 5–33.

———. "The Night the Yankees Burned Broadway: The New York City Fire of 1776." *Early American Studies: An Interdisciplinary Journal* 4, no. 2 (2006): 471–511.

Champagne, R. J. "New York's Radicals and the Coming of Independence." *Journal of American History* 51, no. 1 (1964): 21–40.

Cheng, E. K. M. "American Historical Writers and the Loyalists, 1788–1856: Dissent, Consensus, and American Nationality." *Journal of the Early Republic* 23, no. 4 (2003): 491–519.

Coastworth, John H. "American Trade with European Colonies in the Caribbean and South America, 17990–1812." *William and Mary Quarterly*, 3rd series, vol. 24, no. 2 (April 1967): 243–265.

Conway, S. "To Subdue America: British Army Officers and the Conduct of the Revolutionary War." *William and Mary Quarterly* 43, no. 3 (1986): 381–407.

Countryman, Edward. "Consolidating Power in Revolutionary America: The Case of New York, 1775–1783." *Journal of Interdisciplinary History* 6, no. 4 (1976): 645–677.

———. "The Uses of Capital in Revolutionary America: The Case of the New York Loyalist Merchants." *William and Mary Quarterly* 49, no. 1 (1992): 3–28.

Domosh, Mona. "Those "Gorgeous Incongruities": Polite Politics and Public Space on the Streets of Nineteenth-Century New York City." *Annals of the Association of American Geographers* 88, no. 2 (June 1998): 209–226.

Dubeau, Sharon M. "New Brunswick Loyalists." *Canadian Genealogist* 3, 2 (1981): 106–120.

Engelman, F. L. "Cadwallader Colden and the New York Stamp Act Riots." *William and Mary Quarterly*, 3rd series, vol. 10, no. 4 (October 1953): 560–578.

Fellows, Robert. "The Loyalists and Land Settlement in New Brunswick, 1783–1790: A Study in Colonial Administration." *Canadian Archivist* 2, no. 2 (1971): 5–15.

Fingerhut, E. R. "Uses and Abuses of the American Loyalists' Claims: A Critique of Quantitative Analyses." *William and Mary Quarterly* 25, 2 (1968): 245–258.

Fisher, S. G. "The Legendary and Myth-Making Process in Histories of the American Revolution." *Proceedings of the American Philosophical Society* 51, no. 204 (1912): 53–75.

Francis, George E. "William Paine." *Proceedings of the American Antiquarian Society* 13, April (1900): 394–408.

Gilbert, G. A. "The Connecticut Loyalists." *American Historical Review* 4, 2 (1899): 273–291.

Gilje, Paul A. "The Baltimore Riots of 1812 and the Breakdown of the Anglo-American Mob Tradition." *Journal of Social History*, 13, 4 (Summer 1980): 547–564.

Godfrey, W. "Loyalist Studies in the Maritimes: Past and Future Directions." *London Journal of Canadian Studies* 9 (1993): 1–12.

Gundersen, J. R. "Independence, Citizenship, and the American Revolution." *Signs* 13, no. 1 (1987): 59–77.

Handlin, M. F., and O. Handlin. "Radicals and Conservatives in Massachusetts after Independence." *The New England Quarterly* 17, no. 3 (1944): 343–355.

Hanger, George DeLancey. "The Life of Loyalist Colonel James DeLancey." *Nova Scotia Historical Review* 3, no. 2 (1983): 39–56.

Hankins, J. F. "A Different Kind of Loyalist: The Sandemanians of New England during the Revolutionary War." *New England Quarterly* 60, no. 2 (1987): 223–249.

Haskett, R. C. "Prosecuting the Revolution." *American Historical Review* 59, no. 3 (1954): 578–587.

Holton, W. "An 'Excess of Democracy'—Or a Shortage?: The Federalists' Earliest Adversaries." *Journal of the Early Republic* 25, no. 3 (2005): 339–382.

Hood, C. "An Unusable Past: Urban Elites, New York City's Evacuation Day, and the Transformations of Memory Culture." *Journal of Social History* 37, no. 4 (2004): 883–913.

Hull, N. E. H., P. C. Hoffer et al. "Choosing Sides: A Quantitative Study of the Personality Determinants of Loyalist and Revolutionary Political Affiliation in New York." *Journal of American History* 65, no. 2 (1978): 344–366.

Irvin, B. H. "Tar, Feathers, and the Enemies of American Liberties, 1768–1776." *New England Quarterly* 76, no. 2 (2003): 197–238.

Jack, David Russell. "General John Watts DePeyster." *Acadiensis* VIII, no. 3 (July 1907): 287–296.

Johnson, H. A. "John Jay: Lawyer in a Time of Transition, 1764–1775." *University of Pennsylvania Law Review* 124, no. 5 (1976): 1260–1292.

Kaufmann, Eric. "Condemned to Rootlessness: The Loyalist Origins of Canada's Identity Crisis." *Nationalism and Ethnic Politics* 3, no. 1 (spring 1997): 110–136.

Keesey, R. M. "Loyalism in Bergen County, New Jersey." *William and Mary Quarterly* 18, no. 4 (1961): 558–576.

Kettner, J. H. "Subjects or Citizens? A Note on British Views Respecting the Legal Effects of American Independence." *Virginia Law Review* 62, no. 5 (1976): 945–967.

Kim, S. B. "Impact of Class Relations and Warfare in the American Revolution: The New York Experience." *Journal of American History* 69, no. 2 (1982): 326–346.

———. "The Limits of Politicization in the American Revolution: The Experience of Westchester County, New York." *Journal of American History* 80, no. 3 (1993): 868–889.

Kornhiser, Robert. "Tory & Patriot: Love in the Revolution." *Journal of Long Island History* XII, no. 2 (1976): 36–45.

Luskey, Brian P. " 'What is My Prospects?': The Contours of Mercantile Apprenticeship, Ambition, and Advancement in the Early American Economy."
Business History Review 78, no. 4 (Winter 2004): 665–702.

MacKinnon, Neil. "A Death of Miracles: Governor John Parr and the Settling
of the Loyalists in Nova Scotia." *Nova Scotia Historical Review* 15, no. 1
(June 1995): 33–44.

MacNutt, William Stewart. "Our Loyalist Founders." *Humanities Association
Review* 27 (Spring 1976): 120–128.

McKirdy, C. R. "A Bar Divided: The Lawyers of Massachusetts and the American
Revolution." *American Journal of Legal History* 16, no. 3 (1972): 205–214.

Merritt, B. G. "Loyalism and Social Conflict in Revolutionary Deerfield, Massachusetts." *Journal of American History* 57, no. 2 (1970): 277–289.

Morris, R. B. "Class Struggle and the American Revolution." *William and Mary
Quarterly* 19, 1 (1962): 3–29.

Morris, R. B. "Ending the American Revolution: Lessons for Our Time." *Journal
of Peace Research* 6, no. 4 (1969): 349–357.

Narrett, David E. "Dutch Customs of Inheritance, Women, and the Law in
Colonial New York City." *Authority and Resistance in Early New York.* Edited
by William Pencak and Conrad Edick Wright. New York: The New-York
Historical Society, 1988: 27–45.

Nelson, P. D. "British Conduct of the American Revolutionary War: A Review
of Interpretations." *Journal of American History* 65, no. 3 (1978): 623–
653.

Newcomer, L. N. "Yankee Rebels of Inland Massachusetts." *William and Mary
Quarterly* 9, no. 2 (1952): 156–165.

Nolan, D. R. "The Effect of the Revolution on the Bar: The Maryland Experience." *Virginia Law Review* 62, 5 (1976): 969–997.

Norton, Mary Beth. "Eighteenth-Century American Women in Peace and War:
The Case of the Loyalists." *William and Mary Quarterly* 33, no. 3 (1976):
386–409.

———. "The Fate of Some Black Loyalists of the American Revolution." *Journal
of Negro History* 58, no. 4 (October 1973): 402–426.

Peyer, Jean. "Jamaica, New York 1656–1776: Class Structure and Social Mobil-
ity." *Journal of Long Island History* XIV, no. 1 (1977): 34–47.

Potter, Janice. "The Lost Alternative: The Loyalists in the American Revolution." *Humanities Association Review* 27 (Spring 1976): 89–103.

Ranlet, P. "British Recruitment of Americans in New York During the American
Revolution." *Military Affairs* 48, no. 1 (1984): 26–28.

Rawlyk, George. "The Federalist-Loyalist Alliance in New Brunswick, 1784–
1815." *Humanities Association Review* 27 (Spring 1976): 142–160.

Rejai, M., and K. Phillips. "Loyalists and Revolutionaries: Political Elites in Comparative Perspective." *International Political Science Review/Revue internationale de science politique* 9, no. 2 (1988): 107–118.

Reubens, B. G. "Pre-Emptive Rights in the Disposition of a Confiscated Estate, Philipsburg Manor, New York." *William and Mary Quarterly* 22, 3 (1965): 435–456.

Riddell, William Renwick. "Slavery in the Maritime Provinces." *Journal of Negro History* 5, no. 3 (July 1920): 359–375.

Ritcheson, C. R. "'Loyalist Influence' on British Policy Toward the United States After the American Revolution." *Eighteenth-Century Studies* 7, no. 1 (1973): 1–17.

Robinson, T. P., and L. H. Leder. "Governor Livingston and the 'Sunshine Patriots.'" *William and Mary Quarterly* 13, no. 3 (1956): 394–397.

Rosen, Deborah A. "Women and Property Across Colonial America: A Comparison of Legal Systems in New Mexico and New York." *William and Mary Quarterly*, 3rd series, vol. 60, no. 2, (April 2003): 355–381.

Roth, Stacy F. "Loyalist Father, Patriot Son: The Cox Family at Shelburne, Nova Scotia." *Princeton University Library Chronicle* 51, no. 2 (1990): 183–200.

Scobey, David. "Anatomy of the Promenade: The Politics of Bourgeois Sociability in Nineteenth-Century New York." *Social History* 17, no. 2 (May 1992): 203–227.

Stewart, Ian. "New Myths for Old: The Loyalists and Maritime Political Culture." *Journal of Canadian Studies* 25, no. 2 (Summer 1990).

Taylor, Alan. "The Late Loyalists: Northern Reflections of the Early American Republic." *Journal of the Early Republic* 27 (Spring 2007): 1–34.

Thomas, R. S. "A List of Graduates of Harvard who were Tories in the American Revolution, Residing in Massachusetts." *William and Mary College Quarterly Historical Magazine* 7, no. 2 (1898): 76–81.

Tiedemann, J. S. "A Revolution Foiled: Queens County, New York, 1775–1776." *Journal of American History* 75, no. 2 (1988): 417–444.

——— "Patriots by Default: Queens County, New York, and the British Army, 1776–1783." *William and Mary Quarterly* 43, no. 1 (1986): 35–63.

Traister, B. "Criminal Correspondence: Loyalism, Espionage and Crevecoeur." *Early American Literature* 37, no. 3 (2002): 469–496.

Troxler, C. W. "Refuge, Resistance, and Reward: The Southern Loyalists' Claim on East Florida." *Journal of Southern History* 55, no. 4 (1989): 563–596.

Tyler, M. C. "The Party of the Loyalists in the American Revolution." *American Historical Review* 1, no. 1 (1895): 24–45.

234 / Bibliography

Zeichner, Oscar. "The Rehabilitation of Loyalists in Connecticut." *New England Quarterly* 11, no. 2 (1938): 308–330.

———. "The Loyalist Problem in New York After the Revolution." *New York History* 21, (1940): 284–302.

Dissertations

Ashton, Rick J. "The Loyalist Experience in New York, 1763–1789." PhD Diss., Northwestern University, 1973.

Klein, Kim Marie. "Acquisition of Power: The Membership of the New Brunswick Assembly, 1785–1837." PhD Diss., Johns Hopkins University, 1998.

McGrath, Stephen Paul. "Loyalism in Five Fairfield County, Connecticut Towns." MA Thesis, 1975.

Morton, F. W. O. "The Conservative Revolution of Independence: Economy, Society, and Politics in Bahia, 1790–1840." PhD Diss., Oxford University, 1974.

Overfield, Richard Arthur. "The Loyalists of Maryland During the American Revolution." PhD Diss., University of Maryland, 1968.

Villers, David Henry. "Loyalists in Connecticut, 1763–1783." PhD Diss., University of Connecticut, 1976.

Yoshpe, Harry. "The Disposition of Loyalist Estates in the Southern District of the State of New York." PhD Diss., Columbia University, 1939.

Websites

Bergen County Deeds (Book S: 167) Bergen County, New Jersey, Recorded 12 Sep 1803–10 June 1813, Recorded at Hackensack. Abstracted by Pat Wardell, 1998. http://files.usgwarchives.net/nj/bergen/land/deed-s.txt ac.

Classification of American Wealth: History and Genealogy of the Wealthy Families of America. http://www.raken.com/american_wealth/encyclopedia/Mrs_Astors_400.asp.

DeKalb, *New York Town Historian.* http://dekalbnyhistorian.org/CooperLetters/cooperindex.html.

Folts, James D. "The 'Alien' Proprietorship: The Pulteney Estate During the Nineteenth Century," *Crooked Lake Review*, Fall 2003. http://www.crookedlakereview.com/articles/101_135/129fall2003/129folts.html. Grantbook Database, Provincial Archives of New Brunswick, Harriet Irving Library, University of New Brunswick. http://www.lib.unb.ca/gddm/data/panb/search.php.

Reference Dept/Morris County Library, *Morris Turnpike Company, 1801–1851*, November 2009. http://mcl.mainlib.org/historic.html.

Saint John Free Public Library Primary Source Documents. http://dev.hil.unb.ca/Texts/philologic/vvv.html.

Index

DePeyster, Frederick *(continued)*
familius, 116, property in New
York, 85; prosperity in New
Brunswick, 56, 96; reputation, 82,
109; retirement, 108–111, 136–138,
148, 158; return to New York, 6,
56–57, 61–62, 64, 85–87, 96, 158;
silver plate, 208n24, Sugar Island
dispute, 54, 184n69; trading with
Abraham, 88; ward of William
Axtell, 24; wealth, 66, 101–102,
111, 116–118, 121–122, 126–127,
129, 131, 134; will, 120–121,
208n24; worldwide trade, 87

DePeyster, Frederick Jr, 1796–1882:
apprenticeships, 118, 128, 154;
business, 138; civic institutions,
128; death, 128, 156; education,
117, 128, 133; enthusiasm for New
York, 131; estate management,
156; family, 65, 109–110, 113,
145; inheritance, 121; law career,
155–156; marriage, 109, 155;
military items, 146; Philadelphia,
130–131; philanthropic and social
organizations, 131–132, 156, 158;
wealth and success, 111, 156,
158–159; without the k, 135

DePeyster, Frederick, 1731–1773
(Frederick's uncle, the "Marquis"),
19

DePeyster, Frederick Augustus,
1790/2 – 1868: apprenticeship,
118, 122; childhood, 57–58,
65, 95, 113–114; death, 157;
inheritance, 113, 121; marriage,
157; sailing captain, 156–157;
sailing career, 122, 125, 132, 140,
156; success, 158

DePeyster, Frederick James, 157
DePeyster, Harriot Charlton, 61, 69
DePeyster, Jacobus. *See* DePeyster,
James A.
DePeyster, James, 1791–1797 (son of
Abraham): 61, 67
DePeyster, James, Jr., 1755–1755: 18,
20, 23, 25, 30
DePeyster, James A. (Jacobus),
1726–1799: 5, 127, after the
Revolution, 29, 33; avoiding
persecution during Revolution,
23; bankruptcy, 17–18, 20, 63,
190n33; death, 73; debtor, 14;
exclusion from wills, 20; loss of
ships, 172n9; management of
Frederick's property, 30, 56, 85,
195n1; marriage, 12; merchant,
11–12; taking care of family, 115;
treason trial, 13
DePeyster, James Ferguson, 1794
–1874: education, 117; family, 65,
113, 157; inheritance, 108, 121;
marriage, 157; merchant, 138,
157–158; military service, 122,
125; philanthropy, 158; society,
128, 134–135; St. Croix, 134;
Washington, DC, 129–130; wealth
and success, 158–159
DePeyster, Joanna Cornelia, 79, 158,
205n123
DePeyster, Johannes, 9–10, 171n1,
172n2
DePeyster, John Watts, 155–156
DePeyster, Joseph Reade: after the
Revolution, 30; Canadian exile,
31–32, 62; Counter-Petition, 43;
death, 47, 182n47; family, 18,
114–116, 118; land allotment in

33, 51; merchants and landowners, 52; military settlement, 44, 52; seperation from Nova Scotia, 47–49, 54; trade, 55

new colony. *See* founding a new colony

New Ireland, 41

New Jersey, 10–11, 24, 26, 28, 30, 32, 75, 85, 92–95, 119

New Orleans, 87, 102, 104–105, 108, 138, 141–143, 145–147, 149–150, 158

New York: anti-Tory laws, 26–27, 86; Atlantic trade, 15; British occupied, 5, 8; Citation and Trespass Acts, 28; colonial government, 16, 22; complicated loyalty, 9; cotton market collapse, 144; dependence on slavery, 154; disease, 95; diversity of residents, 15; Dutch tradition, 12; economic turmoil, 102; evacuation of Loyalists, 2, 29, 34–36, 39; French and Indian War, 14; government, 9; home of the DePeysters, 2, 5–6, 8–9, 29–30; Loyalists, 4, 21, 23, 25–27, 136; marriage practices, 109; occupation by American Army, 22; post-revolutionary turmoil, 2; Provincial Congress, 22–23; response to Treaty of Paris, 26–27; revolutionary committees, 22; Revolutionary War, 15, 21–23, 86, 161; Royal Assembly, 22; society, 127; State Legislature, 89–90, 106, 128; mercantilism, 9, 11, 13, 52, 87–88, 101; waterways, locks and dams, and canals, 91

New York Bread Company, 97–98

New York City Chamber of Commerce, 144

New-York Historical Society, 5–6, 11, 102, 111, 119, 156

New York Hospital, 131

New-York Insurance Company, 92

Nicholas Society, 111, 156

Non-Importation Act of 1806, 101, 104

Non-Intercourse Act of 1809, 80, 101

Nova Scotia, 31: harsh winter, 34–37, 47; loyalist evacuees, 34–39; partitioning, 40–43, 46–49

Odlin, Woodbridge, 151

Ogden, Aaron, 93–94

Ogden, David B., 93

Ogden, Jacob, 93, 114, 138

Ogden, James DePeyster: apprenticeship, 123, 138; break with Robert, 150; cotton merchant, 141–145, 147, 150; childhood and education, 114, 116–117, 138; death, 144; family name, 139; inheritance, 119–120, 140, 144; merchant, 91, 108, 124–126, 132–133, 138, 154; opinions on war, 124–125; stranded in Europe, 123–125, 139–140, 210n40, tourist, 125–126; wealth and success, 144, 158–159; young man of wealth, 140

Ogden, John, 93–94

Ogden, Josiah, 93

Ogden, Samuel, 93

opposition party. *See* Lower Covers

Otsego County, New York, 60

silver plate, 208n24

slavery, 10, 51, 64, 66, 96–97, 113, 152–154, 183n60, 201n61

smuggling, 11–13, 89, 98–101, 104–105, 109, 196n8, 203n99

social elite, *See* Loyalist elite

Society for the Prevention of Cruelty to Children, 156

South Wales, 71, 73

Spencer, George, 13

St. Croix, West Indies, 76, 127, 129, 133–136, 138, 144–145

St. Croix river, 38

St. James Park (London), 71

St. John, 35–38, 43–57, 60, 63–66, 87, 94–95, 98, 100, 102–103

St. John River, 36–38, 44, 52–54, 94, 103

St. Mary, Georgia, 134–135

St. Patrick's Day. *See* Evacuation Day

St. Petersburg, Russia, 139

Stamp Act, 14

Stamp Act Congress, 15

Stamp Act Riots, 15–17, 21

steamboats, 141–142, 146

Steer, Samuel, 146–148, 150

Sugar Act, 14

Sugar Island dispute, 54, 184n69

Sully, Tomas, 131

supercargo, 91, 123–124, 139–140, 151

Supreme Court, 130

Sweden, 124–125, 139

tar and feathers, 26, 85

Tenefly, New Jersey, 119

Third Great Turnpike Company, 92

tobacco, 105, 108, 141–142, 150, 153

toll roads. *See* turnpikes

tombstone, 67–68

Tory-baiting, 26

tourism, 125–126, 129–132, 211n51

trade: Amsterdam, 98; Atlantic, 15; Brazil, 150–152; Canadian, 98, 101; China, 156–157; United States, 21, 61, 80, 101–102; West Indies, 13, 55, 76, 86–88, 104, 133

trading with both sides during war, 88

Treason Act of 1351, 13

treason trial. *See under* DePeyster, James A.

Treaty of 1703, 150

Treaty of Ghent, 126

Treaty of Paris (1783), 2, 6, 25–27, 29, 32, 86, 104

Trespass Act (1783), 28

Trinity Episcopal, 12, 14, 80

Troup, Robert, 90, 197n27

Tryon, William, 22

Turnpikes, 91–92

Upper Covers, 52–53

Union Hall Academy, 117, 138

United States: banking and monetary system, 107; cotton exports, 141; culture, 148; Loyalists, 2–3, 6, 25–26; relations with Britain, 95; trade, 80; trade with Brazil, 150, 152; trade with Britain, 15, 55, 61, 86, 101, 141; trade with the West Indies, 49, 86, 88; War of 1812, 104

Van Cortlandt, Cornelia, 76

Van Cortlandt, Jacobus, 11